M

W

Thinking
with
Your Soul

Thinking
with
Your Soul

Spiritual Intelligence
and Why It Matters

RICHARD N. WOLMAN, Ph.D.

Harmony Books ⚭ New York

Published by Harmony Books, New York, New York.
Member of the Crown Publishing Group.

Random House, Inc. New York, Toronto, London, Sydney, Auckland
www.randomhouse.com

HARMONY BOOKS is a registered trademark and the
Harmony Books colophon is a trademark of Random House, Inc.

Printed in the United States of America

Design by Barbara Sturman

Library of Congress Cataloging-in-Publication Data

Wolman, Richard.
Thinking with your soul : spiritual intelligence and why
it matters / by Richard Wolman.—1st ed.
p.   cm.
1. Spiritual life.   2. Multiple intelligences.   I. Title.
BL624.W65 2001
291.4—dc21   00-044846

ISBN 0-609-60548-8

10 9 8 7 6 5 4 3 2 1

First Edition

To my wife, Peggy, beloved believer,

who helped in every way imaginable

Contents

Preface

WRITING a book is one of the most isolated yet connected experiences one could imagine. Isolated, because there are no other courts of appeal than the self, the inner ear that assesses the harmonics of word and concept for authenticity, rejecting tone after tone for sounding hollow, superficial, or pedantic, yet occasionally feeling hope rekindled when a phrase says what is truly intended with just the right balance. Writing, like any creative act, demands a series of moral choices—is that word, that passage, *right* or is it *wrong?*—that tax even the most lenient of consciences.

But never can one feel more connected than in the writing process. There is the obvious teleology, the final cause or purpose of writing; creating a work for others to read, appreciate, enjoy, applaud, condemn, reject, critique, appraise, whatever the final judgment may bring. The opportunity to talk with friends, colleagues, scholars who have ventured into this world of spirituality, whether in text or in person, is inspiring and nourishing. The research on which the book is based and that formed the motive for the enterprise has taken me to places I could never have discovered otherwise, and introduced me to people who have traveled the spiritual path in their own personal, sometimes private, sometimes public ways.

Writing a book teaches me about Chaos Theory.[1] The theoretical notion that the fluttering of the wings of a butterfly in Arizona influences the energy distribution of the world in unpredictable ways sounds trivial at one level; but in the context of either large amounts of cosmological time and space or very specific unconscious subliminal stimulation, such alterations can take on extraordinary significance.[2] My sense is that we all enjoy and suffer from the fact that "everyone and everything is connected to everyone and everything in one luminous organism of sacred responsibility."[3]

Acknowledgments

Now these are the names
—EXODUS 1:1[1]

THESE are the names of those who directly and consciously influenced this project. These names are this book. They are here in person, in spirit, by decades, by conversation, by gesture, comment, or glance. They are the anchor tower of the heart; the sources following the text are the anchor tower of the intellect. The design and resilience of the span between is mine.

In appreciation, I offer my deepest thanks to:

Patty Gift, my editor, whose vision enabled this project to be launched and who has encouraged me with her insight and enthusiasm.

Jenny Bent, my agent, whose persistent intensity is remarkable. Jenny supported, convinced, cajoled, demanded, and enjoyed with enthusiasm, patience, good humor, and a maturity beyond her years.

Katherine Davis and Rupa Roy, those friends and colleagues who helped begin this investigation with my wife, Peggy, and me, when years ago we sat in our conference room thinking of "spiritual" items for the new inventory.

xii ~ ACKNOWLEDGMENTS

David Thorne for his support of the development of the Psycho-Matrix Spirituality Inventory and for his generous assistance in taking it public.

My friends and colleagues who contributed time, energy, critiques, enthusiasm, skepticism (just the right amount), and tolerance: Dan and Holly Burnes, Marian Ferguson, Howard Gardner, Susan Harris, Lawrence Kushner, Susan Lee, Steve Molinsky, Rebecca Rosenblum, Keith Taylor, Dora and Arthur Ullian, and Drew and Laura Westen.

My parents, Jack and Mildred, of blessed memory, who in very different but complimentary ways, fostered and encouraged in me a spirit of inquiry.

My family, who are "required to take me in," and who added love, support, and thoughtful consideration and effort to their obligation: Baron, Susan, and Steven.

My children for being here, for providing inspiration, editorial acumen, faith, and affection: Josh and Rachel and Sarah and Ken and Dave and Dan.

My grandson, Sam, born May 5, 2000, for literally being published before me, thereby providing existential perspective.

RNW
Cambridge, Massachusetts
15 August, 2000

Thinking
with
Your Soul

Introduction

THIS book is based on my belief that each of us possesses spiritual intelligence, and that we have the capacity to think with our souls. The term *spiritual intelligence* may at first seem contradictory. The word *spiritual* evokes images of sacred experience, of the soul, of questions about the meaning and purpose of life, of subjective and personal reality. *Intelligence,* on the other hand, connotes the mind at work. Analytic problem-solving, computation, and scientific understanding of the workings of the external world are processes most often associated with contemporary views of intelligence.

Is it possible to fuse spirituality and intelligence into a new creation? I think it is. Spiritual intelligence is our human capacity to ask ultimate questions about the meaning of life; and to experience simultaneously the seamless connection between each of us and the world in which we live. The subjective world, with which spirituality deals, and the objective world, which intelligence seeks to comprehend, both reside within each of us. We need a language to describe sacred experience that can point to commonalities of encounters with the ineffable, but which is not burdened with religious or ideological overtones. We also need a methodology for studying, learning about, and understanding our spiritual selves and the intelligent ways in which we can live our spirituality.

In my opinion, spiritual intelligence is part of the normal—in the statistical and psycho-social sense—life of us all. Even those who voice unflattering views of anything they consider "spiritual" can, with a little prodding, begin to have insight into their own spirituality. Once embarrassment and inhibition fade, we witness the flowering of spiritual awareness in the most unlikely (by conventional distorted standards) individuals.

My research into the nature of spirituality forms the centerpiece of this book, built around the methodology of the Psycho-Matrix Spirituality Inventory, or PSI.[1] The PSI is an eighty-item inventory designed to help people assess the focus and pattern of their own spirituality. This research instrument has been used with more than six thousand men and women in an effort to objectively study spiritual practice and experience. In this book I will describe my creation of the inventory and the findings of the research. In particular, I discovered seven factors that together comprise the spectrum of spiritual experience and behavior. Those factors may be described briefly as follows:

1. Divinity: the sense of connection to a God figure or Divine Energy Source

2. Mindfulness: awareness of the interconnection of the mind and body, with an emphasis on practices that enhance that relationship

3. Intellectuality: a cognitive, inquiring approach to spirituality, with a focus on reading and discussing sacred texts

4. Community: the quality of spirituality enacting connection to the community at large, whether in charity or politics

5. Extrasensory perception: spiritual feelings and perceptions associated with nonrational ways of knowing, including prophetic dreams and near-death experiences

6. Childhood spirituality: a personal, historical association to spirituality through family tradition and activity
7. Trauma: a stimulus to spiritual awareness through experiencing physical or emotional illness or trauma to the self or loved ones

These factors encompass the range of spiritual experience reported by this large representative sampling of people.

When you take the PSI for yourself, you will get a picture of your personal pattern of the dimensions of spirituality represented by the seven factors. Like your fingerprints, this pattern is similar to, but unlike the configuration of any other person. Understanding your spiritual style, as well as your spiritual strengths and limitations, can help you see yourself more clearly and improve your interpersonal relationships. Insight into our own behavior or internal experience and empathy for the experiences of others is crucial for daily living and for psycho-spiritual development. As a psychotherapist, I encourage careful listening and self-reflection in my patients—and in myself—because I believe that understanding the context and meaning of our actions frees us to make conscious choices, rather than enslaving us to respond reflexively to life's demands.

What works in the psychological world can, I believe, also work in the world of spiritual experience. Developing spiritual intelligence and finding a language with which to articulate ineffable and deeply moving moments provides a release of spiritual energy for many people who take the PSI. Such personal spiritual discoveries also create the possibility of dialogue with others about difficult-to-discuss concerns and personal beliefs. Some people back away from such discussions, or from invitations to try the Inventory, with statements like, "Oh, no, thanks, I'm not really very spiritual; that's not really my thing." When such individuals do take the Inventory and receive their personal reports, however, they are drawn into spiritual conversations by the power of their deep and personal experiences. These conversations are eloquent reminders that we are all spiritual, and only need the proper stimulus to evoke relevant thoughts, ideas, and feelings. Memories long buried are sometimes re-evoked. Personal reflection on the value of human interrelationships and the connection to a larger life force emerge spontaneously, sometimes to the person's surprise and joy. People who begin to share their own spiritual histories are often surprised by the force of their feelings—both positive and negative. In some cases the process is one of opening old wounds about religious conflicts that have healed insufficiently and have lain dormant for years. In others, the conversation inspires a feeling of homecoming and renewed dedication to spiritual practices that used to bring pleasure but have been shunted aside by the rush of daily life.

I find that many people have a willingness and need to discuss matters of life, death, and meaning with someone who is psychologically and spiritually open and lends a willing ear. For example, I met an old friend, Ron, at the tennis court. (All names used in the vignettes and examples throughout this book are fictitious, but refer, sometimes in composite form, to actual people.) I hadn't seen him for two years. He and I began to talk about the PSI and the work I was doing in this area of research. Before long, we were discussing his own concerns about spirituality and the fact that his thirty-five-year-old son was still having severe epileptic seizures, which would require yet another round of surgery. His concern for his son's welfare, the quality of the young man's life, and the overall meaning that the effects of the affliction were having on his child were palpable. We played for a short while, but spent most of our time together that afternoon focused on the role of spiritu-

ality and its relation to physical and emotional healing in
and in his son's world.

The next day, as I was walking to the library, I unexpectedly
met Sandra, a friend and former classmate of mine from the third
grade, whom I see from time to time. She recognized me before I recognized her. Sandra's weight and appearance had changed dramatically because, as I learned, she was just recovering from surgery for
a brain tumor. Once again, the issue of spirituality emerged as
we discussed how close Sandra had come to death. "I feel grateful
for every day," she told me. For us human beings, ultimate concerns are never far from consciousness. We don't have to look to
the esoteric to find the spiritual. Everyday life supplies ample
reminders of how fragile life is, and how thoroughly interrelated
we all are.

I recount these stories because I want to be clear about the fact
that spirituality and spiritual intelligence have their greatest application and most profound relevance in day-to-day activities, such as
how we interact with friends or treat others in our families, or the
ways in which we feel our work is meaningful. Sometimes we
encounter a cynical, narrow view of spiritual intelligence. From this
perspective, spirituality may be seen as a caricature of New Age
"seekers" sitting in dreamlike meditation, or chanting and beating
drums. Another view associates spirituality primarily with devout
religious practice. The latter would be far removed from the experience of average people who go to school and to work, and try to
live decent, moral, and caring lives with little fanfare, but take
very seriously their responsibility for their own well-being and
that of their families.

In the first part of the book, we will examine spirituality at the
beginning of the new century, looking at how spirituality perme-
ates every part of our culture and our national and international

then go on to examine ways in which spiritual-
of ultimate purpose and meaning currently
lture, politics, education, and the application of
iology.

hip of spirituality to science and technology is
particularly important because of the unprecedented moral choices
created by the application of new knowledge. We live in an age in
which the mysteries of the fundamental building blocks of life are
being decoded, as we marvel at the completion of the Human
Genome Project. We can shape the reproduction of our species
through *in vitro* fertilization and selective reduction of pregnancies, or with genetic engineering. We can extend life with technological intervention, but cannot guarantee its quality. We live in
an age of rampant epidemics in which more than 50 million people
have been infected with HIV/AIDS and at least 16 million have
died. South Africa alone has 4.2 million people with HIV. A redis-
tribution of resources could have substantially reduced these
numbers.[2] It is my contention that spiritual intelligence is the
foundation on which these moral choices rest. Understanding spiritual intelligence and how to apply it to daily life can enable us to
improve the quality of all our relationships, with one another and
with the world we live in.

To gain a better understanding of the intelligence component
of spiritual intelligence, we will examine the historical notions of
intelligence and some current theories that guide intelligence
research and its applications in education. Intelligence—and the
tests that immediately spring to mind—is a concept that requires
careful analysis. The theory of the existence of something called
intelligence, research about this human capacity, and the application of intelligence testing have been *raisons d'être* of psychology
for decades. This pivotal concept relates to traditional notions of
mental function. Some psychologists, including Howard Gardner,

professor of education at Harvard University, expanded the original idea of a singular intelligence into the theory that we each possess a variety of intelligences.[3] I will explain how intelligence can be understood in relation to spirituality. Once the cultural, political, and philosophical background of spirituality has been described, and the concept of intelligence has been clarified, we will proceed to the research itself.

In the next section of the book, because of the intensely personal nature of an investigation of spirituality, I will trace some relevant steps on my own path. As a psychologist, I know that there is usually some conscious or unconscious "flight plan" that brings us to any destination where we find ourselves. Each of us can look back on his or her life to see the direction of that path. Perhaps you wonder about your own life and its meaning, direction, and purpose. This investigation into the nature of spirituality has helped me become more aware of the spiritual needs that guide our thoughts and activities. I hope it can help you, too.

In the middle of the book, I invite you to take the Psycho-Matrix Spirituality Inventory, score it, and find the ways in which you can apply it to your life on a daily basis. You may find that much of what you know and believe about your own spirituality is confirmed; but I hope that you will also find new ways in which you can enhance and improve your own experience and your personal expression of spirituality.

The last part of the book examines each of the seven spiritual factors and describes some of the possibilities of meaning for various outcomes. Each of these chapters is presented with a different emphasis, some focusing on the application of the spiritual profile at work, some on personal relationships, some on individual growth and experience. I have tried to enhance this explanation with the use of examples of real people who have taken the PSI, and with whom I have been fortunate enough to establish a spiritual dialogue.

Many books on spiritual topics have appeared in the last few years. Why another book on spirituality? What new perspective can my approach offer? I believe that an empirically based investigation of spirituality can help overcome the major rift between science and spirituality by demonstrating that subjective experience of the sacred can be objectively and reliably measured. Creationism and natural science, for example, may best be understood as existing in two separate realms of existence, but personal experience—as opposed to theory—is universal.

With or without a scientific theory, every one of us is conscious, and therefore constitutes a complete subjective reality. Each of us has his or her own personal knowledge and way of being in the world. The words *scientific* and *spiritual* are linguistic descriptors, artifacts with which we communicate our thoughts, ideas, and concepts. Eating breakfast, going to a wedding or a funeral, or changing a baby's diaper are simply acts of living. It is theory that divides the world into separate categories for purposes of analysis. This book seeks to describe the individual spiritual world that forms the subjective and experiential underpinnings of these constructed conceptualizations and theories.

In an increasingly complex and materialistic world, understanding spirituality can also provide us with a new kind of tool for coping better with the challenges of our practical lives. Psychological insight enriches our appreciation of the unique dimensions of individual differences with respect to personality. Similarly, spiritual insight can illuminate unique dimensions of sacred and ineffable experience and thereby enhance opportunities for personal growth.

I also believe the findings of this research can help people develop a language that will foster dialogue about humankind's most compelling quandaries. With an objective measure of spirituality, we can describe individual spiritual expression and help create dialogue between people. Without a methodology of understanding the spirituality of someone else, people might otherwise pass each other by, thinking that their private spiritual selves are too personal and idiosyncratic to share without opening themselves to ridicule or embarrassment.

The approach I take in this book uses a different perspective from other recent works on the subject. Rather than create a lecture or sermon format in which I tell you what spirituality is, how you should understand it, how you should use it, and what role it should play in your life, you tell me about your experience of the spiritual realm. Your stories inform the process of understanding spirituality from your own perspective. You can then use your stories to provide the point of view most relevant to your individual experience. The intent with which I offer this research and speculation is not to advise on such personal and private matters, but to join with you in the search for meaning, and to share the pleasure of new discovery. My research provides the basis for guiding our investigation; our collaboration is the basis for a spiritual dialogue. A longtime friend and colleague once told me, "Love is shared work."

Research on spirituality brings the objective to the subjective, the world of science to the realm of sacred knowledge. I approach the investigation of the spiritual world of another with respect and trepidation.[4] Each of us has a unique way of using spiritual intelligence. In looking for commonalities among people through scientific inquiry, it is important that we do no violence to the delicate privacy with which we guard this spiritual part of ourselves. At the same time, it is equally important to find the sacred threads that bind us and may join us to a transcendent reality.

CHAPTER ONE

Spirituality Today

We live in a spiritually hungry time. The intense spiritual activity in recent years has a tradition that reaches back, in this country, to the turn of the last century. At that time, spiritual consciousness resonated with the Transcendentalist visions of Emerson, Whitman, and Longfellow. One has only to reread Whitman's poem "I Sing the Body Electric" or Emerson's beautiful description of the Over-Soul to evoke the outlook of the time.[1] William James attempted a scholarly analysis of religious motivation and experience in his classic work *The Varieties of Religious Experience*.[2]

Whatever the cause, however, be it the dawn of the new millennium, or the materialism that many of us in our Western culture hope to subserve to the question of ultimate meaning, spirituality in one form or another touches every aspect of contemporary life. In this chapter we will briefly examine the manifestations of the current preoccupation with spirituality in terms of our current social and psycho-spiritual attitude, and the popular culture. From an historical perspective I will address what I consider to be the motivation that drives a good deal of today's spiritual interest. Finally, I will focus on important applications of spirituality in education and science, including metaphysics and bioethics.

Social and Psycho-Spiritual Perspective

I N THE industrialized, technology-driven countries, spiritual journeys and quests for the meaning of life—the moral path, the center from which understanding and inner peace flow—are on the minds of many. There is also no doubt that from an historical and social perspective the time is right for this reentry of spirituality or religious thinking—in some cases the "old-time" variety—into the current political scene.[3] Religion is resurfacing with legislation enabling the Ten Commandments to be displayed and discussed as part of the daily lives of children while they are in school. In one state (Michigan), publicly funded charter schools encourage prayer and Bible studies, even though they face lawsuits from the American Civil Liberties Union. Attendance at churches, synagogues, and temples of every denomination is at an all-time high. A recent Gallup survey of American religious beliefs indicates that a consistent percentage of the population—63 percent—continues to practice traditional religion, 90 percent state that they believe in God, and 44 percent of the population attends some form of religious worship each week.[4] The study also concludes that there exists an era of "customization" that highlights the diversification of religious and spiritual practices, but preserves the fact that Americans are "more religious/spiritual than ever." It is not unusual to find mixed marriages in which a blend of both religious traditions of the couple are further refined into contemporary practice designed for raising children who would, for example, celebrate both Christmas and Chanukah and practice meditation as a form of relaxation. Asian and Buddhist-based worldviews have influenced Western thinking to the point where now the interplay between East and West has blurred distinctions once thought to be sacrosanct.

Cultural and philosophical cross-fertilization is another manifestation of this new attitude of spiritual open-mindedness. The poet Roger Kamenetz describes such a cross-cultural adventure in his remarkable tale, *The Jew in the Lotus*.[5] This story tells of the journey made by a group of American rabbis and Jewish scholars to the residence in exile of the Dalai Lama in Dharamsala, India. The Dalai Lama faces the dilemma of keeping his people, the Tibetans, cohesive as a spiritual culture, after their country has been taken over and their religion suppressed. He sees his situation as similar to that of the Jews, who, driven from their land, still managed to maintain a peoplehood through thousands of years of persecution and wandering. The Dalai Lama believes that the spiritual glue which holds a people together in times of stress and physical displacement is the persistent struggle for the preservation of ritual, language, and hope. Kamenetz's documentation of the encounter between the spiritual East and the spiritual West articulates the degree to which the two worlds are more similar than different. As a result, the enactment of spirituality has become, for many practitioners, an amalgam of both cultures and both traditions.

To illustrate, one need only notice that many thoughtful Western teachers and practitioners have adopted some of the spiritual practices and rituals developed in the East. The most prevalent forms of spiritual practice are meditation and focused breathing. In many stories of the creation of the world, it is the breath which is the closest analogue to spirit or to the soul. In the Judeo-Christian Bible, the book of Genesis recounts how God breathes life into his creation. *Ruach*, spirit, is the breath of life. The Christian concept of the Holy Spirit is the personal infusion, or breath, of the consciousness of God. In the Upanishads, breath is the vital connection between the internal, individual world and the external, transcendental world of Ultimate Reality. The widespread acceptance of the connection between breath and spirit makes the translation easier from one spiritual tradition to another.[6] This experiential correspondence means that if one is on any kind of spiritual quest or is looking for spiritual growth and development, the movement between cultures and traditions presents little in the way of obstacles. This fusion of spiritual understanding makes the study of spirituality, using an objective measure such as the Psycho-Matrix Spirituality Inventory, all the more meaningful, because this investigation highlights what may be thought of as the universal underpinnings of spiritual consciousness and experience.

Consistent with seeking a variety of spiritual experiences, spirituality in our time employs a journey or traveler's metaphor. This journey motif is similar to searching for the Tao, or the Way, a direct result of the influence of the Buddhist philosophy. Sociologist Robert Wuthnow's analysis of spirituality in America in the late twentieth century emphasizes that we have become a culture of spiritual seekers for whom the process of exploration and discovery is more important than "dwelling" somewhere in a community of like-minded spiritual souls.[7] The mind-set of a traveler is that of an adventurer, one who seeks new knowledge, understanding, and wisdom, and for whom the Truth is yet to be revealed. The mind-set of the dweller is that of one who has found the source of knowledge and now must mine it for golden wisdom, all the while refining the product of one's labor. For both, the questions of ultimate meaning are paramount, and both may be viewed as part of the spiritual experience. The value of the study of spirituality from an objective point of view is that it includes both styles of spiritual experience and treats them as different, but equally valid, ways of knowing.

At the same time, spirituality is identified with the idiosyncratic, self-reflective, and self-disclosing subjective world. For the roots of this tradition, we can look back to Saint Augustine, who expressed his own religious concerns in his *Confessions,* written sixteen centuries ago.[8] Augustine fused his personal narrative voice with the human search for transcendence: "Truth it is that I want to do in my heart by confession in Your presence, and with my pen before many witnesses." Augsutine elevated the self to a central position in the spiritual and theological dialogue, setting the stage for centuries to come.

Whether we view spirituality as a quest across cultures and traditions, or as an introspective journey within, a defining characteristic of the modern form of this concept is that we focus on an extraordinary amount of self-improvement. Seeking becomes identified with finding a better way, with leading a better life. This urge is not new. Spiritual or moral self-improvement has been with us since the prophets of the Hebrew Bible. Clearly, spiritual self-help must encompass more than physical attractiveness or the avoidance of disease. Looking good and feeling good satisfy our social and physical needs. Those who want more in terms of the quality of their lives, their contributions to the well-being of others, and their connection with a larger transcendent reality, express this need in terms of meaningful practice and work. In my view, the drive for spiritual self-improvement is basically a desire for self-actualization rooted in a hoped-for personal epiphany, understanding, and a peacefulness with the world in which we live.

Correlated with the relentless search for new and more satisfying experiences is an explosion of opportunities for spiritual

growth and enlightenment. An unprecedented open-minded attitude on the part of many, particularly the young, is a result of the
democratization of knowledge, enhanced by the development of
the Internet. At the touch of a keystroke on a home computer,
descriptions of almost every kind of religious practice or spiritual
experience, no matter how arcane or obscure, are available. No
methodology is summarily shunned, no belief system discarded
out of hand. Traditional religious institutions are augmented with
a remarkable panoply of blends, rearrangements, and re-creations
of belief, practice, and ritual.

As a result of the spiritual and religious "menus" available to
us, we now live in a time of personalized spirituality. One can piece
together or combine any and all mind, body, and soul activities in
order to design a practice that "works for me." If we look at the
process from a mountaintop perspective, we see a landscape filled
with new, exciting, and sometimes frightening spiritual mutations
and recombinations. This array of choices and possibilities can be
confusing and disorienting, because traditional guideposts no longer
exist. Consequently it is important to have a methodology like the
PSI, through which we can study, understand, and implement a
consciousness tailored to individual spiritual needs.

The Popular Culture

As we embark on the new century, a wide variety of social
and cultural trends heralds the resurgence of spirituality.
Books such as *The Road Less Traveled, Conversations with
God, The Soul's Code, Care of the Soul, The Cloister Walk, The Seven
Spiritual Laws of Success, The Art of Happiness, The Path to Tran-
quility, The Seat of the Soul, How to Know God,* and the extensive
Chicken Soup for the Soul series (through all its iterations) have

made the best-seller list week after week. The Dalai Lama recently capped a successful U.S. tour with an appearance in Central Park in New York City attended by hundreds of thousands of followers and interested citizens.

Magazine cover stories on spiritual subjects abound: *Time* featured "Jesus on the Web" one year, and the next year asked, "Does Heaven Exist?" A recent *Life* issue asks, "When You Think of GOD, What Do You See?," *Newsweek* ran a story titled "The Mystery of Prayer: Does God Play Favorites?," and *U.S. News and World Report* asks, "The Bible: Is It Real?" and "Why Did He [Jesus] Die?," while *TV Guide* has devoted several issues to exploring God on television with shows like *Touched by an Angel, Providence,* and *It's a Miracle.*

Hollywood has responded to the fascination with life everlasting in the films *Ghost* and *What Dreams May Come.* The relationship between angels and humans was explored in *City of Angels,* and between Death itself and the requisite attractive human character in *Meet Joe Black.* Conversations with the spirit world through the consciousness of a child were the subject of *The Sixth Sense,* the popularity of which made it one of the top ten Hollywood money-makers of the last decade.

The popular and folk-music worlds are in synchronicity with the rest of the culture, and featured artists reach out musically with their voices tuned to the times. Jewel sings "Who Will Save Your Soul?," and her subsequent album, *Spirit,* topped the charts. Joan Osborne's "[What if God Was] One of Us," Alanis Morissette's "Baba," and Madonna's "Shanti/Ashtangi" reveal the current of spiritual themes in mainstream pop music. Madonna, whose name alone and psychic ear to the vibrations of the culture continue to show a high level of perceptiveness, discusses her recently discovered relation to the ancient Jewish mystical tradition of Kabbalah: "It's about realizing how small my life is in the big picture."[9]

Contemporary folk mainstays Kate and Anna McGarrigle plain-
tively ask, "We have a will and we have muscle; a soul and a face /
Why must we die?" And after Cindy Bullens, a self-described
"straight ahead" solo artist, lost her eleven-year-old daughter to
cancer, her music took on new meaning and purpose. Her new
album and its title song, "Between Heaven and Earth," speak to
the fragility of life, and to self-examination and healing.

The spiritual search for shared creative knowledge and understanding applies to world music as well. This music has echoes
that may have existed before the Silk Road of the trade routes
across Eurasia, as part of the world of the nomadic peoples that
created families of musical connection. Yo-Yo Ma, the internationally acclaimed cellist, turning his attention to music that is
"wandering," but has roots in China, Hungary, Sarajevo, and
Appalachia, noted:

> But no matter how much one absorbs by wandering, there's
> always going to be a piece missing, and that's the piece that
> comes from having roots. The best that music can do is to show
> both. It's the balance between them that will create something
> meaningful, because ultimately that is what we are struggling
> with forever. It's the human dilemma and at the same time, it
> embodies a continuing human spirit.[10]

Customized Spirituality

SPIRITUAL searching appears in another form in the current
scene at conferences and other large-scale gatherings. The
exponential growth of conferences that focus on the topic of
spirituality per se is as remarkable as it is varied. At a recent one,
two hundred women drummers from Vermont set an energized

tone for the evening, followed by a rousing gospel-style rendition of spirituals from a member of Sweet Honey in the Rock, an African-American women's group of international renown. Elsewhere, vibrant choruses of gospel music from urban and usually sedate suburban settings send out messages of faith, praise, and redemption. Spiritual cruises in the Caribbean and to Alaska and the Middle East feature speakers who present workshops that have a spiritual dimension or personal growth message, and cover such topics as forgiveness, past lives, intercessory prayer, near-death experiences, emotional and physical healing, enhancement of personal creativity, the prediction of the future, yoga, and "life after life."

Conferences, workshops, and retreats function as an alternative to worship, particularly for those who have lost faith or trust in traditional religious institutions. These communal experiences seem to satisfy a deep need and longing of the participants, who appear to be thoughtful, sensitive individuals in search of a personal path specifically tailored to their own psycho-spiritual preferences.

People I meet at such conferences, as well as many of my students, patients, and colleagues, complain about religion's lack of relevance to modern life. These same people will readily acknowledge a spiritual need in their lives, but complain that traditional religious thinking alienates them from the "spirit" they want to find in their worship or in their experience of sacred moments. Religion, for many of these people, denotes a set of moral rules and commandments to live by, making it clear what is acceptable and what is unacceptable in the sight of God. In the West, the most famous set of rules is the Ten Commandments—probably still the best such rules ever devised—which direct us as human beings in the art of civilized living. Transgression of the Commandments creates the external need for punishment and the internal experience of guilt. The edifices of institutional religion have been built on these fundamental concepts for millennia.

For many who seek a spiritual connection, however, the problem with traditional forms of religious expression is that those forms are encrusted with rules, obligations, and directives that may be unrealistic when applied in today's world. One of the most obvious examples is the Catholic Church's position on birth control and abortion, namely that those acts constitute murder, the taking of a life, and are to be condemned no matter what the circumstances. Many Catholic-born people retain their identity in the tradition, but fashion their own form of acceptable behavior on such fundamental issues as these. In an age of personalized living, having an external set of rules imposed on one's life is too much of an authoritarian burden for a large segment of the population. As the Gallup Poll findings suggest, a large number of us insist on individually customizing our spiritual and sacred activities and expressions.

Organized religion presupposes a more strict adherence to prescribed principles and directed behaviors. Because spirituality is the umbrella concept under which religion is a subset, there are myriad individualized ways to be spiritual and thereby to gratify spiritual needs. Some of the people with whom I spoke during the gathering of the research data indicated that their solution to the problem of feeling the constraints of religion was to participate in that part of religion that was comfortable for them and ignore the rest. They enjoy their religious affiliations with churches and temples, use them for a community of like-minded travelers on life's path, and appreciate the instruction and practical ritual afforded to their children. They feel that children need the concrete experience of ritual, and the traditional symbols and practices of religion can still hold deep emotional power. The "Christmas spirit," for example, is an integral part of anyone whose heritage is remotely Christian, even if the holiday has become for many primarily a cultural and economic experience rather than a religious one. Spirituality in contemporary culture is a designer spirituality, tailored to the needs of individual tastes and preferences. Unlike the experience of spirituality and religion of former times, which yielded to preexisting molds and structures and to which personal need and taste were subordinated, current spirituality has reversed the situation entirely. It is now the spiritual that must fit our needs, or be discarded like a suit of clothes that neither fits nor is any longer stylish.

Historical Perspective

THE QUESTION of what motivates this return or resurgence of spiritual activity in our time calls for an historical overview that, I believe, reveals the underpinnings of this phenomenon. The rise of modern physics in the early part of the twentieth century raised questions about the nature of space, time, energy, and the universe itself. In my opinion, however, the most significant events impinging on the experience of personal spirituality began with the naked viciousness and brutality of the First World War, a deeply traumatic experience for mankind. The trauma of this war was barely integrated into the common psyche when World War II erupted, concluding with a literal "big bang" and the revelation of systematic human torture and degradation on an unprecedented scale. In my view, the geopolitical context from which these wars emerged, and the reordered thinking into which they evolved, changed the nature of humankind's relation to the world. These events undermined people's belief and confidence in the power of any religious institution or any enlightened belief system to provide comfort and meaning.

Our postwar generation inherited the memories of those nightmares. By the mid-sixties we were living in our own heart of darkness. The historical sweep is poetically summed up in Billy Joel's anthem of innocence: "We didn't start the fire / It was always burning. . . ."[11] The baby boomers and their children, who now seek spiritual meaning and direction, were weaned on the murder of their young, handsome, and brilliant president; the murder of his visionary brother; the murder of one of the century's most significant men of peace; and the murder of their hopeful democratic ideals by a war that today even its most virulent supporters agree was a fraud and a national disaster. From a psychological point of view, it is as if our culture were just beginning to shake off the effects of a massive post-traumatic stress syndrome. We still show signs of a classic symptom of the malady, psychic numbing, reinforced by a daily cartoon continuation in our movies and media of the war we all watched with our families on TV. The hope for more humane human relationships, however, signals to me a reawakening of a loving rather than a self-protective stance in the world.

As a nation we have also suffered the loss of the prestige and symbolic power of the leadership of our government. After the merciless carpet-bombing precipitated the humiliating end of the war in Vietnam, we witnessed our nation's presidency bookended with impeachments for immoral behavior; one for political corruption, the other for personal corruption. As a symbolic statement of the state of mind with which we approach institutions of any kind, I submit that the general attitude is one of mistrust, derision, and cynical avoidance. No wonder, then, that the search for meaning in life has taken on such a personal and individualized vector. The need for spiritual enlightenment to combat chaos and violence and provide some sort of inner peace has never been more profound.

Our Interconnected World

AN IMPORTANT aspect of spirituality today is the intersection of spirituality, education, and science, which has a direct impact on each of us individually and on all of us collectively because our lives are interwoven as part of humanity. What each of us does in life affects countless others. Our moral decisions have a profound influence on the lives of people we know, as well as on those of people we don't. The "neural net" model of artificial intelligence, a model that seeks to mimic the neural structure of the human brain with its literally billions of interconnections, is a useful analogue to understanding how the awareness of one another's spiritual and moral perspective is important. The "recursion" model of artificial intelligence searches through enormous possibilities of data and combinations, or sequences of choices such as those involved in the creation of a computer program like "Big Blue," which plays chess against world masters. Big Blue, however, doesn't know enough to come in out of the rain. The neural-net model, though, is a learning model, one in which each exposure to new information literally grows the tree of connections and interconnections in a structure similar to that of the vast network of the human brain, which is the physiological basis of the human mind. It is those interconnections that make it possible for us to think in patterns and to be constantly aware of and in contact with our internal and external world.[12]

Our brains—and therefore our minds—like our social world, are a web of interwoven cells, any one of which can, in a nanosecond, influence other cells that then affect thought and behavior processes. At the micro neurological level and at the macro level of personal and social relationships, we humans are literally and figuratively wired to one another. This interconnection, once the province of mystics and biblical prophets, has become an accepted fact of daily life, and includes those who describe themselves as very aware of the energy that affects us all, as well as those who consider themselves nonspiritual because they are rooted in practical reality.

Additionally, as part of this interconnection, the pervasive development of technology, the exponential growth of the World Wide Web, and the undeniable reality of multiculturalism force us to accept—on a daily basis—the power of the realization of Marshall McLuhan's prophecy of an electronically linked "global village."[13] Nelson Mandela, former president of South Africa and winner of the Nobel Peace Prize, writes,

> . . . the economic fate of a country is not solely in its own hands. In the globalized world in which we live, events in one corner of the planet can have an immense effect upon the fortunes of others far away and not at all involved in those events. . . . Together we all live in a global neighborhood, and it is not to the long term benefit of any that there are islands of wealth in a sea of poverty. We need a globalization of responsibility as well. Above all, that is the challenge of this new century.[14]

It is inescapably clear how thoroughly intertwined each of us is with a multitude of other human beings on the planet. How I perform as a teacher, and whether I am able to impart to my students a sense of the value of learning and respect for the individuality of others, is based on my beliefs and values. How you raise your children and provide them with an appreciation for the sacredness of each person affects them and the people they meet for the rest of their lives. What a politician does with the responsibility he or she has been given when surpluses of money arrive in the state or national treasury reveals individual values. Is the money used for the benefit of schools or of the poor, or does it help to offset tax benefits for those who need them least? Many large corporations whose manufacturing processes have significant and negative effects on the environment now take responsibility for their actions and seek to minimize damage done. Even the largest tobacco company of them all, Philip Morris, has finally broken its long-standing policy of denial with an admission on its Web site that cigarettes do cause cancer.

In short, the infinite ways in which each of us impacts the lives of our fellow human beings are guided and shaped by our spiritual points of view, and then enacted through our moral choices. David Hume, the eighteenth-century British empiricist philosopher, claimed that he was awakened from his philosophic slumber in order to show that morality is based in experience and custom, rather than in faith or reason. Perhaps we are awakening from a spiritual slumber in order to understand our morality and set sail for a more promising land.

Spirituality and Education

SPIRITUALITY is now a significant part of the current national and international preoccupation with the quality of life for both children and adults. As one of the important applied areas in which spirituality affects our lives, education holds the key to the future. The quest for more meaning in daily life appears openly in the lives of children and young adults, and is often provided by their teachers in school. In most cases, teachers are careful not to focus on religious ideology or to espouse any specific doctrine. Educators do speak, however, about reinstilling in the spirit of education an awareness of life's mysteries, of its purpose and meaning, and of sacred experience that captures a child's "natural" sense of wonder.

Spiritual awareness is on the minds of many educators. Parker Palmer, senior associate of the American Association of Higher Education, describes the hidden "inner curriculum" that many teachers have used for years, and are beginning to explore overtly in their classrooms, through which they hope to articulate the spiritual dimensions of learning:

> By spiritual I mean the ancient and abiding human quest for connectedness with something larger and more trustworthy than our egos—with our own souls, with one another, with the worlds of history and nature, with the invisible winds of the spirit, with the mystery of being alive.[15]

College campuses, always an important barometer of the current concerns and interests of the next generation, are also experiencing their own resurrection of interest in questions of morality, the spirit, religion, and the meaning of life. The most popular undergraduate course at Harvard University last year was a lecture course titled "The Bible and Its Interpreters," with an enrollment of 853 students. Classes in ethics and comparative religion continue to be oversubscribed at nearly every major university in the United States. Medical education also reflects the demand for spiritual awareness on the part of students, in this case those who will be part of the healing profession. Harvard Medical School, as well as medical schools at Stanford, Duke, Johns Hopkins, Columbia, and others, have introduced courses on spirituality and healing that tend to be some of the most popular in the curriculum; and undergraduate and graduate programs in psychology are now beginning to include discussions in their classes on the usefulness of spirituality in psychotherapy.

Teaching spirituality or addressing deeply emotional religious issues in schools is, however, never a smooth or easy road to travel. Some schools are eagerly pursuing the spiritual side of education, while others struggle with the opposite issue of how spirituality or, more specifically, religion interferes with education. There are schools, for example, that face the question of whether to even teach established scientific theories such as evolution or the Big Bang, because those theories[16] clash with the beliefs of religious fundamentalists who hold that anything but a literal reading of the Judeo-Christian Bible is sacrilegious.

Teaching evolution to schoolchildren was the issue in the famous Scopes trial of 1927. In that trial, a Tennessee schoolteacher was convicted of teaching Darwin's theory of evolution to his high school students. The Tennessee law that prohibits this part of the curriculum has been challenged successfully in appeals court after appeals court, including the Supreme Court of the United States, but the issue does not go away. The constitutionally guaranteed separation of church and state is still a basic tenet of educational policy in this country, but is currently under a barrage of assaults by religious groups who seek to reinstate what I think must be termed anachronistic thinking.

The Kansas Board of Education recently instituted a policy stating that because evolution is only a scientific theory, it need not be taught in biology classes, nor indeed in any of the science curricula, in that state's public schools.[17] The policy provides that any student who is uncomfortable with evolution or related parts of the educational program does not have to study or take tests on this portion of the science courses. By law, alternative assignments must be provided.

The Kansas school board also has no problem (although the Supreme Court of the United States does) with the inclusion of "Creation Science" in the school curriculum. Based on a literal reading of the Judeo-Christian Bible, Creation Science holds that

God created the world in six days and rested on the seventh; and that this creation took place five to seven thousand years ago, rather than over the billions of years required by current scientific theories. Fundamentalist Christians believe, therefore, that this view ought to be included as one of the theories of the origins of our world that children should learn in school.

The creationists have not been clear about how they want to handle the fact that there are two different creation stories in Genesis—and a few other inconsistencies that make a literal reading problematic. The information is in the Bible, they say, and it should therefore be part of every child's basic educational experience. In the words of one school committee member, "Just because something's in the Bible seems a poor reason to keep it out of the classroom." Or, from another, "I don't think we expected creationism to be in there [the biology text], but there was just page after page of evolution."

The first amendment of the Constitution guarantees the separation of church and state. This separation is also currently under attack by lawmakers pressing for the inclusion of religious teachings in public schools. Their hope is that these venerable moral teachings will somehow help curb the high level of violence that now plagues suburban as well as inner-city schools. While the Congress of the United States refused to pass a gun-control law seeking only to establish a few days' waiting period prior to purchase of a firearm, it simultaneously passed a bill allowing the Ten Commandments (without specifying just whose commandments they would be) a place on public-school walls. Confusion on these issues is the order of the day.

Spirituality and Science

T HE APPLICATION of science and technology can create powerful and sometimes conflicting dimensions of spirituality. Science and spirituality are two of our most basic ways of looking at the world. Science reveres the factual testability of hunches and hypotheses. *Objectivity* is the scientific watchword. If a statement about the world can be measured or tested empirically and replicated with the same results by others, then we can accept the reliability of the claim. Theories in science are never ultimately proved beyond a shadow of a doubt, but hypotheses are confirmed with a larger and larger probability that a given event occurred by some process other than accident or chance alone. The world and reality are "out there" for the scientist—a world waiting to be described, understood, and made predictable by measurement and by the consensus of other minds using similar methods.

Yet for spirituality (and for its subset, religion) it is faith, not empirical evidence, that establishes the unshakable truth of a particular worldview. No one was present when the universe was formed, but to those who believe, there is no question that God formed the world out of nothingness. The dawn of each day, with the perfectly predictable sunrise, or the first cry of a newborn constitutes the empirical proof that the hand of the Supreme Being is still active in the day-to-day workings of creation. The subjective world is the reality of the spirit and of the spirit made manifest. Internal peace, the understanding of the inevitable nature of death, and the interweaving of all living creatures creates a reality that is as solid as any geologist's rock or as powerful as any physicist's atomic nucleus.

Recently a debate was held in a science center classroom at Harvard University on the question of the existence of God.[18] One of the debaters, from the scientific side, contended that the human experience of faith can be reduced to an anomalous activity of the brain's temporal lobe. (Among the symptoms of temporal-lobe epilepsy are a heightened sense of religiosity and visual and auditory religious experiences.) Science views the origin of matter and the cosmos, the source of the fundamental forces of nature, and the underpinnings of human consciousness as enigmas that can be solved with clearer theories, exacting neuroscience, and more powerful computers. The opposing view—spirituality—insists on a supernatural presence in our natural reality. From this perspective, moral action is a question of intentionality and of adherence to values and standards of choice embedded in and transmitted by a tradition or precedent based on a premise of faith.

Of more interest than the points scored in the debate is the fact that it took place at all. Historically, such a debate would have been considered heresy by theologians and superfluous, in this century at least, by the scientific community. Patricia Hampl, poet and professor of English at the University of Minnesota, states the contemporary view: "Our culture doesn't worry, as the Psalmists did, that God doesn't listen. We suspect that He doesn't exist. Or rather we feel we can *decide* if God exists."[19] This debate on the existence of God and the person-centered decision process underscores the remarkable elevation in contemporary culture of the Self—rather than objective science—as the arbiter of the factual basis of what the renowned philosopher and theologian Paul Tillich termed the "ground of being." In Tillich's view, ultimate existential reality, or the meaning and purpose of life, focuses attention on the fundamental source from which all life emanates. Contemporary thinking gives precedence to the individual and his or her idiosyncratic determination of what constitutes ultimate truth. It is because of the supremacy of Self that people can decide not only what combination of belief and practice suits them, but also whether belief or practice is necessary at all.

The split between science and spirituality may be seen as the difference in how fact and reality are determined. Personal reality adjudication, for example, also reinforces the now unconsciously accepted metapsychological position, articulated by Sigmund Freud, that God is the projected creation of the human psyche. According to Freud, earliest family life was characterized by and scarred with acts of patricide. "Primal" sons banded together to rid themselves of the powerful "primal" father. In following this fundamental instinct, the phylogenetic basis of the Oedipal complex was created, because the sons were then free to pursue their mother. In Freud's view, this act of incestuously driven murder was not without consequence. The deed created a powerful feeling of guilt in the sons, who sought to overcome their discomfort with this act of aggression and the anxiety of retribution for their crime by resurrecting their father in the form of God.

> The primal father was the original image of God, the model on which later generations have shaped the figure of God . . . therefore the displacement of man's will onto God is fully justified. For men knew that they had disposed of their father by violence, and in their reaction to that impious deed, they determined to respect his will henceforward.[20]

No thinker has elevated man to the position of determining the existence of God more than Freud. Caught between science and religion, psychoanalysis only intensifies the debate on the origins of the idea of God versus the fact of God's reality.

The debate on whether God exists also highlights the almost axiomatic separation of what the paleontologist Stephen Jay Gould has termed the two "magisteria" (domains of authority in teaching) of science and religion. Gould holds the view that the debate we have been discussing is really no debate at all, because the two worlds of science and spirituality can live totally separate, side by side in peaceful coexistence: "I do not see how science and religion could be unified, or even synthesized, under any common scheme of explanation or analysis; but I also do not understand why the two enterprises should experience any conflict."[21]

Gould's vision of two worlds, one of science and one of the spirit, underscores the epistemological reality of the two areas. Epistemology deals with the origins, nature, methodology, and limits of knowledge, and in this case, the claim is made that these two areas essentially come from two different worlds. The domain of science is defined by subjecting theories, and the empirical data that support them, to the test of falsifiability. This is the test that proves the defining limit of a theory, or demonstrates the case in which the theory simply does not provide an adequate explanation of the data, such as the fatuous theory that some races are intellectually and morally inferior to others. On the other hand, the domain of the spirit, of faith and religion, is based on evidence both empirical and nonempirical, namely those events that can be physically seen, such as the birth of a child, as well as those that can only be intuited, such as the felt spirit of a recently deceased loved one. The result, however, is a theory that is testable and falsifiable only by the presence or loss of faith.

A problem arises, however, when Gould and others postulate these two independent worlds of knowledge. They seek to escape an existential paradox by simply stating that religion and science live on different sides of the metaphysical tracks: "We still cannot draw moral messages or religious conclusions from any factual construction of nature."[22]

In my opinion, there exists a *necessary* overlap of the two realms. Why is the overlap between the worlds of science and spirituality necessary, or even inevitable? Because science, by its relevance to, and presence in, the personal and social lives of us all, exerts an inescapable gravitational pull on our moral consciousness. The questions that are posed by the possibilities of science and technological development present choices so compelling that it is impossible to remain an intellectual or moral bystander.

As a student at Brandeis University in 1962, I attended a speech delivered by David Ben-Gurion, then prime minister of Israel. His words were prophetic: "We must bring the tree of knowledge, of good and evil, from the Garden of Eden to the world of science and technology." His vision anticipated the current dilemma and the psycho-spiritual imperative.

Science and Spirituality: The New Metaphysics

I T MAY be that the answer to the question of the relationship between spirituality and science is to be found by developing a new metaphysics. Metaphysics, which is the aspect of philosophical inquiry that deals with the relationship between faith and reason, ponders the nature of ultimate truth. This realm of knowledge was considered for centuries to reign as the "queen of the sciences." At the beginning of the new millennium, though, metaphysics has been dethroned from this exalted position and replaced by an empirical and materialistic worldview, making the gulf between science and spirituality appear ever wider and apparently unbridgeable.

For the scientific community, the capacity to tolerate the split between the two magisteria seems comfortable. Many scientists hold religious convictions, and the dual tracks of reality appear to coexist easily for them. Among religion's true believers, however, for whom science represents either a threat or an insufficient explanation of life, a metaphysics that seeks to discover deeper truths and penetrate the hidden mystery of this life, past lives, and eternal life holds her lofty perch as securely as ever.

The indiscriminate or automatic merging of these two domains would be a mistake. Yet it is necessary to recognize the dynamic tension that exists between science and spirituality. I would even suggest that bioethics is probably the leading candidate for the new metaphysics. Bioethics addresses such issues as the termination of life under seriously compromised conditions; the allocations of medical and technological resources to underdeveloped countries; genetic counseling and the advice to terminate pregnancy as a result of lab tests; organ transplants and a host of other life-enhancing and life-threatening issues that have emerged because we now have technology sophisticated enough to create choice where none previously existed.

Bioethics attempts to enable the two domains of science and morality to inform and complement each other. It deals seriously with the moral and humanistic questions raised by technological innovation, and it searches for a conceptual framework sophisticated enough yet clear enough to contain the biological and moral/spiritual dilemmas of our age. Moral dilemmas become spiritual crises when we realize that any individual choice has implications for us all. The domains of science and spirit are inextricably linked. These two worlds of knowledge will continue to use each other not only to define social policy, but also to bring rationality to the agonizing personal choices individuals must make in the face of often confusing and terrifying realities.

One of the greatest moral debates of the twentieth century, for example, is that which still rages over abortion and reproductive technology. Pharmacological assistance in conception, for thousands of couples desperate to have their own biological children, can produce pregnancies comprising anywhere from one to seven fetuses. Such pregnancies often involve severe risks to the viability of the fetuses and the health of the mother. The first and basic issue in such a situation is whether the parents can accept the termination of any part, or all, of a pregnancy. For some families this course of action is unthinkable and settles the question. In a case from Iowa, the parents accepted the multiple pregnancy as God's will, and miraculously all seven fetuses and the mother survived. If, however, the parents determine that the risks to mother and fetuses are too high to continue with any given pregnancy, they, with the help of their doctor (and possibly their spiritual adviser), must decide on the proper course of action. This choice would include the possibility of reducing the number of fetuses in order to enhance the life expectancy of those remaining. But how does a mother or a father choose for or against "selective reduction"? And of how many babies-to-be? Can a physician learn to become less sensitive to the sound of the intentional stopping of a tiny heart?

Did we ever think that "Sophie's Choice" would become a factor in the obstetrician's office? In William Styron's novel of that title, a young Polish Catholic mother of two is caught in a Nazi roundup of Jews in Warsaw. She finds herself several days later on the train platform at Auschwitz, clutching her four-year-old son and two-year-old daughter. "Choose one," screams a Gestapo guard, "or else they will *both* be killed." I submit that any mother's choice to abort a fetus is an agonizing moral dilemma that exacts a psycho-spiritual toll, no matter what decision is made. It is the role of the new metaphysics to create a dialogue and guidance for moral choices such as this in situations for which few or no spiritual or moral precedents exist.

Moral questions wrench and test our spiritual consciousness daily. How long *should* we permit an aged and infirm parent to live, and with what quality of life? How *should* we calculate the economic and emotional cost to the family, or to the compromised individual? The United Nations was proud of the pinpoint accuracy of its missiles fired at targets in Baghdad, as was NATO with its air strikes on Belgrade. Too often, however, the target also included innocent civilians. How many precise surgical bombings *should* we inflict, even though the surgery is a success but the "patient" dies? *Should* health maintenance organizations be morally permitted to refuse to care for their sickest members because the cost would affect the profit margins of the whole enterprise and thereby allegedly compromise care for all? Science often remains silent on these and other moral questions, but the current cultural consciousness will not let religion or spirituality be reluctant bystanders on questions of the application, use, misuse, and abuse of scientific knowledge.

Complex moral questions require complex analysis. Sometimes the answer is a simple solution, determined by clear beliefs. In a world such as ours, however, answers must be weighed in a balance that contains many points of view and competing realities. It is my belief that an awareness of one's own spiritual center is the best guarantee for a thoughtful and compassionate approach to the life-affirming and life-threatening issues of the day. The research findings on spirituality and the methodology for personal spiritual insight that I present here constitute a step in the direction of a self-understanding that can serve as the basis for informed moral choice.

A study of spirituality leads inevitably to questions of personal experience. For several years now I have discussed my research on spirituality in lectures to my classes, in presentations at conferences, and in personal conversations with colleagues and friends. I am invariably faced with the same questions: "How did you get interested in studying spirituality? What led you into this area of research? What is *your* religious or spiritual background?" None of my other research has ever prompted these kinds of inquiries.

These questions were motivated by more than the other person's curiosity about my "spiritual journey." They were driven by my student's or colleague's desire to compare and contrast his or her own journey with mine in order to create a dialogue, a sharing of personal histories. Everyone with whom I spoke had a story to tell, a spiritual story.

CHAPTER TWO

A Personal View

We live in an autobiographical age. Personal history and stories, memoirs and tales of individual triumph or disaster, are the social, literary, and psychological currency of our time. No book on spirituality is complete without the requisite autobiographical road map of how the author traveled through a variety of transmigrations of consciousness to arrive at the point of looking back and sharing wisdom with those whose psycho-spiritual travels have just begun. The personal description I present here, however, is less about imparting wisdom than it is about relating some of the events in my life that helped bring me to this point of creating a scientific investigation into the world of spirituality.

I have been fascinated by stories since I was small. I remember sitting on the street corner when I was six, surrounded by the big kids with their legs and baseball gloves draped over their bikes, all of them listening in rapt attention as I spun out fantasies that captured their imaginations. I remember, too, sitting with my tiny grandmother (my mother's mother) in her ancient, musty, fragranced apartment, listening to her stories in Yiddish punctuated by an English word or two that I could understand. But I kept nodding, and she kept talking. (In retrospect, I see that this was my first experience of using the therapeutic nod reflex that keeps conversation active.) She told me stories of the old country, of my grandfather, whom I knew only briefly, and of the pain of the murder of her firstborn when the family lived in Tennessee.

In 1950, by the time I was ten, there were more stories, and they were frightening. My cousin Itzick, a terrified and shaken seventeen-year-old, showed up at my paternal grandparents' Passover Seder. "Who is he?" we asked. "What happened?" We learned his story. Itzick's mother had bribed a farmer and put him in the back of a farm wagon so that he could pass through the guard posts around the small Polish town of Trouvitz in which he lived. When he returned home after having hidden in the woods, he discovered that his entire family had been executed by Nazi soldiers. He ran all night, and literally never stopped for two years until the liberation of Europe. I began to think about his life and about the horror he had survived.[1] Soon after, I started reading books about Jews caught in the Nightmare.

On the surface, my daily life was quite normal—I delivered my newspapers in the early morning, went to school, played sports, and met my first girlfriend at summer camp. But at thirteen, death began to haunt my world in a tightening circle. My paternal grandfather died the week of my bar mitzvah—joy and sadness, always mixed. One of my favorite aunts died of cancer at a young age, and my paternal grandmother died when I was a sophomore in high school. I struggled with the idea of death. I thought about Itzick's family, about the millions herded into extermination. The thoughts were made real and poignant by the tales of heroism in the Warsaw Ghetto, as well as by the graphic images of degradation contained in the photos of the Holocaust. I felt a fascinated, terrifying connection to the heroes and the victims. The meaning of suffering preoccupied my mind. There were so many good people in the world. Why must they die for nothing? Old age and infirmity I could understand, but the untimely and unfair losses that occurred for no reason made no sense to me.

When I was sixteen I had a job in the local delicatessen. Every weekend I loaded the bagel bin for the early-morning customers, sliced "just a little over" portions of corned beef and salami, and chatted with the store owner, who became my friend. Mark Salinger was a Polish Jew who had blue eyes, a twinkling smile, and an almost artistic number tattooed on the inside of his forearm. He came in at four-thirty every morning and worked nonstop. One day he started getting bruises on his arms. The subcutaneous bleeding had, in a cruel twist of fate, leached into the area next to the awful and awe-full string of numbers. Before long I was visiting Mark in the University Hospital, where he struggled in vain to overcome his leukemia. To survive Auschwitz and die like this? I just didn't get it.

In my senior year at high school, I had an inspiring English teacher, Milton Flocken, who taught me how to write and not to be ashamed of loving books and poetry. I made an eerie repeat visit to the University Hospital cancer ward that year to say goodbye to this man, too, whom I had come to admire and care for.

These two deaths struck me hard. I felt disoriented by the random nature of suffering. Two good people, one of whom suffered immeasurably and was then cut down in the prime of his life; the other of whom had led a relatively normal and peaceful life as the young and vibrant father of two small children, and was also taken. My own sense of meaning was challenged by this experience with death. What could I believe in?

I kept reading—psychology, philosophy—looking for answers and listening to the stories. My family had a friend, Marvin Fox, an orthodox rabbi and professor of philosophy who introduced me to the wonders of Plato. We read the *Phaedo* together, the dialogue in which Socrates questions the evidence for the immortality of the soul, as he himself is dying. In one of the most moving scenes in all Western literature, Socrates can only speculate on the after-life: "Well then, . . . let us suppose that there are two sorts of existences—one seen, the other unseen."[2]

In my junior year of high school, searching for some kind of spiritual comfort, I settled into being a relatively observant member of my religion, though I made the necessary accommodation to also observe the required attendance at football games on the Sabbath. Big Ten football is the true religion of Midwestern America.

Although Dr. Fox was an ordained rabbi and a good friend, I developed a distaste for and a mistrust of the clergy in general. To me, institutionalized religion was necessary for ritual, but I found that it could also be petty, bureaucratic, even mean-spirited. A case in point: When my friend David's mother died, David wanted a cer-tain rabbi to officiate at her funeral because he had been her per-sonal friend for many years. The rabbi in the synagogue to which his family belonged, however, was insecure enough to feel threat-ened by David's mother's friend, and told him, "If you want your mother buried in the street, then let the other rabbi speak. Other-wise, the people in our temple will be in charge, and I will offici-ate." Other experiences of the politics and of religious infighting with the clergy thoroughly convinced me that the meaning of life was not to be found in any institution that could breed and house such hypocrisy.

I left for college fully iconoclastic. Initially intimidated by the intellectual power of my professors and classmates, I finally gained the confidence to challenge and learn from scholars like Herbert

Marcuse and Léo Bronstein, who helped me find my way back to the issues that had been haunting me for years. My nagging questions about evil and injustice in the world just wouldn't go away. One of my favorite but most troubling courses, a study of the book of Job, was taught by a learned Bible scholar, Nahum Glatzer. Job continues to endure suffering, while all his friends and family believe that somehow, somewhere he must have transgressed. Why else, they speculate, would anyone have to go through this torture? But Job knows that he has been a faithful believer and has lived on the path of righteousness.

I was stunned by the power of the "Voice out of the whirlwind" that thunders, "How dare you ask? Where were you when I laid the foundations of the world?" The conclusion of the story is that man essentially has no right to question the will of God. The presence of evil in the world is beyond the capacity of any individual to comprehend, and follows no coherent plan. This answer was painful, but with the exception of some unquestioning faith, I decided it was probably also correct.

After college, I decided to try to bring my preoccupations with ultimate issues "back to earth," and enrolled in a graduate program of clinical psychology. More stories. These were interesting, in fact fascinating, because they were stories based on real lives, stories of people who had been led into their own misery and self-destruction by internal forces out of their conscious control. At last there was a way to find the truth behind the appearance, a way to find out why misery and suffering and pain really happened. When psychoanalysis and psychology are accused of having replaced religion, I believe it is because of their claim to ultimate truth—both hidden and to-be-revealed—a territory that religion jealously and fiercely guards.

Sometimes my patients experience the therapeutic process in religious terms to the extent that they feel they are in some kind of (imagined) all-knowing presence. A young man whom I have seen for several years remarked on his significant progress in treatment, "I know that I am much better, but how did it happen?" I replied that he needed to believe in magic to understand fully, because no one knows for sure. The image of the shaman, an intermediary between this world and supernatural worlds, who uses magic to heal and see beyond, has continued in other cultures to answer the human need to be known and understood. This image of the healer, once reserved for traditional medicine and the clergy, is now becoming part of our own culture in the form of less overtly exotic, but just as mysterious, practitioners of mind/body healing and students of the placebo effect.[3]

During graduate school, I met and married a wonderful woman and settled down to a life of academia, which included teaching, research, and perfecting my skills as a psychotherapist. I am fortunate to have had many excellent teachers and colleagues who shaped my thinking in terms of psychological theory and clinical practice. At the University of Wisconsin, I investigated the nature of transference with Joe Kepecs, using a subliminal experimental technique; I learned family therapy with Carl Whitaker as my co-therapist; and I wrote about the development of emotions in children with Bill Lewis. Not one of these therapists, though, ever openly addressed the spiritual dimension in himself, his patients, his research, or his teaching, except maybe to disavow the need for, or the scientific respectability of, spiritual thinking. In those days it was fashionable to ignore or even eschew any reference to spiritual or religious motivational belief systems, conscious or unconscious, that might direct or influence behavior. Religion was seen as either neurotic or psychologically compensatory, if it was ever discussed at all, and I was inclined to agree with that view.

Sometimes, though, life has a funny way of turning one's attention back to ultimate issues. Within the first four years of the beginning of my professional career, I experienced the immediacy and wonder of the birth of two of our four children, the untimely deaths of both my father and father-in-law, and the war in Vietnam—a war brought to us in gory detail each evening on the six-o'clock news. No matter what my colleagues or the psychological theories of the day offered, I found myself back in the world of joy and suffering, trying to cope with the overwhelming psychic shock and the possible meaning of it all. Judaism, the religion of my birth, provided some structure and badly needed ritual in times of greatest joy and distress. My focus continued, however, on looking for the meaning behind the appearances—both in my own life and in witnessing the courageous struggles of my patients, whose stories were filled with pain that was never far from the surface.

My dissertation adviser, Ed Barker, who had been part of the humanistic subgroup of the American Psychological Association, taught me that there were some psychologists who spoke to the issues of the spirit and nonbehavioral aspects of the human psyche. There were scholars like William James, Carl Jung—who broke with Freud over this issue—Eric Fromm, Victor Frankl, and Rollo May, to name a few of those who came to be known as the humanistic psychologists, but who remained in the minority and out of the mainstream of academic psychology and psychological research.

My own research activities in the area of child development investigated the means by which children develop language with which to express their emotions. I also conducted studies on the process of transference in psychotherapy in order to understand the intersubjectivity of this relationship—in other words, the process by which "I see you seeing me," which is the basis of empathy. In retrospect I can appreciate the fact that working with children brought me closer to the phenomenological basis of experience.

Children experience the world directly, having not yet developed the tools for interpretation. At the same time, my research on the perception and awareness of others helped me understand the process of psychological connection between people, which forms the core of human survival.

In the mid-1970s I discovered the world of the child-custody dispute. I had worked with families in therapy, but had never encountered a world so fractured, so rashomonic in its core. (The term *rashomonic* is derived from the famous film *Rashomon*, directed by Akira Kurosawa, in which each of four self-confessed eyewitnesses to a murder tells a different, though credible and internally consistent, story of the events.) I remember asking a judge about the children whose "best interests" were allegedly being protected. "Whatever happens to these kids?" "We don't really know," he said. "If they don't show up in court again, we have no idea." "Someone ought to find out," I replied. Two years later I received a federal grant to investigate the effects of custody disputes on children and their families.[4]

The psychic suffering inflicted on the children whose parents were divorcing and fighting over their custody made a strong impression on me. I began to treat these families who had lost their emotional and moral rudders, and the research grant provided the opportunity to gather empirical data and study these remarkable socio-legal events. From a research perspective, the custody dispute is fascinating; from a humanistic point of view, it is horrifying. Every possible interpersonal and intersystemic conflict occurs. Rarely are anyone's best interests served by this process, but with research findings I believed it might be possible to effect, or at least recommend, change.

I realized in working with these families how powerful "nuclear family fission" could be, and how directionless and lost so many of the parents and children had become. Without some overarching sense of purpose or meaning, there seemed to be little one could do to save these parents and children from themselves. I began to get the feeling that some other force besides psychological insight—if even that could be achieved—was necessary to achieve change and a modicum of personal well-being for parents and their children.

I sensed this need to grapple with ultimate issues in my individual psychotherapy patients as well, and began asking them to describe to me their religious heritages or the moral belief systems that guided their actions. I was fascinated by the results of this exercise. One woman, Samantha, a gifted writer in her thirties, was a junior in an East Coast college when she received a call from her family in the Midwest. Her father, a fit, active professional, had suffered a heart attack during his morning jog, and she was to come home immediately. Samantha was extremely close to her father, and of course she took the first flight home she could get.

When she arrived, her mother told her the horrible truth. Her father had died. The hospital had already transferred him to the funeral home, and he was to be buried the next day. The funeral was closed-casket. Samantha never saw her father's body. He basically evaporated from her life. She had no way to integrate this experience into her psyche, and by the time I started to see her, she was suffering from what is technically termed "unresolved grief reaction." This kind of loss is so devastating that we can begin to understand the nearly fanatical drive to bring home the remains of soldiers who die on foreign soil, or to recover bodies from natural disasters or airline crashes.

Samantha dreamed of her father on a regular basis. In those dreams he was alive, they talked, then he left, then he would reappear. Questions of life and death plagued her, and even though her family was churchgoing, there was nothing in the conventional liturgy and ritual that could comfort her. Samantha was angry with her father for dying, angry with God for taking him, and angry with herself for not being with him to say good-bye.

These ultimate issues in her life were not being dealt with in a way that had meaning for her. The standard psychodynamic therapy that I offered could not help her with the depth of what can only be called her spiritual pain. Only by exploring Samantha's religious heritage and her personal beliefs about the nature of life and death, and by permitting her the spiritual space in which to experience the existential terror of a loss of this proportion, was I finally able to reach her and help her begin to heal.

Samantha had been a regular member of her religious community before her father died, but now she found little comfort or solace with this group. Her isolation left her feeling alone and friendless. As we focused the treatment on how furious she was with life, with the people she loved and on whom she could no longer depend, and with me for not making the situation better, Samantha began to come out of her aloneness. "Have you given up your relationship with God, now that you have left your church?" I asked one day. "No," she said. "I still feel the presence, but in a different way. God is now just around me all the time." Samantha was able to forgive herself and re-create her spirituality in a personal and comforting way as she wrapped herself in her connection to God. For her, this process incorporated her love for her father and the continuation of his presence as part of an internal reality.

The work I was doing with patients began to influence my teaching as well. My psychotherapy supervisees were amazed by the information and the energy they tapped into when they asked their patients about religious or spiritual issues—even though at first they were a little surprised at my asking whether they had inquired during the initial interviews about their patients' spiritual lives. I explained to my students that most people are very conscious of the beliefs that shape their lives, and are eager to talk about them. I didn't abandon my commitment to my own belief in unconscious motivation, but I felt that by enlarging the scope of my own orientation I had added a new dimension to my comprehension of the psyche of the person who had turned to me for understanding, empathy, and guidance.

As my reading and thinking pressed at the edges of conventional psychological research, the limits of traditional academic psychology were becoming more and more apparent to me. There is, to be sure, a growing interest in matters spiritual on the part of some psychologists. A recent survey of a sampling of members of the American Psychological Association indicated that assessment of the religious backgrounds of patients is considered useful, and some of the respondents commented that they use religious concepts with their patients or even recommend participation in religious activities as part of their therapeutic interventions.[5]

As it is currently taught in universities and practiced in clinics and private offices, however, psychology too often leaves questions of the spirit unaddressed or dismissed. One of the most widely used and respected introductory psychology texts in the country, in its 1999 edition, does not even mention the word *spirituality* or discuss any of the research related to it.[6]

Matters of the spirit must be addressed if a thorough understanding of individual psychology is to be achieved. My students and patients often remind me that transcendent issues of morality press on the consciousness of each of us. Many say that traditional psychological or religious approaches to life's most profound issues are so unfulfilling that they have turned to alternative forms of treatment or healing. Some are drawn to acupuncture, herbal medicine, or meditation. One of my patients recently told me that in addition to his psychotherapy he had visited a "doctor of Oriental medicine" who had prescribed rattlesnake venom to help with his psychological difficulties as well as his rather serious blood disorder. This incident reinforced my view that the mental health community may have little interest in the world of spirituality, but our patients do. It is incumbent on us, therefore, to address this need.

At a personal level, the growth of my first two children and the arrival of two more brought me in touch with the cycles and rhythms of life. I reestablished my ties to institutional religion, though I was reluctant and skeptical at first because of my earlier experiences, but eventually I became more trusting and grateful. I discovered in Lawrence Kushner a remarkable rabbi I could admire and from whom I could learn. His writings on spirituality moved me deeply, and his personal warmth and encouragement to me and my family have added to the impetus to follow my curiosity in this complex—yet simple—world of spirituality.

My research interests in the area of spirituality began to crystallize. I thought I could synthesize my awareness of the suffering of countless individuals, and the work I was doing with my patients to help them incorporate their religious and spiritual beliefs into their personal psychological insight. I began reading more extensively in the area of humanistic (or what has come to be called transpersonal) psychology. I also found myself discussing the limits of reality and speculating on the existence of the astral plane with a deeply mystical artist, my friend Hyman Bloom. Recently I attended a variety of conferences on spirituality and healing, presented by such diverse institutions as the *New Age Journal* and the Harvard Medical School. At these conferences I heard literally thousands of uses of the word *spirituality,* including spiritual healing, spiritual growth and development, spiritual relationships, and the "seven laws of spiritual success."

Everyone I spoke with agreed to talk about spirituality and their spiritual practices, but when I questioned them, few could say what spirituality meant to anyone but themselves. As a social scientist, I was dismayed by the imprecise and potentially dangerous or misleading notions of spirituality that I encountered. I was also intrigued by the complexity and significance of the problem of understanding spirituality. It seemed to me that what was needed was a more thoughtful and objective exploration of spirituality in general.

I began searching for some way to "measure" spirituality— though I realized that such an undertaking might be considered either profane or grandiose. It seemed a natural step to ask the question of definition, seeking a commonality of accepted meaning. When I realized that there existed many measures or questionnaires of specific religious belief, but none that I could find on spirituality itself, I decided to create my own measure of spirituality. The company I founded, PsychoMatrix, was oriented toward education, research, and testing of personality. For the new measure, I decided to use the existing technology of test construction and orient it to the world of spirituality.[7] The result was the PsychoMatrix Spirituality Inventory (PSI).

The creation of the PSI was my first step in studying the mysterious and challenging world of spirituality. With this new measure, I was able to tap into a vein of consciousness that included knowledge and experience on which many people were willing to share their views and discuss their personal beliefs in great detail. Finding the seven spiritual factors described in the introduction to this book encouraged me to continue my research and to find a context to which it could be tied. I believe it is crucial in conducting any research to have a conceptual framework that orients, guides, and ultimately helps explain findings that the research may uncover. Without a theoretical context, these findings are often difficult to understand or to generalize beyond what may have been an accidental positive or interesting result. I had developed a new tool for investigating a highly complex and multifaceted phenomenon that, with the help of my participants, I was calling spirituality.

There were now more new and exciting questions to be answered than I had started with. Where does this spiritual knowledge come from? Is it learnable? Does everyone have it, or is it relegated to only a few particularly constituted individuals? How does spiritual knowledge relate to other kinds of knowledge? Other knowledge we usually categorize under the rubric of some kind of intelligence or intellectual functioning of the mind. I wondered, was it possible that the knowledge and experience of spiritual events could be understood as a kind of intelligence in its own right? To address these and other questions, it is necessary for us to review and examine existing theories of intelligence in order to determine whether spiritual knowledge fits in with any established conceptions of intelligence, or whether spirituality may require a paradigm of knowledge all its own.

CHAPTER THREE

Intelligence

Theories of intelligence have served as cornerstones of psychological science since the nineteenth century. A brief overview of the development and elaboration of these theories can help us understand what place, if any, the knowledge and experience of spiritual events have in the pantheon of intelligences that currently exists. If, as I have proposed, spiritual intelligence is an intelligence in its own right, then understanding this phenomenon is possible only in the context of a conceptual framework that encompasses other intelligences and ways of knowing the internal and external world. In this chapter we will examine some of the defining characteristics of intelligence in general, so that we can see how spiritual intelligence differs from, or builds upon, the theoretical models of intelligence proposed by others. For this purpose, the most relevant theorists of intelligence are Howard Gardner, who proposes eight separate and unique intelligences (and recently another "half" of an intelligence, which, as we shall see, is crucial to our discussion)[1] and Jack Mayer, Peter Solovey, David Caruso, and Daniel Goleman, who conduct research on and write extensively about the concept of emotional intelligence.[2]

Over three-quarters of a century ago, an assemblage of educational psychologists participated in a symposium on the nature of intelligence.[3] At that time there was controversy with regard to the existence of a general intelligence capacity, *g,* which could be measured and used for comparison among individuals. IQ tests, originally developed by Alfred Binet, were used to predict academic performance, and specifically to assist in the remediation of those children who fell short in their abilities. In Binet's words, *"après le mal, le remede"* (after the illness, the remedy follows).[4]

Sixty-five years later, in 1986, developmental psychologists Robert Sternberg from Yale and Douglas Detterman from Case Western Reserve University repeated a symposium on the nature of intelligence, noting that while the 1921 symposium had focused on psychometric issues—the measurement of intelligence—the latter concentrated on information processing, cultural context, and their interrelationships.[5] The current application of the theory of intelligence began in 1870 with Francis Galton, to measure a hypothesized innate capacity called general intelligence. Today psychologists and educators focus on the processes by which people understand their worlds, how they manage the myriad cognitive and emotional tasks that we associate with "intelligent" behavior, and how the culture in which they live can actually dictate what is considered intelligent behavior.

If I live in the United States, for example, it is very important, culturally, socially, and professionally, to be seen as one of the "best"—in my social class, in my age group. Anything that I can do to show myself in a good light will be helpful and rewarding.

To be average is the kiss of death. Standing out indicates a high level of intelligence. If, on the other hand, I am Dutch and living in Amsterdam, the last thing I would ever want, socially, academically, or professionally, is to be seen as trying to achieve status by advancing my talents and abilities. To be average is a socially desirable goal; to be aggressive and self-promoting is regarded with severe social censure. Intelligence is therefore not only the capacity to solve word problems on standardized intelligence tests, but is also the ability to read and respond correctly to social cues and expectations. In some cultures, for example, visual-spatial abilities may be more highly developed than verbal strategies. Time allocation and "management," a highly prized skill in industrialized culture, can have a very different value—even a negative one—in rural or less "developed" cultures.

The many years of research and theorizing about intelligence and its existence as a singular innate capacity, its modifiability, its function in human behavior, its relevance to a successful life, its capacity for multiplication into a variety of intelligences—even its location in the brain—have generated more controversy than resolution. Accusations of racism accompany claims for the innate nature of intelligence, which allegedly accounts for some populations to be genetically driven to lower social status. Proposals for the multiplicity of intelligences have been labeled a mere collection of talents, not intelligences. The once immutable "aptitude" that was measured by the Scholastic Aptitude Tests (now termed the Scholastic Assessment Test, a name change attributable to the misuse and misapplication of the aptitude concept) can now be easily elevated with training and the help of preparation counselors.[6]

In spite of theoretical disagreements, however, we do currently find significant advances in understanding mental functioning in the areas of cognitive development, information processing, localization of cognitive difficulties or abnormalities, and understanding of the transmission of cultural knowledge. Neurological evidence suggests specific functions of separate areas of the brain for a variety of cognitive processes. Traditional views of intelligence that defined this elusive force primarily in terms of analytic and verbal reasoning abilities now include other abilities, both physical and emotional. It is now accepted that the concept of a general factor of intelligence has been replaced by the reality that there are many ways of being intelligent—even if some theorists do still wish to collect all smart, clever, insightful, and creative mental activity under one name.

Intelligence theory, according to Robert Sternberg, can be conceived of as a series of basic "metaphors of mind" that have guided and continue to guide research and speculation about how we know what we know, and how we think about and experience our world.

> . . . research into the nature of intelligence is a scientific endeavor which is guided by a somewhat motley collection of models or metaphors. Each metaphor generates a series of questions about intelligence, which the theories and research seek to address.[7]

Examining these metaphors will make comprehension of spiritual intelligence easier. We also thereby pay homage to the various schools of thought that have guided intelligence research and theory for over a hundred years.

The "geographic" metaphor, one of the earliest conceptions, addresses such questions as "What form does a map of the mind take?" This metaphor presents a static model, seeking to describe intelligence as certain primary mental abilities that account for individual differences; and it asks how well each of the factors of intelligence can predict such outcomes as grades in school. This view is most readily associated with psychologists who wrote early works on the nature of intelligence, like Spearman, Thurstone, Guilford, and Cattell.

Sternberg's "computational" metaphor addresses this question: "What are the information processing routines (programs) underlying intelligent thought?" His metaphor analogizes the mind to the workings of a computer, and looks for the process (as opposed to the static geographic model) by which information is encoded, stored, or retrieved. Instead of differences, this metaphor focuses on similarities between people and commonalities of data management. Computational thinking might, for example, focus on the way in which stimuli such as sights and sounds or events are encoded into memories.

The "biological" metaphor inquires, "How do the anatomy and physiology of the brain and the central nervous system account for intelligent thought?" This metaphor describes speed of information processing and localization of function in the brain. Recent research on the lateralization of thought, thinking with the left brain and feeling with the right brain, falls into this category.

A fascinating series of experiments, demonstrating the biological metaphor, was reported by Roger Sperry, Michael Gazzaniga, and others in which the brain is literally cut in half by severing the corpus callosum, the bundle of nerve fibers that connects the left and right hemispheres of the brain.[8] This surgery was performed in order to try to diminish severe seizure activity in epileptic patients. When these patients were examined with psychological testing, it was clear that each half of the brain could exhibit its own knowledge, but in different modalities. The left hemisphere is known for its ability to process analytically, whereas the right brain processes information holistically. In some experiments with "split brain" patients, the left hand literally fought with the right hand in trying to accomplish simple tasks, such as putting on a pair of pants. Levy, Jensen, and

Eysenck are the psychologists most known for their work under the umbrella of this metaphor.

The noted Swiss psychologist Jean Piaget emphasized the genetic or developmental unfolding, through stages, of the human capacity for knowledge of the self and the world. Piaget uses an epistemological metaphor to underscore his well-known hierarchical theory. This metaphor asks, "What are the structures of the mind through which knowledge and mental processes are organized, and how do they develop over time?" Piaget's view of intelligence emphasizes an equilibration of information processing. The mind absorbs new information with a dynamic between *assimilation* (taking in new data) and *accommodation* (adjusting, through comparison, existing mental structures to the new information). For example, a young child cannot comprehend that a given amount of milk in a tall, skinny container is the same as that in a short but wide container. As the child's mind matures and she proceeds through the next stage of development, she can "understand" that the amount of milk is the same in both containers.[9]

The mechanism of influence of the external world on the internal world of the individual is the substance of the "sociological" metaphor, and has been highlighted by Vigotsky and Feuerstein. Children in different social groups, for example, have different conceptions of intelligence depending on their families, their peer groups, and their experience with the public educational system. A classic study of social perception and its relation to knowledge and visual perception is one in which children from poor neighborhoods were compared with children from affluent neighborhoods and asked to draw the physical size of U.S. coins—nickels, dimes and quarters. The drawings of children from the disadvantaged social class consistently drew coins that were larger than those drawn by the advantaged group.

Finally, in an attempt to create an overall synthetic view, Sternberg and Gardner have each adopted the "systems" metaphor, which asks, "How can we understand the mind as a system in a way that crosscuts all the other metaphors?" This meta-metaphor features the interaction of multiple systems of intelligence, and also addresses the establishment of multiple intelligences. Sternberg proposes his own "triarchic" model that views intelligence as a series of progressively higher-order executive mental functions, a kind of mental government with different levels of organizing systems.

Gardner, however, proposes a radical reformulation of intelligence. His metaphor is that intelligence is neither a unitary function that we can measure with a simple metric, or traditional, intelligence test, nor is it a hierarchical arrangement of mental functions. Gardner views intelligence as a collection of multiple intelligences, each associated with distinct abilities, each capable of performing a unique set of functions. Gardner postulates eight (and a half) relatively autonomous intelligences, each operating in different spheres of life. In this paradigm, he defines intelligence as "the ability to solve problems and fashion products that are of consequence in a particular cultural setting or community."[10]

Gardner has been criticized by some psychologists, including Sternberg, who claim that his theory of multiple intelligences is really a theory of multiple abilities or talents. I believe, however, that Gardner's view takes us to a new understanding of the concept of intelligence and, in fact, reflects more accurately the variety of ways that people have of being smart in the world. I will present Gardner's ideas in more detail so that we can be familiar with the various intelligences he postulates, because I think spiritual intelligence is also a separate intelligence that qualifies for recognition in its own right.

As noted on page 59, Gardner describes eight and a half independent intelligences and their concomitant real-world applications:

1. linguistic intelligence (that of poets, journalists, advertising copywriters, and lawyers);

2. musical intelligence (that of composers, conductors, and instrumentalists, as well as acousticians and audio engineers);

3. logical-mathematical intelligence (that of mathematicians and computer scientists);

4. spatial intelligence (that of architects, geographers, surgeons, and navigators);

5. bodily-kinesthetic intelligence (that of dancers and rock climbers, athletes and jugglers);

6. interpersonal intelligence (that of therapists, parents, and dedicated teachers);

7. intrapersonal intelligence (that of people with keen introspective skills; this intelligence may act as a "central intelligence agency," enabling individuals to know their own abilities and perceive how best to use them);

8. naturalist intelligence (that of biologists, ecologists, and taxonomists);

$8\frac{1}{2}$. existential intelligence (concern with cosmological and ultimate questions of life and death).

Gardner also notes the importance of understanding that intelligences operate in combination, and that individuals are distinguished by their individual and particular "profiles of intelligences." Each profile features its own "unique combination of relatively stronger and weaker intelligences which individuals use to solve problems or fashion products."[11]

As we shall see, the idea of a profile of intelligences is also important in understanding spiritual intelligence. The profile or pattern of spiritual behavior and experience that each individual possesses is important in defining the hallmark of that person's own way of being spiritual in the world.

The description of an individual's spiritual profile is similar to the descriptions used by psychologists to describe individual differences in personality. To be sure, each of us has a personality. But is it better to be an extrovert or an introvert? The question makes no sense, because we realize that each of us is different, and that the patterns with which our personalities are shaped are unique. Whether it is preferable to have one personality pattern or another is more a function of context in which that pattern will be active than a function of absolute standards claiming that one type of personality is superior to another. The same approach applies to spiritual intelligence. Rather than ranking spirituality on a scale that evaluates individual approaches to spiritual dimensions of life, we will use the seven spiritual dimensions and their interactions to describe the characteristic way in which each of us construes his or her spiritual approach to life.

The distinction between evaluation and description of spirituality is critical. Some intelligence theorists claim that one of the defining criteria of an intelligence is its amenability to the psychometric method, the method of measurement from high to low, from less to more. For some intelligences, such as the mathematical or linguistic, the right answer is *the* right answer; that is, a math problem has an accurate solution, and a vocabulary word has a correct definition. It follows, therefore, that the psychometric approach makes sense in assessing the strength of these intelligences. For other intelligences, the matter is not so clear. How do we "measure" musical intelligence or bodily intelligence? Gardner suggests that we use performance criteria. In other words, the demonstration of musical intelligence would be to sing a song or write a melody; of bodily intelligence, to learn a dance step, or to throw strikes over home plate.

Research on spiritual intelligence is young. In addition, spiritual intelligence may never yield to the kind of psychometric approach reserved for a small number of the intelligences. It is my opinion, therefore, that the best we can do in terms of criteria for evaluation of spiritual intelligence is to document the manifestations of this intelligence, and make no claim that someone is high on spiritual intelligence, implying superior performance, while someone else is low, implying inferior performance.

There is a danger in regarding any individual's spiritual intelligence as low or inferior. This problem can best be illustrated when we think of "primitive" cultures and "underdeveloped" groups of people. When we speak of primitive cultures and thereby conclude that the individuals in those cultures are less intelligent, or less spiritually intelligent (no matter what definition of intelligence we are using), we make the mistake of assuming that the experience of the sacred can be quantified in the same fashion as getting the right answer to a series of math problems, which can be rank-ordered from top to bottom. In this context the notion of primitive cultures is often a veiled but pejorative way of condemning other forms of mental activity and preference. It takes little effort to realize that there can be no culture less intelligent and more primitive in its cruel and prejudicial moments than our own.

Theories of intelligence can easily become value-laden, particularly with regard to the notion of industrial, technological, highly developed cultures versus agrarian, nomadic, or tribal "underdeveloped" cultures. What is valuable and intelligent in one culture may be an obstruction in another. Similarly, when we think of spiritual intelligence, the idea that high scores on a particular factor are good or signify a high level of development, while low scores are indicative of low or undeveloped spiritual intelligence, is simply incorrect. I believe that the best we can hope for in the process of defining and articulating spiritual intelligence is the description of individual, personal spiritual behavior and experience, rather than an evaluative ranking of scores from good to bad.

Emotional Intelligence

T HE RECENT popularity of the concept of emotional intelligence is an indication of how ready the academic, educational, and lay communities are to receive a concept that reflects subjective and immediate personal experience in a broader context than traditional—or even improved—views of intelligence. To use emotions in an intelligent way, and to discuss feelings as an important and meaningful part of mental states, has an instant appeal. If, for example, you are depressed, your thinking is most likely not as clear as usual. Emotions are therefore also included in the realm of mental dexterity and problem solving. This view is consistent with conventional wisdom, because everyone somehow intuits that there must be more to the ability to live well in the world than is thought of in the psychology or philosophy of the analytic mind.

Research on emotional intelligence has been active for some time, and is documented in the work of Jack Mayer, Peter Salovey, and David Caruso.[12] Research and analysis of emotional intelligence is also well described in Daniel Goleman's popular work of the same name.[13] Like Gardner and Sternberg, these researchers and theorists of intelligence have developed their own metaphors and standards by which they consider a mental activity as having achieved the status of an intelligence. An intelligence, according to Mayer and his coauthors, must "meet stringent criteria in order to be judged as a true intelligence." That is:

1. An intelligence must reflect performance rather than simply preferred ways of behaving, self-esteem, or other non-intellectual attainments.

2. An intelligence should describe a set of closely related abilities that are similar to, but distinct from, mental abilities described by already established intelligences.

3. An intelligence should develop with age and experience, typically increasing from childhood through roughly middle adulthood.[14]

In other words, every theorist of intelligence has certain criteria by which the authenticity of that intelligence is judged. In the case of emotional intelligence, Mayer et al. claim that in order to qualify for membership in the intelligence world, any new intelligence must meet the standard of being a set of abilities, reflected in performance. These abilities should interrelate with each other in a way that is different from any other known intelligence. Further, to qualify as a true intelligence, this mental process must grow and develop over the life span of the individual.

Some theorists, like Gardner, also require that an intelligence be neurologically distinct from all other intelligences in order to qualify as a separate form of intelligence; it should be related to a specific brain function in a specific part of the brain. Mayer et al., though, make no claim for this neurological condition to be met for emotional intelligence.

Daniel Goleman finds a middle ground. He does not use underlying neurological structures to bolster his argument for the existence of emotional intelligence. Rather, he accepts the existence of emotional intelligence and focuses his presentation on what he considers to be the neurological center of emotion and emotional intelligence, the amygdala. "If you are feeling overwhelmed with emotion," said

Goleman in his recent public television lecture on emotional intelligence, "it's just your amygdala working extra hard."[15]

The amygdala, an almond-shaped structure located deep in the brain, creates the first "instinctive" response to external stimuli: flight or fight, emotional flooding or emotional calm. These immediate and survival-based responses occur well before parallel sensory information has passed through the thalamus (the major information-switching center in the brain) to higher-order cerebral cortex structures in the brain. In other words, any sensation—say, of terror or passion—gets processed by the *entire* brain. Some of the sensory inputs pass through the amygdala and get an instantaneous response from the organism—stay or run, explode or remain calm. The rest of the sensory inputs are passed on to the "higher" brain centers (the cortex) where they can be interpreted more slowly and carefully, before they are acted upon. The cortex is the seat of intellectual and abstract reasoning functions that can reflect on and find meaning in this sensory input, from the mildest and most pleasant emotional arousal to the overwhelming flood of intensity of traumatic experience.

Emotional intelligence, therefore, requires two processes: first, a person must be able to respond to the instantaneous arousal that is a result of the activity of the amygdala; second, this person, within a short period of "reflection" time, must also assess the meaning and quality of his or her emotional response, and act on that understanding in an adaptive fashion. Let's say that a man sees a former lover for whom he still has strong and unresolved feelings. The emotionally intelligent response might be to greet the person and ask about her life, but not refer back to the former relationship unless there are cues that such a discussion would be welcome or appropriate. He might say, "Hello, how are you? How long has it been? Three years? I understand you are married and have a new job." If, however, he also responded to the flood of emotion that surrounds his seeing her and the memories that were released, he might blurt out something very different, such as, "It's great to see you, but it really hurts. I can't believe you got married and changed jobs after all that we meant to each other and went through together!" This response to the powerful emotional stimulus is not better or worse than the first response; it does not come from a lower part of the brain or a more primitive center of thought. The strongly emotional response is a result of the balance of forces in the entire, fully functioning brain.

The dangerous idea of higher versus lower, superior versus inferior, advanced versus backward has made its way to the discussion of brain function at the neurological level, just as we have seen happen at the societal or intellectual level. Goleman, for example, in his discussion of emotional intelligence, quotes neuroscientist Joseph LeDoux about the "emotional" brain, with specific focus on the amygdala as the center of emotions, and then uses the concept of the "primitive limbic system." (The limbic system is a group of structures deep in the brain, including the amygdala, that have been associated with emotion and memory.)

LeDoux, however, considers the idea of the limbic system to be an outmoded theoretical construct, and shows that with the recent advances in neurological understanding, such a system really doesn't exist. In his discussion, LeDoux calls into question the very notion of "higher" and "lower" brain function: "It's an outmoded concept—more poetic than scientific, because the brain structures that form various subsystems or focal centers are distributed throughout the brain."[16]

Once again, the notion of "higher" and "lower" mental functioning creeps into the discussion of intelligence. In this case, the idea of more primitive brain centers has been shown to be a misunderstanding of the way the brain works. In fact, significant information processing and editing occurs at every level of sensory input into our brains.

For example, the eye, specifically the retina, does not deliver to the brain every sensation of light and shape that falls on it. Quite the contrary: the retina edits the information passed through the optic nerve to the occipital lobe for interpretation. The Harvard University neuroscientist David Hubel describes the function of retinal cells and cells in general: "The job of a nerve cell is to take in information from the cells that feed into it, to sum up and integrate that information and to deliver the integrated information to other cells."[17]

Do we say, then, that the eye has its own intelligence? In terms of information processing, one could make the case for a kind of sensory intelligence. To the extent that intelligence requires a subjectivity, a consciousness, then of course the answer is no. Neither the eye nor any other sensory organ has intelligence in the sense that we are using the term. To call the information processing "primitive," however, does violence to the sophistication of our capacity for interaction with the world.

As LeDoux notes, the various subsystems that make up the totality of mental functioning are distributed throughout the brain. Neural cell "processes" are stringlike portions of nerve cells that can be up to three feet long and intersect with each other in billions of interconnections throughout the human brain. These nerve projections reach from the amygdala (deeply embedded in the brain) to the neocortex (areas near the surface). Even though some areas of the brain may be developmentally antecedent because they develop with the growing child, it does not follow that they are therefore more primitive and "lower" in function.

The terms *primitive* and *lower* are, as I have indicated, loaded with cultural and pseudoscientific power. Some of the forms of intelligence that are valued in a society, such as analytic or linguistic intelligence, risk invoking discrimination (racial, cultural, or social) based on a false assumption. For example, since we admit students to selective colleges based on specific forms of intelligence, and since society's doors open most easily to the graduates of those institutions, then we have labeled one intelligence as higher than, or superior to, or more advanced than, another. My focus here on the way in which the brain processes information is meant to show that the notions of "higher" and "lower" really have no meaning except in socially valued terms. Intelligence takes place in all parts of the brain. Modern imaging techniques such as functional MRI demonstrate that the centers of the brain associated with the tasks of thinking and perception are distributed throughout, and are also localized into centers of activity, thereby suggesting that the brain is created in the form of "modules" that pass information from one to another, but not in a hierarchical fashion.

While it is true, for example, that some sites in the brain are associated with such phenomena as vision or language, the brain is also amazingly flexible and plastic. Our brains process aspects of information in a wide number of areas that somehow manage to interconnect and coordinate with one another in order to produce a coherent thought or clear vision. The notion, however, that some knowledge occurs in the (nonexistent) primitive limbic system while other knowledge resides in the higher centers is, according to current research, simply incorrect. My point is that emotional intelligence, for example, is not "lower" in status because it involves deep brain structures. This view also means that verbal and analytic intelligence is not "higher" because it involves the cerebral cortex. The truth is that knowledge occurs all over the brain all the time, producing a variety of ways of knowing about the world that we call intelligences. This approach is particularly important because it prevents the minimizing or trivializing of forms of knowing that have traditionally sustained and given meaning to life, such as music, art, and spirituality.

Problem Solving and Intelligence

G OLEMAN and the other theorists of emotional intelligence take a highly instrumental position with regard to the concept of emotional intelligence. Emotional intelligence, in their terms, becomes a set of abilities or skills. The "ability" to discern the emotion on faces in a series of photos, or the "ability" to discuss emotion, etc., constitutes a similar managerial view. Emotional intelligence, musical intelligence, visual spatial intelligence, bodily-kinesthetic intelligence, and even spiritual intelligence all have dimensions of problem solving associated with them. What is the best way to handle my anger? How should I express my feelings of love? What is the most graceful dance step? How can I feel closer to the Divine Energy Source? How do I make this melody sound pleasant? Those are problems that these intelligences might address. The abilities to solve such problems are also included in the concept of intelligence.

I agree with Gardner, the neurologist Antonio Damasio, and other speculators on consciousness that no one quite knows how the problem-solving process works.[18] With regard to the sequence in logical-mathematical intelligence:

First, in the gifted individual, the process of problem solving is often remarkably rapid . . . and underscores the non-verbal nature of the intelligence. A solution to a problem can be constructed before it is articulated. Along with the companion skill of language, logical-mathematical reasoning provides the principal basis for IQ tests. This form of intelligence . . . is the archetype of "raw intelligence," or the problem-solving faculty that purportedly cuts across domains. It is perhaps ironic, then, that the actual mechanism by which one arrives at a solution to a logical-mathematical problem is not as yet properly understood.[19]

Thinking of the intelligences in terms of problem solving, some well-known and beloved problem-solving scenarios come to mind: the scene in the play *Amadeus* in which Mozart sits down to play the march that the established but relatively unimaginative court composer, Salieri, has written for Mozart's arrival at court. The piece sounds "dull"—or maybe just average—to the listener, until Mozart, with a few shifts and transformations, says, "That didn't quite work, did it? There, that's better," and produces the clear, sparkling *Non So Piu* aria from *The Marriage of Figaro*. Similarly, the San Francisco 49ers' quarterback Joe Montana "finding" wide receiver Jerry Rice in the end zone with a perfect pinpoint pass, by "threading the needle" through twenty other massive bodies scattered over the field between them; and Yo-Yo Ma changing his bowing technique so he could "fiddle" with Marc O'Connor and Edger Mayer to the jazz/bluegrass/Celtic rhythm-derived tunes that O'Connor had written, are all examples of creative problem solving using different forms of intelligence.[20]

The mechanism for creative problem solving in these situations, or even of empathically understanding someone's emotional state as a function of emotional intelligence, is also not well understood. The problem-solving dimensions of spiritual intelligence are best exemplified in facing a moral dilemma, and these processes are equally complicated. Using spiritual intelligence to solve spiritual or moral problems must include basic intelligences plus an intelligence of a qualitatively different kind, because a moral dilemma not only invokes all the problem-solving skills of traditional intelligences; it also requires another level of understanding that includes empathy and an awareness of the larger context of personal interconnection.

Acquisition of Intelligent Abilities

THE DEMONSTRATION of the mental abilities that are crucial to Gardner's basic eight and one-half intelligences, or to emotional intelligence or spiritual intelligence, raises the question of the acquisition of those abilities. Do they appear as a result of inborn traits, or are the abilities the consequence of training? If they are inborn traits, then it could be surmised that some of us have them, and some of us just don't. Often the scholastic debate of nature versus nurture concludes that we all obviously have both nature and nurture influencing our abilities, so therefore the answer must be a mixture of the two. While it will be more useful to focus on the abilities themselves, it is worth considering some of the current theories of origin, because if the abilities associated with intelligence of any kind, or spiritual intelligence in particular, are primarily inborn and immutable, then change can only occur at the cellular or evolutionary level, and the idea of self-perfection or improvement is irrelevant.

The increase of mental abilities has been the focus of recent research on the copying of a mouse gene that is coded for a protein that can facilitate communication between neurons. One popular theory of memory bases its view on the organism's ability to make associations between events like the loss of a loved one and the feeling of sadness. Consequently, if the speed of association can be genetically increased (in this case with mice, but we assume that eventually it can be applied to humans), then mental processing power can be increased and we have a gene for making organisms "smarter."

Intelligence, however, is the result of the complex interaction of a series of genes with an ever-changing environment. To think that there could be a gene for intelligence is to oversimplify, to the point of distortion, the genetic basis of behavior. We are not merely the sum of our genes. The organizing principle that coordinates and directs the development of an organism—a person— from genetic building blocks is not reducible to the genes themselves, any more than the meaning of a poem can be reduced to the number and frequency of the letters with which it is written, or the beauty of a string quartet can be revealed by listing the notes. Even a behavioral genetics adherent like David Lykken at the University of Minnesota states clearly that it is "extremely unlikely that there is a 'poetry gene' or 'music gene,' since complex human behaviors typically have a polygenic basis." It would be equally difficult, then, to postulate an emotional intelligence gene or an emotionality gene.

Because there is so much controversy on the question of innate versus learned behavior, however, it is worth examining in some detail the various philosophical positions that have been associated with these claims, particularly with regard to intelligence. Intelligence can best be defined in terms not only of abilities, but also of traits and skills—some learned and some not. Clearly, Gardner was thinking in terms of inborn traits with regard to multiple intelligences, as were Sternberg and Smith in their work with social intelligence. Goleman alluded to biologically based "givens" when he looked at empathy, but he also acknowledges that empathy can be modeled on how a child is disciplined. When a father says to his child, "Look how you made your friend feel," he is teaching empathy by helping the child focus on the other person.

This behavior is learned through the observation of the behavior of parents, siblings, and peers, and is a crucial part of the socialization process.

The question of the origin of the abilities and traits that are part of intelligence is the subject of lively debate between evolutionary psychologists and other evolutionary theorists. The nature of these abilities is important in understanding the intelligences mentioned so far, and informs the understanding of spiritual intelligence as well.

Current debate exists on the issue of the heritability not only of intelligence, but also of morality and religiousness. This debate is aggressively contested between two basic positions: evolutionary psychologists argue that human behavior is determined by the (inherited) purposeful and adaptational nature of the evolutionary process, while pluralists maintain the belief in the powerful force of the laws of natural selection as articulated by Charles Darwin. The pluralists also claim there is much in the human condition and repertoire of behavior that arrived by accident, the meaning and purpose of which is understandable by design only after the fact.[21]

In other words, there is lack of agreement about (a) whether any mental capacity like intelligence can be inherited in the first place; and (b) even if one can demonstrate inherited characteristics throughout historical or even prehistorical development, there is no *a priori* reason to suppose that these characteristics were installed in human beings by purposeful design, nor can reverse engineering reveal original intention. (Reverse engineering implies that abilities and capacities that we have as humans were either placed there by a designing mind, often attributed to God, or that these human features evolved in an adaptive way in order that— note the intentional and purposeful language—our genetic material would survive. For example, because we see with our eyes and hear with our ears, those organs must have evolved in order that we be able to see and hear.)

Evolutionary psychologists (and sociobiologists) postulate that what we do, how we think, and how we perceive the world have been shaped by the adaptive forces of natural selection, which gives a survival purpose and meaning to human activity. Those who adapt well survive; those who don't perish.[22] Our capacities to live in the world are developed with an adaptation in mind, an adaptation that serves the end of preserving the reproductive capacity of the species. We have eyes to see with, feet to walk with, brains to think with—and ever more complex brains to think ever more complex thoughts. As the sociobiologist E. O. Wilson has suggested, if we have moral or religious inclinations, there must be a survival value to that way of experiencing the world as well.

On the opposite side, Steven Jay Gould, in his attack on the sociobiologists and evolutionary psychologists, promotes the notion that while there can be no question that evolution has shaped, through natural selection, many adaptive features of human thought and activity, there cannot be read into every act some survival purpose that results from adaptive design. Many human and animal features exist by accident, Gould argues, and, therefore cannot be ascribed to some overarching adaptive purpose. The giraffe's long neck is an excellent example of the serendipitous nature of some aspects of evolution, says Gould, insofar as its original function may well have been to enhance survival through combat with other animals, and only later did it become associated with treetop grazing: "Reasons for origins must not be confused with alterations for later use."

From the viewpoint of the Lamarckian notion of evolution, in which one generation or two (compared to the hundreds of generations required for adaptive change in the Darwinian view) can directly influence the subsequent generation, a giraffe's long neck evolved *in order to* treetop graze, and this feature gets quickly transmitted to the next generation. Gould argues that while some *cultural* evolution of values and attitudes may be transmitted in this high-speed adaptive fashion, many fundamental human characteristics like subjective consciousness, or behavior such as sexuality, aggression, morality, and religious feeling cannot change so quickly. While these human abilities may currently have adaptive features, humans may have developed these useful and meaningful features accidentally and not by some preexisting design or some purposeful "in order to" motivation that would explain sudden changes in species.

For example, Gould and the evolutionary biologist Richard Lewontin liken the development of the conscious awareness of mortality to a spandrel, an architectural artifact that is "left over" in the execution of the original design, like the space between an arch and the corner in which it sits. They speculate that this subjective feature of mind may have developed in the human brain as an unintended consequence of the design attributable to natural selection.

> I don't see how a biologist could argue that the human brain evolved consciousness in order to teach us that we must die. Knowledge of death is therefore probably a spandrel—an ineluctable consequence of consciousness evolved for other reasons. But this spandrel may then have inspired one of our defining institutions [i.e., religion].[23]

This argument is aimed directly at the sociobiologists and evolutionary psychologists. Such reasoning is also, of course, anathema to the religious and theological thinking that sees design in nature as the handiwork of God or some purposeful designer of the universe. In the world of religious belief, adaptational features whose survival value for the existence of humankind may not be apparent are readily explained on the basis of faith.

But what of the evolutionary psychologists? Steven Pinker, professor of linguistics at MIT, and a leading proponent of the evolutionary psychologists' position, claims that of course evolutionary psychologists are pluralists, seeing more than one possible outcome of design. His view is also coupled with the notion of adaptationism—the view that the complexity of what has evolved in human experience has evolved for good reason:

> . . . the brain, like the eyes and the feet, shows signs of good design. The adaptive problems it solves, such as perceiving depth and color, grasping, walking, reasoning, communicating, avoiding hazards, recognizing people and their mental states, and juggling competing demands in real time are among the most challenging engineering tasks ever stated, far beyond the capacity of foreseeable robots and computers.[24]

Yet I think that the evolutionary psychologists' hope of explaining human behavior in terms of the "reverse engineering" of adaptive function fails to elucidate either original purpose (who can know the mind of God or the secret soul of natural selection?); or the usefulness of apparently useless (in terms of reproduction of the species) cultural artifacts and activities like Beethoven's Ninth Symphony, Rembrandt's self-portraits, Bach's Unaccompanied Cello Suites, or Michelangelo's *Pietá*.

By their exclusive reliance on adaptation (pluralistic protestations to the contrary), evolutionary psychologists have actually postulated the philosophical equivalent of a theological explanatory system, with the traditional deity or God figure replaced by the sanctification of the theory of natural selection. This point of view is traditionally known as the argument by design for the existence of God—or, better, the "physico-theological proof" (of the existence of God). The philosopher Immanuel Kant, in his *Critique of Pure Reason,* articulated eighteenth-century concepts that sound prophetically contemporary:

> In the world we everywhere find clear signs of an order in accordance with a determinate purpose, carried out with great wisdom; and this is a universe which is indescribably varied in content and unlimited in extent.[25]

If human behavior can be construed in terms of its adaptational "survival value," of a drive toward genetic replication, then many strange (and seemingly immoral or unacceptable) acts of insensitivity, even cruelty, can be easily explained. Pinker's rationale for extramarital sexual behavior is a typical case in point. He basically states that men's pursuit of young women outside of marriage is simply the expression of the evolutionary force from within trying to express itself in the desire to preserve genetic material, and is a function of the same unconscious and evolutionary force that drives males of all the species. Reading the most basic texts of psychopathology or treating a patient with sexual difficulties, however, immediately suggests that this kind of behavior is better explained by psychodynamic psychology than evolutionary psychology.

Other forms of behavior have also been subjected to an evolutionary psychological hypothesis. But it is untenable as well as horrifying to suppose that the recent ethnic cleansing (is there any more twisted term?) program in Yugoslavia be understood as an adaptive evolutionary response. From a purely objective point of view, it might be argued that the evolutionary drive to propagate one's own genetic heritage for future survival somehow justifies this program of predatory and hate-filled rape and butchery. From a moral, humanitarian, compassionate, or spiritual perspective, however, such thoughts are unconscionable. I can only ask, did we learn nothing from the struggle with the Third Reich?

Gould rightly points out that the strictly adaptational—I would add instrumental—view of the evolutionary psychologists tries to explain "everything" and therefore becomes superficial in its application. I am reminded of a children's book that formed the basis of my master's thesis, Maurice Sendak's *A Hole Is to Dig,* in which the world is defined for the small (and developmentally immature) child strictly in terms of function, use, or instrumentality: "Arms are to hug with; lips are to kiss with." This view of the world sounds like evolutionary psychology in terms of its functionality and limited scope. When we apply this utilitarian precept to many of life's most sacred, precious moments, we come up empty-handed. Under this scheme, what is the usefulness or adaptive value of a poem or a string quartet? There is none. This unmechanical, nontechnological view of the world demonstrates by example the convoluted logic endemic in evolutionary psychological thinking.

A more informative and thoughtful approach is suggested by Lewontin, who makes it clear that an understanding of evolution must include the notion that genetic "blueprints" (that seventeenth-century homunculus that is now stored in the DNA of our cells) only work in constant interaction with their environment. In fact, says Lewontin, the basic biological principle is that we create our own environments rather than developmentally unfold into the environment; or find some "niche" in the environment into which we evolutionarily fit.

It is the biology, indeed the genes, of an organism that determine its effective environment, by establishing the way in which external physical signals become incorporated into its reactions. The common external phenomena of the physical and biotic world pass through a transforming filter created by the peculiar biology of each species, and it is the output of this transformation that reaches the organism and is relevant to it.[26]

In my opinion, the nature of human experience quickly transcends the explanatory power of evolutionary psychological theory because the most meaningful dimensions of life cannot be reduced to utility or adaptive function. The ongoing interaction between brain/mind and environment engaged in the dynamic of the creation of meaning, itself a uniquely human act of symbolic process, is useful, to be sure. This usefulness, however, can only be construed to have been engineered for genetic survival purposes through the largest of intellectual stretches.

To say that some things, events, or experiences are meaningful in and of themselves, without reference to utility or instrumental function, is to reaffirm the human experience of truth, beauty, and spirit—that which makes life worth living. We are greater than the sum of our mental "modules," as Pinker describes our brains, which are analogous to computers whose purpose is to process extremely complex information. Information-processing machines (computers) do not have a subjective experience of joy, love, or pleasure. To reduce the mind to this limited dimension simply contradicts the reported observations and understanding of a large segment of earth's population.

My own view of the abilities associated with intelligence and with intelligent behavior is that these abilities are in fact the result of the complex interaction of genes and experience in an environment. These abilities should be correlated with one another, and with preexisting theories of intelligence, and should also demonstrate unique fluctuations in specific and precisely defined settings. For example, the ability to solve a mathematical problem should correlate with the ability to solve an analogy problem, and be connected to a theory of analytical and linguistic intelligence. The ability to recognize the emotional state of your mother should correlate with how well you get along with other people in your class or organization. While it is true that abilities appear to be the most "measurable" way in which to describe intelligences, the theorists that we have examined also include other facets of mental and physical expression as properly belonging to the overall construct of intelligence. These traits include personality characteristics such as extroversion, athletic talent, and artistic giftedness in dance, painting, or music. Traits are not abilities, but reflect a state of being in the world that can be discerned in the particularity of each one of us.

The inclusion of traits as part of intelligence, along with multiple intelligences themselves, make traditional measurement of any intelligence problematic. Because the measurement of these intelligences cannot be reduced to the right and wrong answers reserved for mathematical and linguistic intelligences, it is important to remember that the judgment of whether an individual is using his or her intelligence well is quite subjective. How often have we heard a statement like "The critics loved the movie, but it was a flop at the box office"? What I am suggesting is that in addition to thinking of problem-solving ability as a measure of intelligence, there is another dimension. This quality of intelligence enables us to simply be in the world, connected to others with an implicit understanding that is the ground of our consciousness.

I agree that it is necessary to include the full complement of human personality, creativity as well as problem-solving ability, in order to begin to comprehend the spectrum of intelligences in general, and spiritual intelligence in particular. When we examine the elements constituting spiritual intelligence in the next chapter, it is with the understanding that these components are sometimes measurable in the conventional psychometric sense, and sometimes measurable in the phenomenological sense, that is, as real phenomena that simply *are*.

CHAPTER FOUR

Spiritual Intelligence

Spiritual intelligence is an authentic intelligence that encompasses thinking, conceptualization, and problem solving. Metaphor was useful in discussing the other intelligences we examined, and the use of metaphor will also help us grasp this concept. I propose a metaphor for spiritual intelligence that is twofold, like the theory of light in quantum physics, where light can exist in two physical states, either as a particle or as a wave. Spiritual intelligence is also capable of being in two states, two *mental* states. On the one hand, it can be understood as a state of being, a state in which subjective experience alone is the reality. On the other, it can be conceptualized as a set of discrete abilities and series of actions that each of us is capable of actualizing and performing. The definition of spiritual intelligence that I propose may be stated as follows:

> Spiritual intelligence is the human capacity to ask ultimate questions about the meaning of life, and to simultaneously

experience the seamless connection between each of us and the world in which we live.

In this chapter we will explore the nature of this phenomenon, its origins, and its relation to other intelligences and morality.

What we are addressing is a theoretical construct, a model, relevant only insofar as it allows us to grasp the complex ways we think about, feel, and experience the world. The metaphor for spiritual intelligence raises all the familiar questions: Is it inherited? Is it learnable? Does it depend on the environment and context in which a person grows up? If this intelligence is inherited, can it be influenced, changed, or modified like IQ scores, or the scores on the well-known Scholastic Assessment Tests, both of which were once thought immutable? Recently, of course, scores on these tests have shown dramatic alterations with training, and the effects of cultural influence.[1]

The impact of environmental forces on scores of any number of psychological tests can distort their meaning and interpretation. Because scores on tests can be radically influenced by, and can vary with, the cultural context in which they are given, historical times and the background of the person taking the test, it helps to focus more on the qualities and process of spiritual intelligence than on the outcome of any particular test in terms of a numerical, psychometric result.

The Origins of Spiritual Intelligence

I N MY VIEW, the concept of multiple intelligences that we discussed in the previous chapter makes sense as a way of describing and understanding the diverse learning functions of the human mind. Intelligences of any kind are, like spiritual intelligence, theoretical constructions. As noted earlier, it is improbable that anything resembling an intelligence gene or a visual art or musical gene will be discovered. It is also reasonable to conclude that there is a low probability for the existence of a "spirituality gene." That being said, however, Robert Emmons, professor of psychology at the University of California at Santa Cruz, suggests in his recent work that some evidence does exist that might imply heritability of religiousness.[2] In their recent books, Danah Zohar, Ian Marshall, and Ray Kurzweil also speculate on research about the "God spot" in the temporal lobes that responds to "asking ultimate questions";[3] and, as we will examine in more detail later, researchers like Michael Persinger regard mystical experiences as the product of "transient electrical activity" in the temporal lobes of the brain.[4] We can speculate that some structures are inherited as part of the design of our brains. Still, to say that they contain genetic material that has specific content—content that only makes sense in a cultural context—seems to me farfetched.

Opposing the view of inheritability are also researchers like Kenneth Kendler at the Virginia Institute for Psychiatric and Medical Genetics, and his colleagues, who show in a study of religion and psychopathology that, based on their measures, "personal devotion and personal institutional conservatism were all strongly familial, suggesting the effect of environmental factors."[5] In other words, their studies indicate that the "nurture" component in these studies of religiosity far outweighed the "nature" component that is currently promoted in some circles.

To ask if spiritual intelligence, or musical and emotional intelligences, for that matter, are governed by either heredity or environment exclusively is to miss the point completely. As Steven Rose points out, "minds develop dynamically and coherently as part of the constant interplay of specificity and plasticity that constitutes the living processes that create us."[6] For instance, we all speak our mother tongues without agonizing over whether this ability is innate or learned, genetically determined or developed in the context of culture. The forces that govern language development are clearly both nature and nurture as well as the interaction between the two. Similarly, I believe we can all enjoy the abilities of our spiritual intelligence. Individual differences exist in its expression, just as they exist in all other forms of intelligence. It appears that spiritual intelligence, like personality, is a trait and a capacity granted to the human condition.

Spiritual Intelligence as Part of Current Intelligence Theory

WHATEVER its origin, it seems to me that the most useful approach to the question of spiritual intelligence is to construe it, at minimum, as a way of being part of and experiencing the world in a manner that connects a sense of what is sacred to daily activities and relationships. It can also be thought of along the lines of other intelligences, with active problem solving as one of its defining characteristics. Problem solving is particularly important for theorists such as Gardner, who define intelligence in terms of abilities to solve problems and fashion products.[7] Gardner has specifically ruled out of the kingdom of intelligences a spiritual intelligence that is in any way phenomenologically based. In Gardner's scheme, an intelligence has to involve *doing* something. For the intelligence associated with the kind of *doing* in asking ultimate questions about the meaning of life, Gardner has included a new "half" of an intelligence, called *existential intelligence.*[8] The metaphor that we are using qualifies spiritual intelligence in both dimensions as an intelligence in terms of being in the world in a particular fashion (phenomenology) and in terms of solving spiritual problems. In my view there is every reason, therefore, to include it as a fully functioning intelligence that can be incorporated into Gardner's model.

Spiritual Intelligence and Problem Solving

THE NOTION of problem solving in relation to spiritual intelligence includes examples such as blocked meditation; connecting to another person's essential self; or gaining access to a community for shared ritual and sacred experience. The fundamental problems or questions that spiritual intelligence addresses and seeks to solve, however, are these: What is the meaning of life? Why are we here? What does my life mean on its own and in relation to others? What is the right way to love? One answer from my tradition which has always fascinated me is, "We are a little lower than the angels; and at the same time we are nothing but dust and ashes." It is this questioning of the meaning of existence with which spiritual intelligence has been wrestling for thousands of years. The beautiful and powerful biblical image of Jacob literally wrestling all night with the angel gives us some idea of the depth and historical resilience of this problem.

One of the issues with the problem-solving approach, however, is the question of measurement. Measuring an intelligence is generally thought of in terms of some sort of scale divided in segments from high to low, with high indicating a large amount and low indicating a small amount of whatever the scale measures. The criteria for successful problem solving are usually expressed in terms of speed and accuracy (as in getting the right answer) in comparison with the general population.

Solving spiritual problems successfully, I would argue, is subject to a different sort of criteria. There are no "right" answers, and speed in making a spiritual or moral decision may just as easily imply impulsiveness as high intelligence. I don't know how this kind of spiritually intelligent problem solving can be seen as anything more than a statement of the fact that some issue was successfully solved, producing a feeling of subjective satisfaction; or that the issue remains unsolved, creating a feeling of frustration and confusion. Consequently, rather than a graduated metric, the problem solving associated with spiritual intelligence is described in terms of a clearcut yes or no. I either find a solution to the question of community participation, for example, or I remain uninvolved.

The capacity to solve a moral or a spiritual dilemma is obviously crucial in daily life. The right or wrong quality of the answer, however, does not lend itself to the traditional forms of measurement used in solving a math or information problem, either in terms of analytical calculation or speed of response. It requires a different kind of yardstick.

Spiritual intelligence can be seen as a methodology for solving moral problems. There may be, however, no problem requiring solution, but rather an event to be experienced. In that case, the connection to ineffable or sacred moments reinforces that portion of our spiritual intelligence metaphor as pure subjectivity. Spiritual intelligence does not necessarily require *doing;* it also permits simply *being.* The measurement of spiritual intelligence will clearly require a different sort of process than the analytic or linguistic measurement of other intelligences. For an approach to this psychometric question, it will be useful to examine the ways in which related constructs such as morality are measured and researched.

Moral Development

THE MEASUREMENT of moral development is a field unto itself, and the theoretical underpinnings can be referenced easily in the work of Lawrence Kohlberg and Carol Gilligan in their respective studies of the stages in children's lives through which they believe moral judgment passes on its way to higher and more sophisticated levels.[9] The measurement used in this fascinating and important research is done by assigning an individual to a numbered stage (I through VI) in order to mark his or her level of development of moral consciousness. The stages reflect the quality of mind that the developing child possesses in approaching a variety of moral dilemmas, such as whether it is legitimate to steal food or medicine for a loved one who is starving or desperately sick; and, in Gilligan's insightful work on gender differences in moral decision making, whether abortion is morally acceptable, and, if so, under what circumstances. Her research shows that women use very different criteria from those used by men in making difficult moral choices.

The notion of the "highest" stage under Kohlberg's model—a paradigm that has come to be the standard in the field—namely, making moral choices on the basis of some universal principle of justice, is based entirely on the males who participated in his research. When faced with the painful and difficult moral question of abortion—their own included—Gilligan demonstrates that women do not use an abstract principle of justice in making these tortured decisions. Instead, females use "stage III" thinking, a stage that had been considered underdeveloped by previous standards. Stage III is the developmental stage of making moral choices based on the effect that such a choice is likely to have on other people. This approach is arguably every bit as sophisticated and "developed" as the standard previously set by an all-male group—and possibily more so. The measurement of moral development has its own internal complexity, but there is general agreement on maturational changes over time. For our purposes, it is the developmental sequencing of moral development that is also reflected in spiritual growth.

The developmental criterion for the measurement of all other intelligences is widely accepted. The concept of intelligence implies, at least to the Western scientific mind, a set of abilities that can be reflected in some form of measurement that will show change over the life span of the person. In the world of education, for example, where some kind of measurement is always present, Gardner suggests that we must design schools that work with individual differences and teach to the strengths of the eight (and one-half) kinds of intelligence that his theory proposes. As we have seen, Gardner's position, with which I agree, is that intelligence cannot be measured with one uniform "dipstick" by which we evaluate everyone along the same dimension. The evaluation of whether proposed schools actually work in educating children, therefore, has to be modified to respect the unique qualities of each child. This measurement needs to reflect not only the retention of information, but also a quality of understanding. The measurement also needs to encompass the developmental sequence of quantitative and qualitative shifts that occur as the child matures.

Measurement of Spiritual Intelligence: General Considerations

I N MY VIEW, it is necessary to expand traditional forms of measurement of the intelligences associated with education, and also the intelligence we are calling spiritual intelligence. The new measuring unit I would include is the quality of understanding, because understanding demonstrates how an individual connects disparate elements of a problem and then uses this synthesis in new situations. Understanding also satisfies a subjective need of involvement in the context from which the problem arises.

There is a fundamental dimension to learning that has been underemphasized and often ignored, namely the motivational power of the experience of understanding that results in subjective pleasure or satisfaction. Understanding takes a person through the process from contextually being part of the problem to being part of the solution. Understanding means that new knowledge is incorporated into the self in such a way that it can readily be applied to a novel situation, and the process of personal comprehension feels good when it is completed. Another term for this form of learning is insight. The smile of pleasure and the deep sigh associated with an "aha!" or "oh yeah, I get it" moment is the signal of satisfaction of understanding.

Why does understanding feel good? Think back to times when you have had the experience of understanding accompanied by pleasure. For example, solving a difficult word problem or a crossword puzzle resolves cognitive tension and conflict. That feels good. Understanding that something is basically true and right and solid about yourself, about someone you love, or about the world you live in also feels good. This feeling of pleasure is important, because it helps us recognize the powerful desire that drives intelligent behavior, a desire that seeks the pleasure of competence and mastery. I believe that this same process of challenge, followed by understanding and a feeling of pleasure, applies to spiritual intelligence. The pleasure that drives spiritual intelligence is described in many forms, often in the sense of oneness with other human beings or all of living creation, or of connection to a larger whole, to a greater and transcendent consciousness. A consistent report of mystics like Meister Eckhart, Saint Teresa of Avila, or the Ba'al Shem Tov are feelings of bliss and ecstasy associated with the loss of boundaries between self and God, self and the world. To date, no one has come up with a way of measuring the pleasure associated with any of the intelligences.

There have been attempts to measure the effects of some religious attitudes and spiritual behaviors. In his work, Robert Emmons reports that a group of undergraduates who were asked to reflect on the gratitude they felt in their lives showed more positive attitudes toward life and had fewer physical symptoms than did the control group. Emmons contends that spiritual intelligence consists of at least five "core characteristics": (1) transcendence, (2) heightened consciousness, (3) endowing everyday activity with a sense of the sacred, (4) using spiritual resources on practical problems, and (5) engaging in virtuous behaviors (such as forgiveness, gratitude, humility, compassion, and wisdom); and he postulates correlation between personality features and individual differences in the way people organize their spiritual skills.

Spirituality need not, therefore, be viewed as an ethereal and otherworldly consciousness, but has wide implications for day-to-day living. Emmons continues:

Spiritual concerns influence the way in which people construe their world, pursue strivings, and regulate their behavior in day-to-day living. This pragmatic approach to spirituality offers a perspective on spirituality that can counter the mistaken belief that spiritual states of mind are somehow on another "plane of existence"—a state of being that is phenomenologically valid, but has little relevance for problem solving and goal attainment in concrete life situations.[10]

Spiritual thinking and activity clearly do not have to be relegated to another level or plane of existence. There is good justification for the notion that spirituality is rooted in daily life, because spiritual consciousness pervades our perception of the world. This relationship to the world does not require induced mental states or spectacular circumstances; all that is necessary is the fact of being alive. People notice and do things every day that are sensitive and compassionate, with no need to seek meaning behind every deed.

Intelligence: A New Definition

SYNTHESIZING the previously described views of intelligence from Gardner, Sternberg, Mayer et al., Goleman, and Emmons, and adding this important and fundamental subjective dimension of pleasure—a pleasure I would call psychophysiological because it affects body and mind—I propose an expanded definition of intelligence, including spiritual intelligence, that adheres to the following sequence: *noticing, knowing, understanding, action.*

Noticing

Intelligence begins with *noticing*—perceiving and sensing an event in the outside or inside world. Noticing presupposes the ability and capacity to experience—see, hear, feel, touch, taste, smell, and otherwise sense—that something is happening. In addition to the usual and obvious use of our senses, there are significant other modes of awareness of the world around us that are often overlooked. The orienting reflex, for example, enables us to respond automatically to subtle changes in the environment.

The orienting reflex is one over which we have no conscious control. This reflex forces us to respond to any novelty in our environment. Examples of the noticing power we (and other species) are born with and use in a constant unconscious fashion include the startle of a deer to some change in sound or smell; the instant awareness that something is wrong when we see a frightened child's or spouse's face; the alert "third ear" that a mother uses to distinguish a cry of hunger from a cry of danger from her child playing in the other room; the instantaneous millisecond adjustments that a downhill skier makes to every bump in the trail at seventy miles per hour; or the subtle awareness that something is wrong in our bodies before the diagnosis comes back from the lab and is articulated by the physician. How often have we heard someone say, "My doctor didn't have to tell me something was wrong. I already knew it"?

Given this concept of noticing, of sensing or of perceiving, I would suggest that we, as humans, possess the ability to notice experiences commonly described as spiritual, i.e., a sense of transcendence, and a connection to a larger context of meaning. This noticing would include the phenomenological level referred to by the philospher Maurice Merleau-Ponty as the "flesh of existence";[11] or what Alfred North Whitehead describes as "perception in the mode of causal efficacy," namely, the innate sense that one is a part of the world in seamless fashion, and that any self-awareness or self-consciousness would constitute a separation from the very ground of being.[12] This experience of flow between each of us and the world is the state of mind Lawrence Kushner terms the "invisible lines of connection."[13]

This basic level of noticing or perceiving is clear when we realize, for example, that a baby does not "think about" his mother. For the baby, she simply *is*. The child "knows" reflexively that his mother is the source of life, of nourishment, of well-being. This perceptual mode applies also to our sense of being in the world, insofar as none of us normally questions the solidity of the ground on which we stand or (under daily circumstances) the usefulness of the air we breathe.

Can we, as conscious beings, step back and know "about" our world and divide it into animate and inanimate, good and evil, healthy and sick? Of course. The perception that results from this separation, however, is related to intelligences other than spiritual intelligence, and can be described from alternative perspectives. The intelligences associated with stepping back or self-consciousness are better described as analytical intelligence or reflective intelligence. Reflection in any of the forms of intelligences may be conscious or unconscious. But perception is not conscious, it is automatic.

· Spiritual intelligence implies a perception beyond, a transcendent connection with a larger universe of meaning, and it is certainly not conscious. Spiritual intelligence begins with the ability, basic to us all, to sense—to see, hear, feel, touch, smell, and reflexively respond to—that which is an extension of us and of which we are an extension; what we call our world. Perception of the spiritual, of the sacred, has been reported since reporting began. In the Hebrew Bible, we learn of Moses' epiphany at the burning bush; we follow the Israelites on their Exodus from Egypt as they perceive the Lord in the form of a "column of fire and cloud" leading them to the Promised Land; we encounter the visions of the prophets Isaiah, Ezekiel, Jesus, Mohammed, Buddha, and the mystics down through the ages.

In our own time we hear reports of "near-death" experiences, of the vision of "white light" and the reconnection with departed loved ones. Are these experiences spiritual, or are they hallucinations, wish fulfillments, perceptual distortions, temporal-lobe anomalies? Does it even make sense always to categorize them in quasi-scientific jargon, since such jargon can be more dismissive than instructive? I don't think so. I think we have to understand

and accept that these reports describe direct experience. Psychology and neurology can help us further understand the individuals and their experiences, but we must guard against reducing those reports to a diagnostic category. It is neither instructive nor accurate to negate individual reports of spiritual phenomena in this fashion. We know that van Gogh was diagnosed manic-depressive. His art is nonetheless beautiful. El Greco had astigmatism, which caused his vision to be distorted. Does his painting lose any of its power? Dostoyevsky was epileptic. Does that explain why Tolstoy said that if he were banished and in exile, with only one book, it would be *Crime and Punishment*? My point is that spiritual intelligence transcends diagnostic reification and categorization, and must be seen in its own terms.

In the minds of those who report their spiritual experiences, there is no doubt of the authenticity and the sacred quality of their perceptions, and the clarity of meaning associated with those perceptions. Individuals from the world over, comprising the most diverse and randomly representative of statistical samples, cling fast to the reality of their personal and immediate perceptual experiences of spiritual events. The subjective reports that poured in, along with the objective data, in my request for responses to the PsychoMatrix Spirituality Inventory, are compelling in their emotional power and visual clarity.

Many people with whom I have spoken, not only those involved in my research, are able to provide elaborate, picturesque, lyrical, and compelling narratives that have no hint of distortion or psychopathology. It is my firm belief that these spiritual perceptions, rooted in daily experience, form the basis of spiritual intelligence. This perception qualifies as a set of abilities distinguishable from—yet possibly correlated with—those commonly associated with other forms of intelligences: visual perception of emotion, auditory perception of harmonious sound, kinesthetic perception of graceful or coordinated physicality, and mathematical or verbal perception of symbolic relationships.*

Knowing

The second critical step in formulating a definition of intelligence is *knowing* that an event or experience occurs and *synthesizing* or *juxtaposing* that knowledge with past experience or internal standards. For example, knowing that a tone is being sung in the right key involves knowing the pitch and being able to reproduce it; or running from a potential menace involves being in an emotionally charged situation in which one must decide how much danger is present. These instances both require using perception and then synthesizing those perceptions and juxtaposing them with similar images or memories in order to make a decision. This process is the familiar compare-and-contrast method, in which the present moment is matched with previous experiences, and if the match is close, as in the case of trauma or emotional flooding, the memory and reliving of the original experience takes place. Comparison occurs both at the cognitive and the emotional level, with knowledge as the result.

Once a spiritual perception occurs, the experience can end there, or it can be subjected to conceptual elaboration and the creation of spiritual knowledge or meaning, with the result of taking action in response to that new meaning. To use an analogy from emotional intelligence, one might perceive emotion; I see a smiling face, or hear a loud and startling voice, or see arms open wide and gesturing to me. From the perception I conclude, based on an educated guess from previous perceptions, that the smiling face is happy or pleased; that the loud voice is angry; that the gesturing arms are loving and inviting. When I respond to the voice or the open arms, I learn whether my guess was correct and thereby create new knowledge that I add to my personal database about the world.

In terms of spiritual intelligence, a useful example of this aspect of the definition of intelligence might lie in a moving tale I recently heard from a woman named Julia, who shared a remarkable experience. A middle-aged mother of four teenagers, Julia was coming home after having been out shopping with her sister. It was early evening, and as she came over the crest of the hill near her suburban home, she saw the "flashing lights, blue and red and yellow, and thought, 'Please God, not one of my children—or anyone's child.'" To her horror, her seventeen-year-old daughter had been thrown out of a dune buggy and was being rushed to the hospital with a severe concussion and with internal injuries. In the emergency room, Julia spoke to her child as the girl lapsed in and out of consciousness. "My back, it's killing me," she moaned as she thrashed about and managed a few coherent words. Julia told me that when she finally went home for a rest, she prayed to God "that I could take my daughter's pain." For the next three days, Julia lay in bed with severe pain in her back, and when she was finally able to return to the hospital to visit her daughter, the child's back was no longer hurting her.

To return to our concept of spiritual intelligence: Julia certainly had perceived and noticed the traumatic event that had befallen her daughter. The knowledge that followed was the certainty of what her daughter was feeling, and she "instinctively" did something about it. She knew what was going on. She knew what she had to do. Did this mother consciously plan to absorb the pain of her daughter? I think not. Her response, both intelligent and spiritual in nature, reflexively invoked her experience with prayer and her sense of the Divine. Julia told me when we were parting, "Be careful what you pray for."

Understanding

The third phase of intelligence is the specific instance of *understanding* in which conceptual elaboration into knowledge of spiritual experiences provides insight into their meaning. Conceptualization includes comprehending spiritual perceptions and embedding them in some kind of cognitive/emotional context. Sometimes this knowledge can be frightful, because of the power and suddenness that is associated with these events. This terror is graphically portrayed by the little boy in the movie *The Sixth Sense*. He has no context but fear in which to house his overwhelming perceptions of the spirits of people who have died and are trying to reach out to some source of communication. How is one able to understand, to incorporate in the usual patterns of conscious thought, a near-death experience, or a mystical experience of the connectedness of all living beings?

The understanding that accompanies conceptual elaboration results in the subjective experience of a spiritual event. Reflection upon this internal mental state is analogous to seeing the meaning in a particular passage of poetry, or knowing that a piece of music sounds beautiful, or understanding that one is disappointed, happy, or in love. A student of mine described his experience of peacefulness at the top of a mountain, an experience that engendered a kind of knowing different from that which accompanies daily experience. When people report near-death experiences, for example, they often say, "It was very bright and peaceful. I knew I was not alone." The feelings of many caregivers in hospitals reflect what a nurse working in the intensive care unit at a hospital told me: "I can feel a presence when I care for my patients. There are always questions of why this illness happened at just this time, or why I was selected to attend this patient, and why this person lived to see his family for one last Christmas. It is these moments that convince me that I am not working in isolation, that there is some other power involved."

Sometimes spiritual understanding and this sense of knowing come directly from the body. The connectedness people describe refers not only to the external world, but often emanates from within. Richard Selzer, surgeon and author, returns from the edge of the abyss brought on by Legionnaires' disease, in which he lapsed into a coma and began his painful journey to a place where there was "more than a hint of death." He describes his ascent from the dark pit:

At last the sick man is lifted forth from the tub, clean, calm and sane. Rubbed dry, he is carried back to his room. The hands of the nurse have the physical kindness of big hands, the way they form themselves into a nest. Settled into it, he could laugh out loud. Perhaps he will. He thinks of how, sixty years before, his father had carried him about in his arms. "Now how do you feel?" "Euphoric," he tells the nurse. "You what?" "Phoric. That means being carried. The 'eu' stands for contented. I am happy to be carried." And he feels the heat and the strength of the solid man infusing him, entering his veins; his breathing lightens, his brain clears into a kind of bright amazement. It seems to him that his molecules, which had been in chaotic disarray, have rearranged themselves, fallen into place. It is the true moment of cure.

As for the rest? Well, that's just medical data. The part that can be read from a computer. That doesn't make you well. Arrayed in clean linen, he lies upon the bed.[14]

The data from which spiritual intelligence generates knowledge may come from outside the body or from within, but the process is, in my judgment, the same no matter what the source. The knowledge that is established can be stored in memory and/or acted upon, depending upon one's circumstance and personal choice.

Emotional Satisfaction and Action

The final component of intelligence is the *emotional satisfaction* of an experience comprehended and/or the choice of implementation of that understanding through *action*. As we have seen, an individual understands through conceptual elaboration that perceptions can have meaning, can represent something. A person is therefore able to incorporate that understanding into his experience, and if he chooses, he can then act on the basis of what he knows. Let's use our example from emotional intelligence. You may see a smile, which you can then choose to return, a scowling face, which you can avoid, or an inviting gesture that will prompt you to run to the open arms.

In the case of Julia, reacting to the crisis with her daughter, her action took the form of prayer. The action one takes on the basis of spiritual understanding can obviously come in many forms. It can be action on the outside world, such as feeding the hungry, or praying in community; it can be action expressed in singing, dancing, or personal prayer; or it can be integrated with internal action, such as self-reflection and self-awareness, meditation, or a personal feeling of closeness to—or distance from—God or some divine or transcendent energy source.

Intelligence, Spiritual Intelligence, and the PSI

D IVIDING spiritual intelligence into the four components outlined above, *perception, knowledge, understanding* and *emotional satisfaction/action*, it is possible to analyze the construct of spiritual intelligence and tie it to a developmental sequence over a person's life span. One of Gardner's and Mayer's criteria for the establishment of an authentic and scientifically legitimate intelligence is that changes must be demonstrated over developmental time. The findings of my research also support this notion with respect to spiritual intelligence.

Gardner has suggested, however, that the developmental change associated with spiritual intelligence "is not merely a function of aging. Otherwise we would call 'grey hair' and 'stooping over' developmental as well."[15] Our data support the findings that scores on the PsychoMatrix Spirituality Inventory increase with age for all of the seven spiritual factors. Does this finding mean that individuals become more spiritually intelligent as they get older? Or might it mean that people become more aware of the spiritual dimension of life as they get older, and more open to questions of ultimate meaning. A five-year-old may ask, "What happens to us when we die?" An eighty-five-year-old may ask the same question. Is one likely to be more spiritually intelligent than the other? I would say no. But if we frame the question, "Is the older person more likely to be spiritually conscious insofar as he or she sees the dimensions of life that involve sacred meaning and experience?" then I think the answer must be yes. This fuller awareness is, I believe, the best way to understand spiritual intelligence across developmental time and transformation. Living includes the experiences of being faced with moral choices in a self-reflective fashion, the experience of joy and sadness, of love achieved and love lost. With each of these life events, I would argue, the application of spiritual intelligence is potentially involved in and subject to the maturation of judgment that we associate with developmental change.

Recent research data from the PsychoMatrix Spirituality Inventory show this positive age correlation; i.e., as age increases, so does the report of spiritual experience and behavior, for both sexes, for all seven spiritual factors. This important finding dovetails nicely with the view of the other theorists of intelligence, demonstrating the progression of the development of this mental capacity. On this dimension as well, spiritual intelligence qualifies as an intelligence that corresponds to a unique set of human experiences.

When we consider the developmental dimension, we then encounter the problem of whether any intelligence, if it is an innate capacity, set at birth, can be raised. Is intelligence of any kind, or spiritual intelligence per se, an innate and an immutable personal attribute? I think the notion of spiritual intelligence can best be viewed the way Shinichi Suzuki, creator of the technique for teaching violin to millions of very young children, described the capacity for learning to play music. He observed that by the age of three, nearly every child in the world has mastered the most complex and daunting of tasks, namely, learning to speak his or her mother tongue. Suzuki hypothesized that these children could also, therefore, learn music, specifically the violin, at an equally young age. His program for teaching music has since been embraced not only in Japan, where it began, but throughout the world.

The father asked me to teach his son violin. At that time I didn't know how to train such a small child, and what to teach I could not guess. Such experience I did not have. What way of violin training would be good for a four-year-old? I thought about it from morning to night.

At that time three of my brothers and I had just formed the Suzuki Quartet. One day when we were practicing at the house of my younger brother, it hit me like a flash: why, all Japanese children speak Japanese! This thought was for me like a light in the dark night. Since they all speak Japanese so easily and fluently, there must be a secret; and this must be training.

Indeed, all children everywhere in the world are brought up by a perfect educational method: their mother tongue. Why not apply this method to other faculties? I felt I had made a tremendous discovery. If a child cannot do his arithmetic, it is said that his intelligence is below average. Yet he speaks the difficult Japanese language—or his own native language—very well. Isn't this something to ponder and think about? In my opinion, the child is not below average in intelligence; it is the educational system that is wrong. His ability or talent simply was not developed properly. It is astonishing that no one has found this out before in all these years, although the situation clearly has existed throughout human history.[16]

In my view, spiritual intelligence, like the intelligence required to learn the violin or one's native tongue, can be appreciated as an innate capacity that, with attention, training, and additional life experience, increases over time.

With respect to the PSI and the kinds of measurement that I developed for it, the developmental dimension proved to be one of the most important and interesting findings. Of the thousands of people who participated in the study, the majority of the sample was between the ages of thirty and sixty, and scores changed depending on the age grouping. As people got older, they scored higher on each of the seven factors. It is premature, at this stage of the research, to follow individuals over time to see if and when any particular person changed scores as he or she grew older; but for research purposes, it worked well to have such a large cross-section of the generations and such clear results.

This finding is not surprising. It stands to reason that questions of ultimate meaning and spiritual awareness increase and deepen as a person accumulates more life experience, as a loved one becomes ill and/or dies; or as someone confronts his or her own mortality following a major surgical procedure. An increase in scores on the PSI reflects an increase in spiritual awareness, or at least a willingness to frame one's thoughts, actions, and experience in spiritual terms. It is important to remember that the outcome on the PSI does not define spiritual capacity per se, or the presence or absence of the intelligence we are calling spiritual. The scores are descriptive only. They demonstrate the manner in which a person expresses his or her spiritual intelligence. In this sense, every score on the PSI is an indication of spirituality, based on my often repeated assumption that we are all spiritual.

The Measurement of Spiritual Intelligence: Practical Considerations

THE PSI is descriptive by design, but there is still the nagging question of measurement and the possibility for the use of psychometric qualities similar to the other intelligences we have discussed. What constitutes the differences of some people who seem to be better, more gifted, or more natural at this "spiritual thing"? We would, for example, describe some people as clearly more physically intelligent because they can throw a ball easily and gracefully with little practice or conscious learning. Some other people are musically intelligent and gifted, and can sing with perfect pitch or "pick up" any number of instruments with ease; and some can solve difficult mathematical problems in an eye-blink. Individual differences exist for these intelligences, so why not for spiritual intelligence as well?

A report of recent research conducted by psychologist Diana Deutsch of the University of California at San Diego may provide a clue to this reasonable and perplexing question. The report indicates that most native speakers of languages like Vietnamese or

Mandarin Chinese, which use tones to convey meaning, may have a form of perfect pitch. In addition, the findings suggest that many or even most babies are born with perfect pitch, but lose it if they do not learn a tonal language or undergo early musical training. This fascinating study suggests a human capacity, inherent from birth, that can be developed or stunted by the psychosocial circumstances in which one develops. It is my contention that what may be true for perfect pitch may also be true for spiritual intelligence. Like the other intelligences, spiritual intelligence is part of our human heritage, and can be expressed in a myriad of ways. Do we all develop any human faculty in exactly the same way? Of course not. But are we all capable of basic human enterprises, such as mastery of our mother tongues? The answer is definitely yes. Like many children, Mozart had perfect pitch. Does that mean we can all create like Mozart? Not necessarily. Mozart was also a composing genius. That rare combination of qualities which produce creative achievements is a deep mystery. But can most of us enjoy Mozart's music? I would say definitely. It is probably no accident that the universal tune children love, the one with which Suzuki starts his four-year-olds on the violin, is "Twinkle, Twinkle, Little Star," composed by Mozart himself.

Measurement of clear individual differences in the domain of spiritual intelligence may ultimately have to be qualitative rather than quantitative. In other words, I think we can say that a person has spiritual capacities given at birth, but the degree to which those capacities are developed may be related to exposure, teaching, or family context; and their level of achievement is a matter of opinion or viewpoint. There is no scale that we can develop to assess spiritual intelligence numerically. As a way to approach the question of measurement, it may be useful to examine the concept of musical intelligence. While some aspects of musical intelligence may be measurable by conventional techniques, musicality itself is as difficult to measure as spiritual intelligence, and is subjectively evaluated on a performance basis by the "consensus of knowledgeable individuals" in much the same fashion as spiritual intelligence.[17] There is no accepted yardstick. The critics can pan a performance that the public loves.

Musical intelligence is as much about music as about intelligence. A patient of mine, a gifted young composer receiving his Ph.D. in the music department of a local university, complained bitterly that he didn't feel that he had musical intelligence, but his colleagues did: "They all seem to have a method for composing, but I don't feel that I do." Interestingly, this man kept winning many of the composing awards, and was one of the few in his graduating class to obtain a job in a university music department upon graduation. This discrepancy between his perceptions of his talent and the view of the outside world is another indication of the subjective quality of the intelligences and the difficulty of measuring them. This man would have measured his musical intelligence as quite low. Clearly the competition judges and hiring committees of the universities measured him as very high.

Intelligence or musicality? The statement that "he is very musical" implies he shows strong musical intelligence. *Why* is he musical? Because he feels the music, has a sense of and responsiveness to the rhythms, feels the beat, expresses himself with his voice or his instrument, feels enthusiasm, joy, sadness—the spectrum of emotions—through his music. Musical intelligence overlaps with what we call "musical"—whether defined as trait- or ability-based. It also defines who a person is in terms of how he or she experiences the world. Similarly, bodily/kinesthetic intelligence is synonymous with "athletic ability" or "gracefulness."

In other words, the phrase *musical intelligence* (or *bodily/kinesthetic intelligence,* or *linguistic intelligence, emotional intelligence,* or *spiritual intelligence*) denotes a state of being in the world—a facet of the diamond that is each person—as well as an "intelligence," which is then delineated by a particular skill or abilities set. An integrated description of spiritual intelligence, in my view, incorporates this state of being into our understanding, a quality that defies any standardized form of measurement.

Spiritual intelligence is a particular psychic stance, a mind-set, a frame of reference, and a point of orientation for relating to one's self, to others, and to the world. We know some of the sensory and experiential inputs that have to be synthesized and integrated into established mental schemas for understanding a math problem, a new word, or a musical phrase. Understanding a sacred moment, however, also encompasses both dimensions of spiritual intelligence so that a person could experience a state of being and/or apply knowledge to new situations or solve new problems.

Some people appear to be better than others at accessing the spiritual realm. Here I am defining "better" as seeming to come by it naturally or comparatively more easily, as reflected in such observations as "she just seems to find it easier, she has always been that way," or "he's gifted." If spiritual intelligence resists measurement with traditional psychometric methods, is there any way in which it *can* be gauged? How, indeed, can one ever measure musical intelligence or spatial intelligence, so crucial in art, architecture, and similar endeavors? For some people—"experts" in a given field—it's easy to determine, based on performance, whether an individual "has it" or "just doesn't have it."

When Antonio Salieri was the state composer and conductor in Vienna in the late eighteenth century, his music was considered to be an example of his gifts and, therefore, of his musical intelligence. Once Mozart arrived on the scene, however, the standards for musical intelligence were raised. But by whom? Why does Mozart sound better than Salieri? Can any of these devoutly held discriminations be psychometrically measured? Musical differences, like tastes, can be described, appreciated, and experienced. Aesthetic creativity and appreciation, however, are influenced by any number of subjective judgments, sociocultural forces, and popularities. This variety of impinging variables makes it hard to determine, on any grounds other than aesthetic, the level of a performer's musical intelligence.

Nevertheless, most people agree on who has musical intelligence and who doesn't, and who has bodily/kinesthetic intelligence and who doesn't; and we somehow base our knowledge on what the average (as in normative) experience of music or athleticism is—our own and others'. Some aspects of these intelligences can clearly be objectively measured. We then decide if an individual has been blessed with (innately given) abilities that take him or her beyond the usual and expectable mode. I can throw a spiral pass with a football and hit a five-iron on the golf course, play the piano, or solve a word problem. I can also enjoy and appreciate listening to Beethoven, Gershwin, the Beatles, and Bruce Springsteen; or gaze in wonder at the power of Rembrandt, van Gogh, or Henry Moore. Like many, and by statistical definition, however, I consider my intelligence in these areas rather average.

The question is, how are my abilities in these aesthetic and physical activities to be measured? With regard to education and the measurement of these kinds of intelligences over developmental time, Gardner proposes evaluations in schools that are performance-based. "Show me your painting; let me hear you play your composition; show me the dance you choreographed; show me the logic of your mathematical proof." Teachers then "evaluate" the performance of the student. Does the student work hard and demonstrate dedication and effort? Does the performance demonstrate not only technical ability but understanding as well? And does that understanding qualify as musical, mathematical, or bodily/ kinesthetic (athletic) intelligence?

The same rationale applies to the realm of spirituality, and of spiritual intelligence. Beginning with the assumption that we are all spiritual and all possess a variety of ways in which we express our spiritual intelligence—just as we all have personalities, can all throw a ball, hum a tune, do math, and speak our native language—it follows that some people seem to know more about spirituality than others, are somehow better at it, find it more consistent with their personalities, their upbringing, or general outlook on life.

When experts evaluate and decide on the presence or absence of spiritual intelligence, the process can be as problematic as it is for other forms of intelligence, and based as much on opinion as on absolute standards. Take the example of Mother Teresa. To some she represents the epitome of spiritual intelligence and spiritual expression, devoting her life to caring for and alleviating the sufferings of people least able to help themselves. To others, her rigid stand on abortion and the political regimes she supported mar her image as a thoroughly saintlike person. The evaluation comes down to personal belief and political persuasion.

Assuming we do attempt to measure it, how can a person demonstrate spiritual intelligence? How do spiritual behaviors reveal that fundamental aspect of intelligences, understanding? And what are spiritual behaviors and experiences, anyway? How do we know if Joan of Arc's vision or a sense of merging with the Almighty, as the mystics described, is a sign of spiritual intelligence or a symptom of pathology of the temporal lobes?

Spiritual Intelligence:
Examples and Research

A S AN EXAMPLE of what we think may or may not qualify as a spiritual experience, consider this description by a Japanese psychiatrist of the *amae:* the uniquely Japanese concept of "a sense of helplessness, desire to be loved, to be a passive love object. Those who are close to each other—that is to say—who are privileged to merge with each other—do not need words to express their feelings. One surely would not feel merged with another (that is, *amae*) if one had to verbalize the need to do so."[18]

The psychiatrist goes on to state that Americans feel encouraged and reassured by verbal exchange; Japanese neither need it nor find it desirable. I am reminded of Annie Leibowitz's famous *Rolling Stone* cover photo of John Lennon and Yoko Ono, in which he is naked and fetally curled against her. Classic *amae*. The photo provoked controversy in the West, not only because of the infantile pose, but because the photo was taken the day John was murdered and featured shortly thereafter.

Is *amae* an example of spiritual intelligence? An expression in human terms of psychological merging? *Amae* occurs between two people and, it could be argued, lacks the transcendent nature associated with spirituality. What if it were God or a God figure with whom the merging occurred? Mystics throughout history use the language of fusion to describe such psychic and spiritual events. The human desire for merging, taken to another level, can, I think, be described as spiritual.

Merging and losing boundaries are the focus of research by Paul Siegel and Joel Weinberger at Adelphi University, in which they examine the motivational factor that propels us to be a part of something larger than ourselves.[19] They use a subliminal technique to study the "motive for oneness" in terms of a need to merge with one's mother. This research can, however, be applied to many other contexts, including the spiritual. For thousands of years, religious and spiritual mystics have poetically described the loss of boundaries and their subsequent merging with the One, thereby blending into the God force. The Eucharist, i.e., ingestion and incorporation of the body and blood of Jesus, is a quintessential merging experience. Can we call this act an expression of spiritual intelligence? I think we have to.

Research on merging yields measurable responses. Intelligence theorists are also continually devising new methods of measurement. Emmons implies that spiritual intelligence can be measured by showing the effects of spiritual behaviors. Emotional intelligence theorists demonstrate ways in which emotional intelligence can be measured. For example, a test of emotional awareness presents subjects with a page filled with twenty-five faces expressing different emotions. The task is to identify correctly which emotion is being expressed on which face. The correct identification of emotion is viewed as an index of emotional intelligence. The next issue, of course, is one of prediction. Can these scores of emotional intelligence be shown to correlate with other measures of intelligence, or with practical life events? For traditional intelligence scores on analytical or verbal intelligence tests, the predictions of such things as grades in school have held up well—mostly because they both measure virtually the same thing. As intelligence describes more-subjective qualities such as emotions, however, the studies showing the predictive power of these measurements indicate very modest correlations between emotional intelligence and such things as school success or life satisfaction. Emotional intelligence studies are ongoing, and some of the more promising areas are those in which the relationship between this intelligence and constructs like empathy seem to be strong.

The question must also be asked about the predictive power of a test of spiritual intelligence such as the PSI. Do people who score in the high range perform better as problem solvers, or have a higher sense of morality, than those who score in the low range? Do high scorers have a more comprehensive understanding of life issues or show greater life successes? Recent studies point toward the connection between religious belief—or even the belief in unrealistic expectations—and the course of illness and length of life.[20] The use of spiritual interventions with psychiatric patients is also documented. Does this mean that, like traditional IQ scores, where high equals good and low equals bad, a high score on the PSI can be interpreted the same way? I think not.

In the terms we have set forth here, a high score on a particular spiritual factor means that *relative to the other scores this particular individual achieves, his or her spiritual energy is distributed in a unique pattern of emphases.* Consequently, a high score in intellectuality by one person does not necessarily mean that this person is smarter or even more intellectual than someone else; what it means is that in relation to his or her other scores on the PSI, this individual focuses more spiritual energy on the dimension of intellectuality than on the other spiritual dimensions.

Spiritual Intelligence and Morality

I N MY VIEW, it is venturing into dangerous territory to think about higher and lower spiritual intelligence rather than the patterning of spirituality, particularly because scores generated from such measurement can easily imply higher and lower morality. Consider, for example, a religious fundamentalist who is trained in and committed to a violent attack on nonbelievers who threaten his or her group's religious or spiritual sanctity. This true believer is honored to sacrifice his or her life, if necessary, to the cause. His or her scores on the PSI would probably be very high, including a high score on Divinity emphasizing a close connection to God; a strong sense of Community and empathy for the suffering of others, particularly his or her countrymen; a high score on Trauma with strong degrees of suffering, possibly during incarceration for his or her religious beliefs and past violent behavior; and a high score on Childhood Spirituality, reporting a strong family history of religious activity. This hypothetical person also fully meets the criteria for spiritual intelligence described by Emmons: transcendence, heightened consciousness, imbuing daily life with a sense of the sacred.

For most of us, this extreme case is a disturbing picture of spiritual intelligence, and one that often leads people to rationalize the avoidance of spiritual activities and experience altogether. This resistance promotes the view of spirituality as either the sanctuary of the devoutly religious, the preoccupation of New Agers, or the dangerous and explosive world of militant fundamentalists who consider it an act of the highest spiritual purpose to die in an explosion of a car bomb aimed at infidels.

In order to deal with these (often justifiable) concerns, we must return to the moral dimension of spirituality. Moral sensibility underscores the clear understanding that any action that disrupts the harmonious connection between people, or inflicts needless suffering on innocents or on the environment, is not only immoral but is also a sign of misguided and distorted spiritual intelligence.

Spiritual intelligence is not the same as morality, yet is the basis for it. Each of us uses his or her spiritual consciousness to make moral choices: to decide whether to fight in what we might individually consider an unjust war; to terminate, reduce, or retain a pregnancy; to continue life-support systems for a loved

one whose quality of life has sunk below imagination; or to participate in the protest against prejudice and racial hatred.

Morality as the ability to do "the right thing" means a comprehension of the fact that what I personally do affects others, and I
must be responsible for the choices I make and the actions I take.
The actual choices we make are shaped by a variety of conscious
and unconscious personal, social, and spiritual forces. We classify
such choices as good or evil depending on how they shape our
larger sense of the interconnection of people in our world. Spiritual intelligence is the ground on which morality stands. It is
about relationship: to self, to others, to a transcendent Intelligence
or energy source. Moral choice is the result of the understanding
that spiritual intelligence provides. The fact that conventional
methods of psychometric measurement may be inapplicable to this
kind of knowledge, however, does not invalidate or diminish the
power and scope of its relevance to our lives.

Spiritual Intelligence as a Basic Life Force

SPIRITUAL intelligence is clearly much more than a set of
sophisticated problem-solving abilities. It combines abilities, talents, gifts, and a transcendent interconnection of the
individual human spirit with a larger, luminous universe that is the
source of our being. Spiritual intelligence implies the capacity to
think with one's soul, a total phenomenon that can be viewed as the
human relationship to sacred experience, encompassing the knowing of spirituality through the mind as well as the heart and soul.

Rather than try to evaluate whether a person is highly spiritual
or nonspiritual or aspiritual, therefore, it is more important to
remember that the pattern of scores that emerges on the seven

spiritual factors indicates where the spiritual energy of that person is focused. By spiritual energy I mean the conscious—and unconscious—passion for life by which one is gravitationally pulled in one direction or another. This basic life force exists in us all and reminds us that we are not completely in control of our spiritual energy, any more than we are in control of our feelings of love, hatred, or indifference; or in control of our thoughts, our insights, or our "problem-solving" behavior. We are, in fact, directed *by* our passions as much as we actively direct our lives with passion; and the forces that control our most fundamental relationship to the world have not changed appreciably for thousands of years. A relevant historical perspective on the continuity of "primitive" spiritual consciousness is provided by Maria Torgovnick, professor of English at Duke University:

. . . before contact with Europeans, Indians in the Americas had a different concept of time. For them, the present was simply the unraveling of the past in alternative, "branching" directions, a notion Europeans found mysteriously alien in these "primitive people." But consider all the centuries of debate in the West concerning free will and its meaning—what were these inquiries but imaginings and reimaginings of the relationship between past, present and future? Europeans were likewise fascinated by the Indians' belief in beings who were half animal and half human, and their imitations of such beings in their ritual dances. But what are the minotaur, the satyrs, and the mermaids if not Western versions of the half-animal/half-human beings who haunt many African and Native American traditions?

. . . to dissociate our contemporary Western selves from past Western impulses is to disown patterns of thought from

Platonism through Transcendentalism that have assumed the existence of a spiritual realm at which our senses, limited to the material world, can only guess.[21]

The spiritual passion—of which each of us is capable—lives (shall we say lurks?) just below the surface of daily life and provides the energy source for spiritual intelligence and spiritual expression.

Spiritual passion and spiritual knowing can arise from the body, from the mind, or from mysterious reservoirs of energy. Claims are made that spiritual knowledge is gleaned from past lives or directly from God, and history is filled with countless examples and treasures of creative ineffable inspiration. A spiritual event can occur in a moment of creative insight, coming from sources unknown, and perceived and understood by the mind in a flash. Neil Baldwin, in his biography of Thomas Edison, that icon of American material inventiveness, quotes the inventor on the subject of his deep commitment to "realms beyond": "People say I have created things, . . . I have never created anything. I get impressions from the Universe at large and work them out, but I am only a plate on a record, a receiving apparatus . . ."[22]

Edison fervently espoused the existence of a Supreme Intelligence that acted as a kind of "Master Mind," informing all singular intellects on the planet. We see here the blend of spiritual intelligence and analytic intelligence. Creative intelligence is often described as transcription, taking down dictation from another source, not under conscious control. Jane Roberts describes going into trance and speaking through the voice of an entity named "Seth" about the nature of the world and the personal reality that each of us creates from an individual belief system.[23] Her work prompted and was fed by other "channeling" phenomena, a concept later made popular by the actress Shirley Maclaine. Mozart, almost universally considered the epitome of musical intelligence, described his composing technique as one of transcribing the music in his mind, music that flowed from his pen virtually unedited.[24]

The evaluation of spiritual intelligence is, in my opinion, a fruitless endeavor if we seek to measure one person against another and judge him or her in the same fashion that we measure analytical intelligence, verbal intelligence, or even emotional intelligence. At this point it seems to me that the best we can do is to describe the various ways in which people experience their spirituality and exercise their spiritual intelligence. If we can find a useful way to agree on the concept of spirituality and spiritual intelligence, then we can begin to devise ways in which the construct can be carefully and thoughtfully tested in the arena of empirical evidence.

The Goal of Research on Spiritual Intelligence

M Y GOAL is to document and demonstrate the workings of spiritual intelligence, adhering as closely as possible to actual experience. Most of the research on spirituality or religious belief leads away from experience. For example, if I ask questions like, "How do you know what is spiritual in your life?" or "Do you believe in God?" I press for a self-reflective mental act. This mental act then generates a conscious split in thinking. Self-reflection produces thoughts and interpretations *about* what the person thinks is happening in his or her own thought process. By asking a question in this manner, I force you to leave the experiential data that you have sensed or felt, and cognitively move you to a different level of abstract thinking.

The mental process is different if I ask you just to describe your spiritual behavior or experiences: "Tell me about the times that you pray," or " Tell me if you feel close to or distant from God." In this instance I invoke dialogue because you can respond without reflecting upon the *meaning* of your experience. You respond simply in terms of what you actually *do*. Your spiritual intelligence can thereby be documented in a direct fashion by approaching it as a clear, straightforward report. In addition, meaningful elaborations occur spontaneously when you begin to describe your subjective experience, i.e., how you felt when a loved one died, or what was in your mind when you were praying.

Spiritual intelligence, from this perspective, becomes what the PsychoMatrix Spirituality Inventory measures. The PSI is based strictly on self-reported behavior, activity, and experience. It is an attempt to articulate and specify the concept of spirituality on the most basic and fundamental level of personal mental and physical activity.

Spiritual intelligence can best be seen as a capacity for a particular kind of experience we humans possess, and one for which we also demonstrate certain related abilities. Our task now is to understand how this intelligence can and does influence our lives, how its energy can be harnessed, and how we can come to know ourselves better through spiritual self-reflection.

The point is that spiritual intelligence is not a rare or specialized capacity or set of skills; it is a universal fact of human existence. It is my contention that each of us is spiritual, and that we can seek our own spiritual paths. Each of us makes personal and intimate choices about what we value, whom we love, what we are willing to devote our lives to, and what form our relationship to transcendental phenomena can take. In this manner we shape our individual spiritual relationships to the world.

Spiritual questions, speculations, and beliefs form the basis of life's most significant activities, the most daring and challenging moments of existence. How am I to live my life? What gives my life meaning? What is the way? Who will find me if I get lost? Can I use the guide my parents used, or must I find my own path? Those are the questions we ask in our most private moments, when we feel the smallest in comparison to the universe; or when we feel we are the center of the universe. These are the questions, the values, the beliefs that the PSI taps and uncovers; these are the quandaries that spiritual intelligence seeks to comprehend.

CHAPTER FIVE

Creating the PSI

In order to investigate spirituality, I realized that such research would have to overcome the prejudices created by psychodynamic language and thinking that currently pervade our knowledge of the world. Such research, therefore, would have to reach beyond conventional ways of describing individual behavior, psychopathology, and mental function.

In thinking more about spirituality and how I might approach it as a research problem, some key questions emerged:

~ What defines a personal connection to the sacred?
~ What thoughts, ideas, and practices shape spiritual experience?
~ Are there commonalities in how individuals experience this phenomenon?
~ Do certain types of personalities experience the ineffable in similar ways?

～ How does spiritual experience affect our personal and professional relationships?

～ What role does spirit play in the work we do?

～ Are there evolutionary forces that drive and direct our search for the meaningful and the good?

～ Is there an underlying neuropsychological and neurophysiological structure of spiritual experience?

These are areas in which I think we need to know more. Questions of this kind begin to approach the core of spiritual experience. The problem is, however, that speculation about spirituality often leads instantly and without careful reflection to cosmic, encompassing concepts. Often these notions are vague and ill-defined, views on which it is difficult to achieve any consensus or clarity of meaning. The basis for the research that I wanted to do, though, is that most everyone who talks about spirituality has a spiritual story to tell. These personal and often moving accounts constitute a body of subjective knowledge that forms our oral tradition of the transmission of spiritual history, and is the raw data from which any meaningful research must begin.

Using the wide range and frankly beautiful subjective reports of spiritual experience, was there some way, I wondered, that spirituality could also be empirically examined? If spirituality could be investigated in a systematic fashion, then it might be possible to find ways for people to make use of their own spiritual experiences as well as the spiritual experiences of others. People could see themselves reflected in other people, and appreciate and respect any perceived differences.

To generate the PsychoMatrix Spirituality Inventory items, I consulted with family, friends, clergy, other psychologists, academics, writers, musicians, and poets to address the notion of what they thought might be usefully included in a group of statements describing spiritual behavior and experience. With help from my staff at PsychoMatrix, I developed a tentative set of items that I thought might be considered spiritual. I noticed in the acronym of the Inventory that I had "unconsciously" named it PSI, the name for the mysterious "sixth sense" that psychologists refer to as *psi*. With this extra push, the Inventory seemed off to a good start. I initiated focus groups with students and staff of various publications in the area of mind/body studies on the question of spirituality. Also, in my conversations with colleagues, some of whom were comfortable with the notion and some of whom were not, I sensed what kinds of ultimate concerns and existential issues might be considered spiritual but not specifically religious. For further development of the item set to be used in the Inventory, I also turned to my understanding as a psychotherapist of what experiences and practices might be considered spiritual. From years of clinical experience, I have come to appreciate the power of spiritual forces that can enhance or retard the growth and development of personality. From my work as a family therapist, I have also learned to appreciate the bonding—and explosive—power of spiritual practices, expectations, viewpoints and rebellions in the crucible of family life. Some of the most heated conflicts—for example, in divorce and custody disputes—occur in relation to the sharing and timing of religious holidays, the most symbolic of which (in our culture) are Thanksgiving and Christmas. I have witnessed parents literally and figuratively coming to blows over the question of who will have (halve?) the children on either of these holidays.

Christmas is particularly susceptible to individual, familial, cultural, and symbolic religious meaning and overtones. In one family with whom I worked, Beth, the mother, had a strong emotional investment in Christmas Eve. In her home as a child, this was a time when her family was closest and attended particularly meaningful evening or midnight services that she still remembers. These recollections were made all the more poignant during the pain of separation and divorce. Arnold, her husband, wanted the children with him on Christmas Eve, so that he could be with them when they woke up on Christmas morning to see all their gifts. Christmas morning was, for him, an equally charged and symbolic time that was an overlay of childhood religious and spiritual moments that he remembered with joy. The pain and agony that these symbolic moments possessed for Beth and Arnold reinforced my belief that the creation of any method for studying spirituality in general would also have to be cognizant of the psychological and emotional world into which I was tapping.

The importance of separating spirituality from psychopathology also was an issue in the development of this new measure. How can one be sure that reports of spiritual phenomena are not just some way in which the mind plays tricks on itself? I was partially reassured on this point by a discussion I had with a friend and colleague, a psychologist who is also a nun, and a member of a religious order. She explained the value she attributes to discussing spiritual issues with her patients. This person works with severely psychiatrically disturbed people and, in addition to psychological questions, discusses spiritual knowledge and observance in her group meetings with them. "There is no question that when we talk about God or spiritual feelings my patients can distinguish easily between hallucinations from their illness and the other dimension, call it religious or spiritual." It seemed to me that if psychopathology could potentially be separated from spirituality, then it might be possible to articulate the features of this unique spiritual dimension in some of the items I wanted to include in the new spirituality inventory.

As I continued gathering ideas about what kinds of items I might include in the Inventory, people recounted incredible stories of their near-death occurrences, out-of-body experiences, and other spiritual epiphanies. These people felt they had actually experienced these kinds of phenomena, so it never was an issue to ask if they "believed" that such things could happen. Consequently, because it might mean challenging a personally defined and emotionally charged part of an individual's internal world, it was clear to me that any measure of spirituality that focused primarily on belief was doomed. I decided not to ask general questions such as, "Do you believe in God?" because invoking such concepts might be too difficult for each person to define. This kind of question is also extremely problematic because it can raise issues about belief itself, such as what does "believe in" really mean, is it formal or personal belief, and so on. Specific questions were also ruled out, such as, "Do you believe in the Virgin birth?" "Do you believe that Moses saw a burning bush that was not consumed by the fire?" "Do you believe that there is a bright light and a pathway to another realm of existence?" "Do you believe that the earth is part of a 'Gaia mind' that encompasses a total harmonic, psycho-spiritual, ecologic system?" Rather than use ideological questions that could cause endless controversy and theological sophistry, I decided to concentrate my efforts on understanding spiritual practices and psycho-spiritual experience.

The items I finally chose for inclusion were, therefore, based not on belief but on actual experience and behavior. By using an item that could be answered as something one does or feels or senses, I deliberately sought to overcome any religious or ideological undertones in the inventory, and obtain a more direct view of spirituality:

～ I forgive others for their hurtful actions.
～ I feel the connectedness of all living beings.

~ I think about returning after death in a new life-form.
~ My prayers have been answered.

These statements, and 76 others in the same format, evolved into the PsychoMatrix Spirituality Inventory. Responses to the items are statements of psycho-spiritual fact, in terms of whether you do something or whether you have a particular experience, rather than endorsements of beliefs.

The PSI is an inventory based on self-report. Unlike some psychological measures, in which the meaning of answers is hidden from the subject or is inferred by the administrator of the test or questionnaire, this form has both strengths and weaknesses. It captures individuals' conscious experience of their behavior; but it leaves open the question of *why* they do what they do. The notion of motivation is important to understand, but it was my belief that with research this formative, it was preferable to begin with straightforward items requiring little if any interpretation.

Inventories similar in form to the one I created often use a five-point scale for answers. The PSI, however, uses only four answer possibilities in terms of frequency: "never," "seldom," "frequently," and "almost always." On a five-point scale, the midrange, "sometimes," is usually an option. Many people who take the Inventory want to know why this is not included as a choice. I deliberately exclude this category, because I feel it is important for those taking the Inventory to make a definitive statement one way or the other, rather than fall into the defensive posture of using "sometimes" as a default answer.

How Well Does the PSI Describe Spirituality?

THE VALIDITY of any assessment technique is first of all reflected in the degree to which the instrument, in this case the PSI, actually relates to what it says it is assessing. As an example of how a widely used concept might be tested, let's look at self-esteem. How do we know that a test of self-esteem actually measures self-esteem? The only way that the relevance, usefulness, and accuracy of such a test can be established is to determine first what is meant by self-esteem. What do we mean when we use the term, and what have other psychologists or social scientists been referring to when they have used it? Second, it is necessary to determine whether the items in a particular test are reflective of the concept in question. In other words, do the test items look as though they are part of the established meaning of self-esteem? If one knows what others have said about self-esteem, do the items in this particular test seem to reflect to the trained observer what is meant by self-esteem? A good example is an item that reflects pride in personal accomplishment. Given what we know about self-esteem, this item and others like it would fit well into any new measure of the concept. Finally, it would be necessary to check to determine whether the scores on this new test bear any relationship to other measures that might reasonably be related, such as popularity with peers or success in school.

Establishing any kind of validity with a new measure of spirituality would similarly have to propose items that bear some resemblance to the concept in question. The concept is spirituality. In order to make any sense at all, the items must at least be consistent with general notions of spirituality. This is the reason that I spent so much time and energy investigating what kinds of items would be implied by the general concept of spirituality, and why it is so important to include as wide a net as possible. Once items are selected, the question then is: Do they have enough relevance to spirituality that most people would agree that, yes, they seem to stem from this one particular concept? This initial "educated" impression is known in psychological parlance as *face validity,* which means that the items or questions that constitute a test or psychological measure "look like" or "on their face" seem to be the kinds of items that one would customarily associate with the topic.

The actual items of the PSI are based on common associations with the word *spiritual.* This concept includes traditional ideas of God, a Supreme Being, or a Transcendent Energy Source; items that reflect ideas about natural phenomena and the beauty and power of nature; and items that relate to health and healing practices or mind/body experiences. Because illness is such a powerful stimulus for spiritual thinking, I thought it crucial to include this crisis-stimulated aspect of spirituality in the item pool. "There are no atheists in foxholes" is an historic aphorism from World War II. Today this might be stated, "There are no atheists in operating rooms." Relevant items about illness and healing were, therefore, included in the form of asking people if they had experienced serious physical or emotional illness themselves, or witnessed it in people they loved or with whom they were close.

To acknowledge the specific religious or ritualistic aspects of spirituality, items that pertain to prayer and meditation were included. Spirituality may be thought of as encompassing religion or religiosity, because it is clearly a broader and more comprehensive phenomenon than the latter. Spirituality also pertains to a person's attitude and stance toward the outside world, the world of social organization, and to the view he or she has of past, present, and future. As a result, items about participation in community, childhood exposure to spiritual practices or ideas, as well as statements about near-death experiences, became part of the final version of the Inventory as it was rolled out for its first test flight.

Who Participated in the Study?

T HE PSI was pilot-tested on 714 individuals who were taking part in conferences oriented toward and focused on mind/body awareness, healing, spiritual practices, and consciousness and self-empowerment. These participants came from every walk of life and lived in all parts of the country. They were nicely representative in terms of geography, socioeconomic status, and educational levels. More than half had attended and completed college; many were professionals such as lawyers, doctors, and teachers; many were office workers and individual business owners; some were retired. In age, they spanned eighteen years to eighty. A large percentage were women.

This sample was obviously self-selected on the basis of interest in and inclination toward matters spiritual, and seemed a likely group to respond at least favorably, if not scientifically, to the new measure. In doing any research, it is most useful to start with a population that promises the greatest likelihood of success in showing the results the researcher hopes for. In colloquial terms, if you can't get results by studying the choir, chances are the results aren't in the congregation, either. I also asked those individuals who participated in this pilot portion of the research to share, in writing, their subjective descriptions of important or personally transformative spiritual experiences. The responses to this invitation were moving and profound descriptions of spirituality, as in the case of Diane, a mother and a professor of history at a liberal-arts college in the Midwest:

At age eleven, my son was diagnosed with a pinealoma, a tumor on the pineal gland. It was inoperable by position, and malignant. From the beginning, my prayer was not for healing his body. Somehow that seemed to be taking on a posture of knowing more than God about how things should be happening. My prayer was to see this as God's will and accept it as such.

After a year of brain surgery to install a ventricular shunt, then replace it twice, doctors felt that [my son's] condition had not been much improved and that he had twelve to eighteen months to live. In that lowest point, I had a dream that I equate to a near-death experience: I was in a beautiful meadow, walking toward a small stream only two or three feet wide. As I came near, I saw a huge rock on the other side. Standing next to the rock was a brilliant light being that I immediately recognized as a Christ Consciousness. The love, warmth, acceptance, and caring coming from that light were impossible to describe. Then a communication more than words spoke to me, saying: "As much as you love him, don't you know I love him more and I would never do anything that would really hurt him?" I released my worry and concern and trusted that an all-loving power was controlling events. It has changed my feeling about my children and my parents, as well as my friends. Incidentally, my son is alive and well twenty-five years later.

Diane's description of her experience is remarkable to me. It is filled with love, anxiety, faith, trauma, and a transcendence that became her epiphany. I was unprepared for this kind of depth of expression. This clarity and freshness in the memory of a transformative experience or moment was repeated by others who responded to the PSI as well. I realized that I had tapped into a remarkable reservoir of spiritual consciousness. I turned back to the objective data with enthusiasm and the hope that I might capture in the numbers and statistical analysis some of the qualities that these personal reports had so elegantly articulated.

Findings from the Pilot Study

Once the data from the original pilot group had been gathered, the statistical process of factor analysis began. Statistical questions basically ask, Are the thousands of responses (in the case of the PSI, 74,970 [105 × 714] responses) given to the spirituality items on the Inventory scattered in a random fashion among the 714 people? Or was there some grouping of responses that could be clustered into an identifiable pattern called factors? The statistical process of factor analysis finds these groupings—or factors—if they exist. In a pilot study of this kind, it is common to find one, maybe two, factors that are clusters of responses that have some statistical consistency, and are generated from the fact that the people who gave the responses did so in some consistent, identifiable fashion.

Astonishingly, *seven* factors emerged from the statistical analysis. This finding is remarkable because it demonstrates that it is possible to find commonalities of response to a group of statements that are chosen from a conceptual framework of what spirituality ought to look like or might look like. To achieve this result on the first factor analysis—a result that was upheld by subsequent factor analyses—demonstrated an even greater sophistication of the construct of spirituality than I had anticipated. Finding these factors meant that I could now proceed into a much wider field and investigate with confidence the spiritual experience of people in a way that permits comparison between groups and individuals. I felt confident that the PSI was a functioning measure of the construct we call spirituality.

Naming the Factors

ONCE THE statistical process revealed seven factors, it was necessary to decide what to call them. Factors emerge from the analysis as a collection of items. The researcher must inspect the items in the cluster and try to determine what qualities they have in common, and then find a name that is inclusive of the meaning associated with as many of the items as possible. As I inspected them, I saw that each of the factors had a distinct quality. The first cluster included those items that were concerned with God or a Supreme Being, prayer, and the feeling that human beings are here for a purpose. I chose to call this factor Divinity. The second cluster contained items that included activities of meditation, careful eating, and the use of exercise regimens. I chose to call this factor Mindfulness. Naming the other five factors with a similar process, I chose Intellectuality, Community, Trauma, Extrasensory Perception, and Childhood Spirituality. All seven factors are presented in more detail below.

The major finding of the study was that spirituality could be studied at all, and that seven relevant factors emerged from the data analyses. Other findings of the pilot study, and of subsequent studies as well, showed that scores on all factors are correlated with age. As age increases, so do factor scores. This makes sense when we consider that as people get older, they accumulate more life experience, experience the loss of loved ones through death and divorce, are likely to have had more illnesses, and to have struggled with the spiritual education of children. While some people reported disaffection with spiritual thinking as they advanced in age, the majority reported an increase. This finding was statistically significant, meaning that the probability that this correlation would have occurred by chance alone was less than 5 percent.

Another interesting finding of this early research was that women showed higher factor scores than men, in a statistically significant fashion. Does this mean that women are more spiritual than men? Not necessarily. What the finding may mean is that women are more comfortable using spiritual language in describing their inner lives than men are. We hope that further research will shed some more light on this question.

I published the findings from the pilot study in the *New Age Journal* in the fall of 1997. With the article, I included a copy of the PsychoMatrix Spirituality Inventory and invited the participation of the magazine's readership. Thinking that several hundred might respond, I was delighted by the thousands of responses that poured in. From this enthusiastic and wide-ranging response, I concluded that the desire to speak about, share, and understand these unique, intense, and transcendent moments of life is extremely powerful. I also learned that this strong urge to communicate either everyday or peak experiences is often held in check by embarrassment or social convention. In their subjective statements, many people revealed how they had never dared to share this kind of information before.

With the influx of thousands of new respondents to the PSI, I had a tremendous amount of new data to continue my investigation. Statistical analyses continued to support the findings. In addition, I expanded the representative nature of the sample to include people who may not have already identified themselves as interested in spirituality or alternative forms of healing. I began to include the PSI in my classes with college students, and to give it to psychologists who work in chronic care clinics. I also administered the PSI to medical patients undergoing chemotherapy or treatment for hypertension, to physicians and nurses, and to a group of prisoners in Massachusetts involved in an emotional literacy program. In short, the sample comprising this spirituality research is now more representative of the population at large.

The Seven Factors

D ESCRIPTIONS of the seven factors of spiritual practice and experience are elaborated in the following pages. With each description I also include the meaning associated with different scores that someone might receive after taking the Inventory. Once again, it is important to state that the terms *high, moderate,* and *low* are descriptive only. The natural reflex is usually to think that "high" means "good." In this scoring paradigm, however, high is neither good nor bad. Sometimes high is positive, sometimes negative. Think, for example, of high anxiety or high blood pressure. Conversely, low is also not bad or good. Under some circumstances, low means a positive and useful state. Low stress, low cholesterol, and low debt are useful examples that come to mind. The terms *high, moderate,* and *low* are merely a statistical convenience. The purpose of the numerical notations is to locate each person's responses in relation to the responses of every other person who has taken the Inventory.

It is also important to point out that someone who might score low on all factors is not low on spiritual intelligence, and therefore is not necessarily nonspiritual or aspiritual. A low score on Divinity, for example, is described as a commitment to the practical, to the here and now. That commitment is a belief in, and an orientation toward, the value of the pragmatic and utilitarian approach to life. Is this belief spiritual? Yes, most definitely, because *spiritual* means the existential center of one's relationship to the world.

FACTOR ONE: DIVINITY

This factor is associated with the sense of, or intuitive knowing about, a Divine Energy Source, Higher Being, or the feeling of awesome wonder in the presence of natural phenomena.

High Score. Individuals who obtain a high score on Divinity demonstrate a strong awareness of, and connection to, a Higher Being or Divine Presence, often when experiencing the beauty and power of nature and the arts. Such individuals report a feeling of closeness to God or a "Transcendent Energy Source," praying at specific times of the day, and being comforted by blessings. They also report having had their prayers answered, and having used angels for guidance. A high score on Divinity may indicate a strong commitment to such activities as praying for the recovery of a loved one. High scorers sense the sacredness of others, are convinced that humans are "here for a purpose," and often report having experienced miracles.

Low Score. Individuals who obtain a low score on Divinity demonstrate a pragmatic approach to life, with little need of reliance upon any form of Higher Being for peace of mind. For example, such individuals may deeply appreciate the power and beauty of nature or the arts without reference to, or awareness of, a Divine Presence. These people feel most secure in counting on themselves, family, and friends for support and nurturing in times of calm or crisis. They also tend to rely more on scientific explanations for illness and catastrophic events. Rather than holding the conviction that humans are "here for a purpose," low scorers are often more naturalistic in their ideologies.

FACTOR TWO: MINDFULNESS

This factor includes activities associated with attention to bodily processes such as conscious eating, regular meditation with focused breathing, and exercise like yoga or t'ai chi. This factor also pertains to alternative or integrative health practices.

High Score. Individuals who score high on Mindfulness set aside time for contemplation and self-reflection on a regular basis. They often report that meditation has been a meaningful part of their lives, and may also practice yoga, t'ai chi, or other relaxation techniques. High scorers on Mindfulness also pay close attention to the foods they eat and to the physical status of their bodies. These people use a variety of foods, vitamins, and dietary supplements to energize themselves or alter their internal physical balance to ensure optimal psychophysiological function. A high score on Mindfulness also indicates an individual who is affiliative, i.e., feels connected with, and seeks the company of, others as an opportunity to share ideas and concerns.

Low Score. Individuals who score low on Mindfulness do not regularly set aside time for contemplation and self-reflection. They report that meditation may be a pleasurable experience; but they may also practice yoga, t'ai chi, and other, more conventional relaxation techniques such as walking, hiking, and other forms of exercise, without necessarily connecting these activities to personal programs or larger contexts of meaning. Low scorers on Mindfulness are not particularly attentive to, or concerned with, the foods they eat or to the physical status of their bodies. These people use foods to energize themselves, independent of their internal physical balance. A low score on Mindfulness indicates an individual who has low affiliative needs, i.e., does not sense a connectedness to, or seek the company of, others as a way of sharing ideas and concerns. Such individuals tend to be comfortable being on their own and pursuing their own activities in a more solitary fashion.

FACTOR THREE: EXTRASENSORY PERCEPTION

This factor encompasses those items that pertain to the "sixth sense" or paranormal psychic events, ranging from receiving phone calls from someone "just as I was thinking about them," to out-of-body or near-death experiences.

High Score. Individuals who score high on Extrasensory Perception often demonstrate a range of psychic awareness that encompasses knowledge outside conventional ways of knowing. They often have the common experience of bumping into someone they haven't seen for years and were just talking about, or of sensing that some event is about to occur just before it does. High scorers on Extrasensory Perception sense the presence of loved ones who are no longer living, and report having conversations with those individuals. A high score on Extrasensory Perception is also correlated with reports of near-death and out-of-body experiences, and the belief in the existence of past lives.

Low Score. Individuals who score low on Extrasensory Perception rarely demonstrate a range of intellectual or psychological activity that encompasses knowledge outside conventional ways of knowing. They almost never report prophetic dreams or prescience of events that they intuitively felt were about to occur. Low scorers on Extrasensory Perception use their intellect and capacity for new knowledge in conventional, pragmatic, but often highly effective ways. They might, under highly charged conditions, briefly sense the presence of loved ones who are no longer living, but do not report having internal conversation or dialogue with that person.

FACTOR FOUR: COMMUNITY

This factor describes social activities that include peers—such as the Parent Teacher Organization—or activities that are on a volunteer basis and charitable in nature, such as working with the less fortunate and socially disadvantaged.

High Score. Individuals who score high on Community are involved with a wide variety of social activities that include other people, such as friends or mentors. They may be involved with charitable organizations, giving generously of their time and energy to the needy or the chronically ill, to homeless shelters or beautification projects. High scorers often attend religious services, consult with clergy or spiritual leaders, and participate in classes, workshops, and conferences concerning spirituality, or are themselves members of a spiritual community.

Low Score. Individuals who score in the low range on Community are seldom involved with the variety of activities that include other people, either as mentors, friends, or the recipients of charitable gifts of time and energy, such as the needy or homeless. Low scorers may attend religious services, but feel more of a sense of individual or family connection to ritual. They consult with clergy and spiritual leaders for personal gratification and psycho-spiritual improvement. They might seek out classes, workshops, and conferences where they focus on learning and new experience to help themselves grow and develop in an independent fashion. Those who score low on Community tend not to spend much time with school, civic, and political activities, or spiritual communities. Rather, they are most comfortable with a smaller, more intimate circle of friends or family, with whom they pursue those activities that provide them with emotional and spiritual nourishment and pleasure.

FACTOR FIVE: INTELLECTUALITY

This factor denotes a desire and commitment to read, study, and/or discuss spiritual material or sacred texts. It also incorporates the active questioning of traditional teachings of religion.

High Score. Individuals who score high on Intellectuality spend a good deal of time and energy reading about, discussing, and studying dimensions of spirituality. These people are intellectually curious and take pleasure in the cognitive and mental activity associated with spiritual experience. High scorers ponder such questions as: the justification for the existence of God or a higher power; the meaning and purpose of life; the finality of death; the reality of individual souls; and the possibility of the immortality of the soul, assuming its existence. They also report thoughts about returning after death in a new life-form. People who score high on Intellectuality discuss spirituality openly and are willing to question actively the teachings of traditional religion.

Low Score. Individuals who score low on Intellectuality focus their intellectual activities on issues other than spirituality. They may be extremely interested in learning and in complex cognitive activity, and their areas of interest may be far-reaching, but these areas generally do not include the spiritual. Low scorers seldom address questions of the existence of higher powers, life, death, and the immortality of the soul. These individuals prefer to examine specific social, political, or moral problems as practical problems to be understood and solved with logic and empirical evidence. They often experience life with enthusiasm, and focus on the concrete here-and-now in a rational and practical approach to the world. People who score in the low range on Intellectuality tend to keep their thoughts about spirituality to themselves, if they have them, and do not usually question the teachings of traditional religion.

FACTOR SIX: TRAUMA

This is the factor that is often thought of as a crisis-oriented stimulus to spirituality. It refers to the experience of illness—physical or emotional—in oneself or in a loved one. At the extreme, Trauma refers to the actual loss of a loved one through death.

High Score. A high score on Trauma indicates personal encounters with physical or emotional pain and suffering. This experience can be the person's own, or witnessing the suffering of someone close. In some cases a high score is correlated with a near-death or out-of-body experience in which the individual leaves his or her body and then returns. High scorers on Trauma have usually had, or have observed, more than one episode of significant illness or injury.

Low Score. A low score on Trauma is correlated with the report of fewer-than-average personal encounters with physical or emotional pain and suffering. This suffering can be the person's own, or witnessing the agony of someone close. Low scorers also tend to report few, if any, near-death episodes or out-of-body experiences in which an individual leaves his or her body and then returns. Individuals who score low on Trauma may be highly sympathetic to the pain of others, but may simply not have been exposed to these types of experiences.

FACTOR SEVEN: CHILDHOOD SPIRITUALITY

Childhood Spirituality is a factor that refers to spiritual experiences that took place during childhood, such as attending religious services or being read to from books like the Bible or the Koran by parents or grandparents.

High Score. A high score on Childhood Spirituality is related to frequent and meaningful spiritual activities early in life. These spiritual moments often are of being read to (from the Bible or other religious texts) by parents or grandparents. In addition, high scorers on the Childhood Spirituality factor usually attended religious services or religious schools as children, and frequently report that their parents or grandparents spoke often of God to them or in their presence.

Low Score. A low score on Childhood Spirituality indicates a relative absence of religious activity in childhood—either positive or negative in nature. Low scores on this factor may indicate extensive and deep ethical and moral discussions with family, but with little if any formal ritual instruction or expression. Family interaction may have included some religious holidays, such as Christmas, Easter, or Passover, but these events were more cultural and ethnic than religious or spiritual in terms of discussion of religious or sacred texts and exploration of the tenets of faith.

With these seven spiritual factors it is possible to describe the spiritual experience of individuals regardless of age, gender, or cultural, ethnic, or religious background. We turn now to the Psycho-Matrix Spirituality Inventory itself, so that you can experience this new methodology firsthand.

CHAPTER SIX

Taking the PSI

N ow that the conceptual background of the Psycho-Matrix Spirituality Inventory is established, it is time for you to take the Inventory and discover your individual spirituality profile. Find a quiet spot, save yourself one-half to three-quarters of an hour, and enjoy the process. The Inventory is thoroughly straightforward. There are no trick questions, no hidden agendas. The Inventory is designed to provide you with a spiritual snapshot of yourself. It is based on your honest and spontaneous responses to the items. When you take the Inventory, make sure you give your own answers without asking for the input of anyone else.

PsychoMatrix
Spirituality
Inventory

ALL RESPONSES ARE NORMAL.
YOU CANNOT PASS OR FAIL.

The Inventory is descriptive, not evaluative. High scores are not good; low scores are not bad. The scores locate your profile in relation to others who have taken the Inventory. As you read on in subsequent chapters, you will be able to match your scores with the detailed descriptions of the Seven Spiritual Factors, and the meanings associated with different scores. You will also find suggestions on how you can address spiritual aspects of your life that you may want to change or improve.

	Never	Seldom	Often (more than 50%)	Almost Always
1 I set aside time for contemplation and self-reflection.	☐	☐	☐	☐
2 Blessings comfort me.	☐	☐	☐	☐
3 I consult with clergy or spiritual healers.	☐	☐	☐	☐
4 I forgive myself for my own failings.	☐	☐	☐	☐

	Never	Seldom	Often (more than 50%)	Almost Always
5 I am aware of a transcendent energy source.	☐	☐	☐	☐
6 My parents expected me to attend religious services.	☐	☐	☐	☐
7 I think about serious physical injury that has happened to me.	☐	☐	☐	☐
8 I discuss spirituality openly with family and friends.	☐	☐	☐	☐
9 When I see a magnificent sunset or sunrise, experience a beautiful day, or observe the structure of a flower or a starlit sky, I am aware of a Divine presence.	☐	☐	☐	☐
10 I use certain foods to calm me.	☐	☐	☐	☐
11 I said my prayers at night as a child.	☐	☐	☐	☐
12 I have witnessed serious illness in people close to me.	☐	☐	☐	☐
13 I exercise with friends or acquaintances.	☐	☐	☐	☐

(continued)

	Never	Seldom	Often (more than 50%)	Almost Always
14 I feel the divinity of people I meet.	☐	☐	☐	☐
15 I think about the effects on humankind of the new millennium.	☐	☐	☐	☐
16 I pay special attention to the foods I eat.	☐	☐	☐	☐
17 I remind myself that human beings are here for a purpose.	☐	☐	☐	☐
18 I have cared for physically ill relatives or friends.	☐	☐	☐	☐
19 I sense that something is going to happen before it happens.	☐	☐	☐	☐
20 I participate in community activities, such as PTO, civic, or political organizations.	☐	☐	☐	☐
21 I discuss the existence of a Higher Being.	☐	☐	☐	☐
22 I sense the personality or the soul of animals like pet dogs or cats.	☐	☐	☐	☐
23 I use my own sense of ethics to guide my actions.	☐	☐	☐	☐

	Never	Seldom	Often (more than 50%)	Almost Always
24 When I hear beautiful music, I feel my body resonate to the melody or rhythm.	☐	☐	☐	☐
25 I think about my soul living beyond my body.	☐	☐	☐	☐
26 I practice yoga, meditation, t'ai chi, or other relaxation techniques.	☐	☐	☐	☐
27 My parents read the Bible or other religious books to me as a child.	☐	☐	☐	☐
28 I feel that my life is directed by God.	☐	☐	☐	☐
29 I like to read books such as the Bible, the Koran, the Upanishads, the Tibetan Book of the Dead, etc.	☐	☐	☐	☐
30 I volunteer time with the needy, the homeless, etc.	☐	☐	☐	☐
31 When I seek a professional consultant, such as a lawyer or an accountant, I consider whether that person is open to spiritual matters.	☐	☐	☐	☐
32 I use relaxation techniques to reduce stress.	☐	☐	☐	☐

(continued)

	Never	Seldom	Often (more than 50%)	Almost Always
33 I read about spiritual matters.	☐	☐	☐	☐
34 I understand the events of life as part of a divine plan.	☐	☐	☐	☐
35 I think about the experience of past lives.	☐	☐	☐	☐
36 I currently practice the religion of my birth.	☐	☐	☐	☐
37 If I feel sick, I remind myself that my body is influenced by my state of mind.	☐	☐	☐	☐
38 My parents spoke to me about God.	☐	☐	☐	☐
39 I pray at specific times of the day.	☐	☐	☐	☐
40 I feel the connectedness of living beings.	☐	☐	☐	☐
41 I attended religious services as a child.	☐	☐	☐	☐
42 I feel connected to my body.	☐	☐	☐	☐
43 I read books and articles about religious questions.	☐	☐	☐	☐
44 I feel close to God.	☐	☐	☐	☐

	Never	Seldom	Often (more than 50%)	Almost Always
45 I feel disconnected from my body.	☐	☐	☐	☐
46 I have witnessed emotional or psychic trauma in people close to me.	☐	☐	☐	☐
47 If someone I love is seriously ill, I say prayers for his or her recovery.	☐	☐	☐	☐
48 I use spirit guides to help me get through crises.	☐	☐	☐	☐
49 I forgive others for their hurtful actions.	☐	☐	☐	☐
50 I attend classes or workshops about spirituality.	☐	☐	☐	☐
51 I sense my own divinity.	☐	☐	☐	☐
52 I feel the presence of a power greater than myself.	☐	☐	☐	☐
53 Scientific explanations give me peace of mind in confusing life situations.	☐	☐	☐	☐
54 I judge others by my own ethical standards.	☐	☐	☐	☐
55 I sense the presence of loved ones who are no longer living.	☐	☐	☐	☐

(continued)

	Never	Seldom	Often (more than 50%)	Almost Always
56 I devote time to a spiritual community.	☐	☐	☐	☐
57 I think about out-of-body experiences I have had.	☐	☐	☐	☐
58 My prayers have been answered.	☐	☐	☐	☐
59 I think about life, death, and the hereafter.	☐	☐	☐	☐
60 I turn to my angel for guidance.	☐	☐	☐	☐
61 Meditation has been a meaningful part of my life.	☐	☐	☐	☐
62 I question many of the teachings of religion.	☐	☐	☐	☐
63 I use certain foods to energize me.	☐	☐	☐	☐
64 Beautiful music, powerful art, or meaningful theater makes me joyful or can even make me cry.	☐	☐	☐	☐
65 I receive phone calls from people just as I was thinking about them, or shortly after.	☐	☐	☐	☐
66 I focus on scientific explanations of the origin of life.	☐	☐	☐	☐

	Never	Seldom	Often (more than 50%)	Almost Always
67 I have experienced miracles.	☐	☐	☐	☐
68 I attend religious services.	☐	☐	☐	☐
69 I choose medical care-givers who are attentive to spiritual experience.	☐	☐	☐	☐
70 I attend conferences concerning spirituality.	☐	☐	☐	☐
71 I have experienced emotional or psychic trauma.	☐	☐	☐	☐
72 I was encouraged to decide about my religious beliefs as a child.	☐	☐	☐	☐
73 I follow a specific ethical code when deciding difficult issues.	☐	☐	☐	☐
74 I think about returning after death in a new life-form.	☐	☐	☐	☐
75 I feel awed by the power of nature.	☐	☐	☐	☐
76 My family encouraged community service.	☐	☐	☐	☐
77 I use alternative therapies such as acupuncture, aromatherapy, or massage.	☐	☐	☐	☐

(continued)

	Never	Seldom	Often (more than 50%)	Almost Always
78 I have conversations with people who have died.	☐	☐	☐	☐
79 My family practiced specific spiritual rituals.	☐	☐	☐	☐
80 I have memories of near-death experiences.	☐	☐	☐	☐

Scoring Your PsychoMatrix Spirituality Inventory

Scoring the PSI is straightforward and easy. Each factor is associated with specific items.

Your score on each item is based on the following scale:

Never = 1
Seldom = 2
Often = 3
Almost Always = 4

Here's How to Score Your PSI

Add up your scores for each item on each factor.

Divide this double digit number by 7. This number is your Factor Score.

Locate your Factor Score in the corresponding grid to determine if your score is described as High, Moderate, or Low. That's all there is to it![1]

FACTOR ONE. DIVINITY

Item	2	9	17	28	34	44	52
My Score							

My total score = _____

My total score divided by 7 = _____

My Divinity Factor score = _____

Divinity Factor Score	Low	Moderate	High
Male	less than 2.2	2.3 to 2.8	2.9 or more
Female	less than 2.5	2.6 to 3.1	3.2 or more

FACTOR TWO. MINDEULNESS

Item	1	16	26	32	42	61	77
My Score							

My total score = _____

My total score divided by 7 = _____

My Mindfulness Factor score = _____

Mindfulness Factor Score	Low	Moderate	High
Male	less than 2.3	2.4 to 2.9	3.0 or more
Female	less than 2.6	2.7 to 3.2	3.3 or more

FACTOR THREE. EXTRASENSORY PERCEPTION

Item	19	25	48	55	60	65	78
My score							

My total score = _____

My total score divided by 7 = _____

My Extrasensory Perception Factor score = _____

Extrasensory Perception Factor Score	Low	Moderate	High
Male	less than 1.3	1.4 to 1.9	2.0 or more
Female	less than 1.7	1.8 to 2.3	2.4 or more

FACTOR FOUR. COMMUNITY

Item	3	20	30	50	56	68	76
My Score							

My total score = _____

My total score divided by 7 = _____

My Community Factor score = _____

Community Factor Score	Low	Moderate	High
Male	less than 1.4	1.5 to 1.9	2.0 or more
Female	less than 1.4	1.5 to 2.0	2.1 or more

FACTOR FIVE. INTELLECTUALITY

Item	8	21	29	33	53	59	62
My Score							

My total score = _____

My total score divided by 7 = _____

My Intellectuality Factor score = _____

Intellectuality Factor Score	Low	Moderate	High
Male	less than 2.3	2.4 to 2.9	3.0 or more
Female	less than 2.4	2.5 to 3.0	3.1 or more

FACTOR SIX. TRAUMA

Item	7	12	18	35	46	71	80
My Score							

My total score = _____

My total score divided by 7 = _____

My Trauma Factor score = _____

Trauma Factor Score	Low	Moderate	High
Male	less than 1.0	1.1 to 1.9	2.0 or more
Female	less than 1.3	1.4 to 2.1	2.2 or more

FACTOR SEVEN. CHILDHOOD SPIRITUALITY

Item	6	11	27	36	38	41	79
My Score							

My total score = _____

My total score divided by 7 = _____

My Childhood Spirituality Factor score = _____

Childhood Spirituality Factor Score	Low	Moderate	High
Male	less than 1.4	1.5 to 2.1	2.2 or more
Female	less than 1.4	1.5 to 2.1	2.2 or more

This completes your Psychomatrix Spirituality Inventory. In the following chapters you will read how your scores describe your spiritual experience using the seven spiritual factors. For those of you who would like to have a written summary of your results on the PSI, you may go to www.psychomatrix.com to take the inventory, have it scored automatically, and receive a personal report.

CHAPTER SEVEN

Divinity

Now that you have taken the PsychoMatrix Spirituality Inventory, scored it, and created your spiritual profile, you have a reflective view in the psychic mirror of the pattern in which your spiritual energy is shaped. We can now turn our attention to the ways in which the PSI can *directly* influence your life. As you look over your scores on the PSI, think in terms of how they might relate to several areas of your life: work, family, personal relationships, and spirituality and worship. Remember, the Seven Spiritual Factors are never static or isolated. No factor stands alone. In discussing each factor, we will of necessity be discussing the ways in which the factors interact with each other in a dynamic and reciprocal fashion. When you examine your individual factor scores and your general overall spiritual profile, focus your attention on the interplay of spiritual energy that each factor contributes. We will use as our first example the Divinity scores and their experiential emphases.

The Divinity factor points to the areas of life commonly associated with spirituality, the dimension that includes a concept of some kind of Divine Energy Source, Transcendent Intelligence, or Higher Power, or God. This factor encompasses traditional religious beliefs and practices, but must not be equated with them. It is also important to remember that no factor, particularly Divinity, should be considered alone. A high or low score on this factor is only one of many ways to experience spirituality or to have this dimension influence the general shape of one's spirituality.

I also want to restate clearly that a high score on any factor is not intrinsically *good;* nor is a low score necessarily *bad.* The score you achieve on any factor simply shows the emphasis you place on that particular dimension of spirituality. This emphasis is reflected in the relationship of your scores to each other, and is also reflected in the larger context of how others generally score on any particular factor. A high score on Divinity, for example, indicates that in relation to your other scores—at least those in a different range—Divinity absorbs a high percentage of your spiritual energy. In addition, this high score indicates that you share that approach to your distribution of spiritual energy with others who do the same with their spiritual energy. Is that a "good" way to experience your spirituality? The question is not valid. A better question is "Is that your way of experiencing spirituality?" The answer to this question is definitely "yes." Once we remove the evaluative component of any testing, it is much easier to appreciate individual differences for what they are, namely different ways of being in the world—nothing more, nothing less.

Applications of the Divinity Factor

O NE OF the dimensions of life in which it might be useful to appreciate and understand the application of the results of your PSI might be at your place of employment. At work, for example, a high Divinity score might be translated into relationships with your co-workers that are supportive and relatively noncompetitive. The high Divinity score also implies that you might seek the deeper meaning of work and may demand that spirit-numbing activity be either eliminated or at least rotated among many different employees in order to combat feelings of meaninglessness and anomie. According to Danah Zohar, "Corporate management must start talking about the spiritual and philosophical questions of our time."[1] A recent issue of *Business Week* magazine featured a lead story about the spiritual transformation of the corporate workplace, and articles from the Harvard Business School reinforce the new view of spirituality's place in corporate America.[2] It is not uncommon to find executives going on meditation retreats, or taking time in the middle of the day when they remove themselves from the office cacophony and select a quiet spot to sit, meditate, and reflect on what they consider to be the higher power that influences the lives of management and employees alike. Some companies include employees in the new approach to work, encouraging thoughtful reflection and the contribution of ideas, as well as acceptance of responsibility for the quality and meaning of work performed.

Service professions are also seeking to incorporate a more humane and thoughtful approach to work. A small group of lawyers in the Boston area, for example, meets on a regular basis to use a "holistic approach to bring deeper meaning to a profession often derided as morally bankrupt." The group—originally consisting of lawyers who were also: a Methodist minister, a mystical Jew, a traditional Buddhist, and a Zen practitioner—recently focused their attention on the issue of forgiveness, "looking at clients in the contexts of their whole lives and mindsets."[3]

Physicians are also being introduced to the dimension of Divinity with their patients. This need has always been part of the doctor-patient relationship, with physicians many times being the only individuals with whom a dying person could or would converse about fears, beliefs, and the meanings of various choices attending the end of life. New attitudes, however, are dictating the formal teaching of this kind of sensitive caregiving with regard to these most personal and difficult issues. The Sloan-Kettering Cancer Center in New York has a program on integrative medicine, as does the consortium of hospitals associated with the integrative medicine curricula at the University of Arizona, Duke, Stanford, Johns Hopkins, Columbia, and Harvard, to name but a few. Many clinics and hospitals now help patients and their caregivers focus on questions of ultimate concern that people face at the end of life. It is understandable that these caregivers are the natural recipients of the desperate hopes, concerns, fears, and anxieties of their critically ill patients and their families, because physicians, nurses, and hospital staff spend such intense and focused time with them. The spiritual dimensions of the Divinity factor come into play in a dramatic fashion under these conditions. Many physicians and staff at hospitals report that their own sense of spirituality is both activated and challenged by their daily interactions with their patients' moral and ethical dilemmas.

A friend who is a rabbi told me of the medical ethics groups she conducts with local physicians. Questions that arise lead quickly to ultimate commitments and beliefs. In one recent meeting, for example, the issue of elective cosmetic surgery was discussed. From the Jewish perspective alone, this rabbi reported, a variety of guidelines could be followed. From the strictly Orthodox point of view, cosmetic surgery is considered by some rabbis to be a desecration of the body. For other Orthodox rabbis, the surgery is a violation of the sanctity of the body, unless there is some larger meaning such as enhancing the beauty of a woman to enable her to have a higher probability of attracting a husband. In short, for this group, cosmetic surgery is permitted if it is tied to the saving or perpetuation of a life. For the conservative and reform groups of Judaism, the standards are governed more by the individual's right to self-determination than by sages' interpretations of the Bible. Interestingly, the position of the reform movement in Judaism is actually less flexible than the Orthodox one, but for very different reasons. Their argument is based on the notion that beauty should emanate from within. If someone decides that she needs plastic surgery, it may be because of a faulty self-concept, reinforced by distorted social standards. This motivation, the argument continues, drives people (mostly women) to seek market-created self-enhancement, and the practice is to be avoided on social/psychological grounds, rather than because it violates a commandment from God.[4] The point is that these issues are (fortunately) being raised on a regular basis, not only by patients but also by their doctors and caregivers.

High Score

I F YOU SCORE high on the Divinity factor, then prayer and a sense of wonder are likely to be your companions as you proceed through life. The meaning of existence comes to you as a connection to a larger transcendent phenomenon, rather than being strictly grounded in the pragmatic concerns of daily life. For some, this connection provides peace of mind in difficult circumstances such as death and serious illness—a subject we shall address directly when we talk about the factor of Trauma. For others, this connection provides an opportunity to escape from the practical demands of the necessities of life and can become an impediment to growth and personal development. You can use your high score to signal the strong degree of spiritual energy that is focused on the dimension of Divinity, and decide how to best implement this commitment in your life.

Your high score on the Divinity factor may indicate that you see your work as a sacred duty, one in which the meaning and purpose of work are revealed in daily endeavor. This view can give a special meaning to your workplace and imbue it with energy and a sense of daily refreshment and replenishment. For those who love the work they do, the workplace can become a haven where they are involved in a labor of love, one in which they feel *called* to perform their daily tasks.

In some corporate business settings, the spiritual direction of the company is set by the CEO who may use his or her strong commitment to Divinity and ethical principles derived from a religious and spiritual background to direct and guide company policy—as in the case of Timberland (a manufacturer of outdoor footwear and clothing) or Tom's of Maine (which makes personal-care products).[5] The use of spiritual concepts in the workplace is growing daily. National and international conferences on the role of spirituality in the world of business are being held on a regular basis. A high score on the Divinity factor implies a willingness to see in work, in business, and in corporate dealings a need for standards based on compassion and nonexploitative practice. You must be careful, of course, as a director or manager, not to impose specific spiritual views on others in the work setting, and to remain open to other points of view. A high score on the Divinity factor only becomes problematic if it implies a rigid and dogmatic approach that could foster intolerance and impatience with others.

A high score on the Divinity factor also has implications for the way in which you might relate to the members of your family. You probably see family as a source of blessed connection, and enjoy those in your family as part of the gift of life. You may experience a strong need for, and commitment to, the transmission of family values and spiritual values. This bond between you and your family is based on love and the feeling of connection to a transcendent life force.

The risk associated with a high investment of energy on the Divinity dimension is that you might become so dedicated to your own sense of the value of certain family relationships and traditions that you lose sight of the needs of others in the family who may not share your perspective, and who would score in a different range on the Divinity factor.

Moderate Score

A MODERATE score on the Divinity factor brings a blend of the two ends of the spectrum. Features of the high score on Divinity, such as interest in and reflection on the nature of God or a Divine Energy source, combined with a here-and-now pragmatic view, are the hallmarks of this dimension. One achieves the best—and worst—of both points of view. This combination can be demonstrated in the workplace or at home. You may, for example, see work as a blend of the sacred and the utilitarian, with high importance attached to your interactions with colleagues.

In terms of family relationships, moderate scorers on the Divinity factor may feel very strong family ties and also deeply believe in the value of the transmission of family values. If your factor score is moderate, it would not be surprising to find you encouraging learning and experimenting with new activities, but modulated by existing structures of family life. It can be very trying, for example, to make the right choices for sleeping arrangements when a college senior brings his girlfriend home for Thanksgiving. There is the tension between traditional values and the modern approach to sexuality, which forces parents to confront their moral and spiritual values and then to try to integrate those views with the outlooks and needs of their nearly grown children. A moderate score on the Divinity factor indicates that you would most likely be willing to make some accommodation to the current mores, while still working at incorporating the value of respect and adherence to personal spiritual tradition.

Low Score

A LOW SCORE on the Divinity factor does not imply that an individual is not spiritual or is aspiritual. It simply means that for this person the world is a place in which one must deal pragmatically, objectively, and "rationally." People who score low on Divinity rely on empirical evidence that can be measured by scientific means, rather than on evidence that may be used to point to a higher energy source or what some call God. It is interesting that well-known scientists and cosmologists such as Albert Einstein and Stephen Hawking have little trouble using the notion of God in their writings and speculations about the nature of the universe. Others, however, like Sigmund Freud, may view the notion of God as a purely human construction, satisfying a psychological need, and for which there is no empirical evidence. In neither case would it be accurate to say that one of these scientists is spiritual, the other not. Rather, it would be accurate, in my estimation, to understand that each experiences spirituality in his own personal way. Freud's passionate commitment to "making the irrational rational" can be easily viewed as a deeply spiritual act, even though he doesn't feel compelled to cast his theory in terms of a Divine Energy Source.

The low score on the Divinity factor signals an attitude toward this dimension of spirituality that is focused on the practical here-and-now aspects of life. If we look at the way in which this attitude plays out in the world of work, you may find that a score in the low range on the Divinity factor implies that you regard your work in pragmatic and utilitarian terms. Work is a job to be accomplished, and you may take great satisfaction in persevering and completing these tasks without necessarily seeing in your work some additional layer of meaning. In these terms, your vocation accomplishes the ends of fulfilling obligations, making the money necessary for living, and feeling good about the fact that you are able to function in a useful way. Work, in this sense, becomes an end in itself and satisfies on its own terms.

A low score does not imply disdain for spirituality, but other people may see it as indifference. It is important for you to remember that a pragmatic approach to life, a focus on the objective facts of day-to-day existence, is but one of many possibilities. For some people, one danger of a low score on the Divinity factor is the implied or overt cynicism toward those who might score high on the Divinity factor and speak of their closeness to God. You might be tempted to view these colleagues as being too soft-headed or easily influenced by otherworldly concerns and therefore not to be trusted with difficult business- or work-related decisions. You must remember not only to strive for tolerance but also for understanding of those with different points of view.

If you score in the low range on Divinity, your family relationships can well be based on the deep pleasure of bonding with others, with a commitment to learning and relating through critical inquiry and scientific or pragmatic discussions. Of particular interest is the dynamic that may exist in your family between one member with a low score on the Divinity factor and another person in your family, say a child, who has spiritual needs and interests.

In one family I work with, for example, a father, Ben, who scored in the low range on the Divinity factor thoroughly enjoys and treasures being with his children. Yet he feels uncomfortable and limited as a parent in answering his eight-year-old son, Tommy's, questions about God or about life after death. Using the findings from the PSI, he can now recognize this difficulty as part of the way he sees the world, rather than as some personal or moral deficiency. Consequently he now chooses to consciously devote more attention to carefully listening to his children with an open mind.

Similarly, Ben's wife, Laura, scored high on the Divinity factor. She was frustrated in trying to comfort Ben during his recent angioplasty and hospitalization, because she put his health in "the hands of the Divine Energy Source," while what Ben needed were careful scientific explanations for his diagnosis and treatment.

My conversations with Ben and Laura in connection with their scores on the PSI have helped them understand the spiritual points of view that define each of them. Rather than argue about forcing the other into a particular way of looking at the world or feeling frustrated with his or her spouse for being "stubborn" or oppositional, both Ben and Laura can now appreciate that each of them has unique spiritual needs which are not consciously under his or her control. Their unique and personal style forms the personality structures and individual patterns with which they express their spiritual intelligence.

If you score in the low range on the Divinity factor, you probably find meaning and fulfillment in a wide variety of activities including work, leisure, and the arts. Your tendency, however, would be to tie those activities to a personal construction of life's requirements and opportunities rather than as an implementation of, or connection to, a Divine Energy Source or Higher Power. The pleasure you feel on a daily basis comes from the practical and present creative acts that make life livable for what it is, without a desire to create larger contexts of meaning.

The Dynamic of the Divinity Factor in Personal Relationships

N O MATTER what score you receive, the role of the Divinity factor in personal and intimate relationships can be extremely powerful and lead either to conflict or growth. Consider the example of William and Brenda, deeply in love and engaged to be married. They have actively discussed nearly everything about their lives except their spiritual beliefs and preferences. William's enthusiastic commitment to his church and involvement with family activities surrounding religious events has always made Brenda uncomfortable, but she has held back her comments, thinking her misgivings might make William angry or push them apart.

At my suggestion, each of them took the PSI as part of their premarital preparations. William's score on the Divinity factor was predictably high; Brenda's was (from William's point of view) disappointingly low. Interestingly, the reverse was true on the factor of Trauma, where Brenda scored extremely high. As we noted earlier, no factor exists in isolation, and Brenda and I examined her scores on the Divinity factor in relation to her scores on the Trauma factor. The two dimensions stimulated memories of her past that she was eager to explore.

As their consultant, I had encouraged this couple to identify the origins of their differences, in the hope of fostering better dialogue and understanding. William and Brenda then began a spiritual (and spirited) conversation in which was revealed the fact that her reticence and even cynicism about spiritual issues was tied to the untimely and painful death of her father from pancreatic cancer when she was eleven years old. Brenda had mentioned this fact to her fiancé, but the deep pain was far from her consciousness, and she treated it as if she had resolved the issue. This loss left Brenda feeling abandoned by her father and by God, and so she abandoned them both.

William finally understood Brenda's resistance to participating in his spiritual life, and the unconscious pressure he was putting on her. Brenda, tearfully acknowledging her pain and self-protection, was now able to open her heart to dimensions of her own spirituality that had lain dormant for years. The couple took their marriage vows with a new appreciation of each other's emotional and spiritual needs and sensitivities.

Experiences with Divinity and the qualities that affect intimate relationships can come from surprising sources in unexpected ways. Linda Weltner, the gifted *Boston Globe* writer, contacted me after reporting the following spiritual epiphany in her weekly newspaper column:

> I can't help replaying in my head one thing that happened the night Jack [my husband] became ill. My husband is a doctor, you understand, and when he comes up with a diagnosis, I always listen. That night he'd spoken to our internist, who'd agreed with Jack's analysis that all he needed was a shot of

Demerol for a terrible migraine. We left the house sometime after 1:00 A.M., heading for a local emergency ward.

I got to the end of our street. I was planning to turn right, but I looked left first, just to check the traffic, and the street was empty all the way to Boston. I couldn't see all the way to Boston, of course, but I could feel the call of that empty road, as if it were summoning me. I remember the moment perfectly. I went to turn right, but something came between me and my conscious intention, and before I knew it, we were headed to the Massachusetts General Hospital emergency room. Within fifteen minutes of our arrival, he was in the hands of an outstanding neurology team . . . preparing for surgery for a cerebral aneurysm . . . We have no words to describe the voice that speaks in silence, the power that shines in darkness, the invisibility that now and then appears to guide us through life's mysteries. No words, that is, but thank You.[6]

This example underscores the unpredictable nature of an experience with a "voice" or a "power" that many individuals describe as their understanding of the Divine. It is important to note that an articulate woman like Linda Weltner chose not to speak of her own intuition, thereby locating the experience of **saving** her husband's life within herself. Rather, she anchored this powerful experience in the external world, and saw herself as a receiver of information and guidance. In my view, this attitude toward knowing is one that defines the Divinity factor—namely, the sense that we are not alone, that forces outside ourselves exist, and that from time to time these forces intervene in our lives. These interventions occur in ways that can be termed fortunate or blessed, and can add joy to our lives; or they can be a source of pain and destruction for which it is difficult to find meaning without the aid of an overarching system of belief.

A recent study reported by Shelly Taylor and her colleagues demonstrated a fascinating relationship between beliefs and the course of illness. In working with men who had AIDS, the researcher found that individuals who accepted the fundamental reality of their disease and all the implications of the nature of their illness did not live as long or with as much satisfaction as did those patients suffering from the same illness who held "unrealistically optimistic" beliefs about the outcome of their illness, or who saw some meaning in the suffering they were experiencing.[7] While the beliefs, optimism, and meaning were not coded for dimensions of Divinity, it is striking to find the data to support the notion that these kinds of mental processes have such a powerful effect on the body and life itself. This interaction between mind and body is the subject of the next chapter.

CHAPTER EIGHT

Mindfulness

The factor of Mindfulness denotes attention, through conscious living, to activities and attitudes that increase the quality of life through improvement of physical and psychological health. One of the hallmarks of Mindfulness is the use of alternative or integrative therapies, dietary supplements, and what have come to be termed *alternative, complementary,* or *integrative* treatment formats for physiological difficulties and medical conditions.[1]

A 1990 study that examined such treatments as acupuncture, chiropractic, meditation, massage, reiki, and the general use of alternative health care in the United States found that patients averaged as many visits to alternative health care practitioners as they did to traditional medical practitioners.[2] This finding is all the more interesting because very few if any of these alternative forms of treatment are covered by third-party insurance, meaning that individuals had to pay for these treatments out of their own pockets—which they did to the tune of billions of dollars annu-ally. A 1997 follow-up study found that the number of patient vis-its to alternative health care providers had eclipsed visits to standard medical caregivers with a ratio of three visits to alterna-tive medicine providers to two of standard care. People are serious about their health, and they will go to great lengths to preserve or improve it. Very often, these visits to alternative caregivers are *in addition* to the visits to regular doctors.

The factor of Mindfulness demonstrates the degree to which your spirituality is bound up with this kind of personal attention paid to yourself and your loved ones.

Mindfulness also implies, particularly for those who emphasize this dimension of spirituality, an acceptance of the seamless flow between mind and body. In this view, there really is no mind *and* body, just mindbody. An individual is viewed as an integrated sys-tem of living in which qualities traditionally viewed as either mental *or* physical interact with each other to such a degree that it is impos-sible and unnecessary to separate or artificially force them apart.

The interaction of mind and body has been documented in many studies, some of the most interesting and puzzling of which include pseudocyesis (false pregnancy). How is it possible that all the symptoms of pregnancy, even to the point of cervical dilation as well as labor and delivery pain, can occur in the absence of a fetus? How does the mindbody "know" when and where to create the symptoms? There are also verified reports of false pregnancy in men—the couvade phenomenon—in which the father's belly swells and labor pains are experienced. (A recent issue of a preg-nancy catalog offering a variety of teaching aids for expectant families included a kind of "pregnancy vest," complete with weighted front, for fathers to wear so they might empathically experience the phenomenon of being "heavy with child.") This process indicates the degree to which ordinary psychological and physical boundaries between people can be lifted. It is as if the mindbody were malleable enough that the connection between people can resemble the connection within a person. The psychoanalytic concepts of wish fulfillment and projective identification (i.e., the psychological process by which one alters his or her own personality by becoming like another esteemed or feared person) do not quite explain the magnitude and precision of these phenomena. Mindfulness appears to tap into a deeper and more fundamental relationship of mind with body that may be initiated with a symbolic representation, but soon becomes a physiological process with its own energy and purpose. There is no question at this point in history that the distinctions philosophers, scientists, and the lay public have traditionally made between mind and body are outmoded and do more to confuse than to explain.

The Mindfulness factor implies careful attention to the state of one's body as an extension of the mind. For example, anyone who has had a serious illness knows the power of pain and "dis-ease" to arouse immediate attention that becomes riveted on the body. The exquisite interconnection of mind with body is also dramatically demonstrated in an elegant series of experiments with patients who experience the sensations—often extremely painful—of "phantom limb," namely the continued perception of the existence of an amputated arm or leg. This example highlights, in a way few other experiences can, the degree to which mind and body are one.

A neurologist at the University of California at San Diego, V. S. Ramachandran, devised a method for helping patients who were experiencing very real and excruciating pain from the cramping and spasm of a missing limb, or of nonexistent fingernails digging into their nonexistent palms. He showed that the map of the human body undergoes transformations following the loss of a limb. This map is located on the surface of the brain (the somatosensory cortex), and contains a location corresponding to every body part.

Once a limb is amputated and therefore can no longer send sensory impulses to the brain, other parts of the body are invoked in the mapping, so that, for example, portions of the face (which is, incidentally, adjacent to the arm position on the map in the brain), actually correspond to the missing hand and arm. Rubbing a cotton swab lightly over the cheek produces the sensation of having the swab run up and down the arm! In this instance the mind has essentially relocated its image and picture of the body to accommodate a new reality, but residual sensations associated with the missing limb are maintained.

To see if the pain of phantom limbs could be ameliorated, Ramachandran devised a technique in which he constructed a visual illusion of both arms being present when the patient inserted the remaining arm in a cardboard box containing vertical mirrors. To his—and the patient's—amazement, the clenched fingers of the virtual hand opened, and the rigid, spasm-producing position of the arm (which was immobilized prior to the amputation) re-laxed. Patients reported that "the pain is gone" when they looked in the mirrored box that provided visualization of two arms instead of one. The pain returned when the patient did not have the aid of the mirror technique until, with repeated use, the mind/ brain remapped the representation of the body correctly. A con-trol stimulus of mild electric shock produced no effect, thereby demonstrating conclusively that it was the visualization of the restored arm and not a suggestion or placebo effect of the experi-menter that accounted for the pain reduction.

What is remarkable in these mind/brain/body studies is the rapidity of the transformation of the brain mapping as well as the plasticity of the human brain circuitry. This plasticity seems to violate the basic tenet of neurology that body image mapping is laid down early in life and remains stable throughout the life span of the individual. These experiments also show that the image and experience we have of our bodies and the interrelationship of vision, motor feedback, and the map that exists in our brains are all part of a *constructed* reality that is malleable and changeable.

Mindfulness implies that the brain does not, as some artificial-intelligence researchers speculate, behave like a computer, with each module of the brain performing a specific job and then passing along the task to the next module. In that model, the sensory nerves in our eyes, ears, and fingers receive input and pass the information along to higher and higher brain centers. Instead, a more accurate model would show that connections in the brain are extraordinarily active and dynamic, and that perceptions are the result of interactions from different levels of the same senses as well as from different senses. "The fact that visual input can eliminate the spasm of a nonexistent arm and then erase the associated memory of pain vividly illustrates how extensive and profound these interactions can be."[3]

The factor of Mindfulness elucidates this deep interconnection of the brain/mind/body. Individuals who score in the high range on this factor are aware of the power of the influence that one system has on another, whether it is the effect of proper diet on a general sense of well-being, or the alteration of brain states through meditation and focused breathing. What makes this factor particularly relevant to spiritual intelligence is that the self-reflection and conscious intentionality of Mindfulness point to a state of mind that produces a sense of transcendence through the mindbody itself. This conscious awareness can make one highly sensitive to both inner and outer psychic and physical environments—a sensitivity that can lead to an appreciation of the "wonder" associated with daily life. A high score on the Mindfulness factor indicates a focused and intentional use of mind/body perceptions. A low score does not imply that the connection between mind and body does not exist for that individual, but simply that conscious, focused spiritual attention is directed elsewhere.

High Score

A HIGH SCORE on Mindfulness most likely is correlated with exercise and fitness programs incorporated into your daily routine. You also may use deep breathing techniques to overcome the effects of anxiety and stress, or to enhance performance by connecting with a different state of consciousness. You may also participate in, or may have initiated, meditation sessions conducted during regular intervals in the day.

A former patient of mine, Kathryn, has to run at least three times a week or she "can't function." It all started three years ago when she decided she was turning into a flabby "couch potato" and needed to get some exercise. She was working long, hard hours at her job as a research analyst for a large investment banking company, and feeling more and more sluggish and depressed. She tried St. John's wort, vitamins, and a variety of health foods, but decided that what she really needed to feel better was to start moving purposively, rather than in the agitated state of anxiety with which she lived most of her business day. To hear her talk now, it's as if the Mindfulness dimension of her own spirituality has exploded into bloom. "I finally learned to breathe," said Kathryn, with a look of triumph in her eyes. "I never knew what it meant to be able to feel my breathing so keenly, and to feel so connected to it. I think it's almost a, well, spiritual [this is a word she has never used in the years I have known her] feeling. Now, if I don't run on a regular basis, my body and mind don't feel right.

It even helps me if I feel like I'm getting a cold or the flu. I can almost sense the activation in my immune system." Kathryn scored high on the Mindfulness factor, a confirmation of the new connection she feels between her mind and her body.

One of the dimensions of Mindfulness that is sure to emerge if you score in the high range on this spirituality factor is the use of alternative or complementary forms of healing. Sometimes an attention to the preparation and consumption of foods and dietary supplements becomes almost a means of purification. Many families are vegetarian or restrict their food exclusively to that which is organically grown. If you adopt such a lifestyle, you may run the risk of being ridiculed by your children who plead for some refined sugar or just one bag of Doritos, but your commitment to careful eating is deep and abiding.

You can use your high score on the Mindfulness factor as a reminder of the influence this aspect has on your personal and intimate relationships. Many people who score in the high range on this factor find themselves attending workshops that emphasize exercise, introspective communication, and artistic expression of intimacy. Their intimate and sexual relationships may be suffused with symbolic and mystical meaning. Attention to physical health is also important, and many high scorers on Mindfulness have become dissatisfied or frustrated with traditional medicine, often because of conditions that become chronic and resistant to the Western pharmaceutical approach.

Martha is a patient of mine who has been disenchanted with her traditional health care providers. For the last ten years, no Western doctor has been able to help her with a chronic sense of fatigue and recurrent bouts of influenza. Rather than hear again that she's the victim of a compromised immune system or probably just depressed (which she isn't), Martha has turned to the alternative and holistic medical approaches. She reads Andrew Weil's self-healing newsletter faithfully, and follows his recommendations of herbal remedies. Martha is now a regular at the acupuncture clinic, has gone to Chinatown here in Boston to purchase a pharma-copeia of unusual (from my of point of view) drugs and herbs, and has had all of the mercury in her fillings removed and replaced with less dangerous dental products. Recently she reported that she feels much better! A lot of her energy has returned. The care and attention she pays to her mindbody has changed the clinical picture to the point where she has now regained the vibrancy and energy she thought was lost. In case you hadn't guessed, Martha scored in the high range of the Mindfulness factor on the PSI.

For those of you who score high on the Mindfulness factor, this dimension of spirituality and worship holds the promise of meditation and self-reflection as part of a daily ritual. The kinds of experiences you might seek include retreats oriented toward yoga, singing, and focused breathing. You see your physical activities as a method for connecting to the experience of transcendence.

Moderate Score

I F YOU SCORE in the moderate range on the Mindfulness factor, you are likely to set aside time during the day or week for exercise and contemplation. This time provides you with an opportunity for sheer physical exercise and camaraderie, which you use for the development of an inner sense of peace or well-being. You choose your foods carefully, but not exclusively on the basis of healthfulness.

Caroline is a Buddhist. Raised in northern California by her counterculture parents, she moved East to attend college. During her junior year she met Brian. The couple fell instantly in love, and were married shortly after graduation. Caroline and Brian moved to New York City, where Brian went to business school and Caroline pursued her studies in Eastern religion and was a mom to a set of twin boys and a subsequent daughter. Brian received his MBA and took over the CEO position of an Internet start-up company. They settled into raising their three children in the Buddhist tradition with a mixture of Brian's latent Catholicism—a concession Caroline made to Brian's insistent extended family.

Seven years ago the family moved to the Boston area. Eighteen months ago, Brian announced that he needed "more space" to work on his own personal development and to follow his dream of travel and artistic pursuits. He took a separate apartment in a downtown complex fifteen miles from the family home. By agreement, Brian continued to visit the children at their home, to be there for dinner and help with homework before leaving for his own apartment.

On the way home from a meditation session at the Buddhist community one day, to prepare dinner for Brian and the children, Caroline discovered that she literally couldn't breathe. "My chest becomes so tight that I can't get any air in," she sobbed. "When he's there, he takes up all the space, there is nowhere for me. We don't fight. We decided that the children didn't need to see us bicker, and we're trying to work out a civilized arrangement. It's not the Buddhist way to yell and scream, but this is killing me. My energy is essentially gone, and I can't sleep. And I noticed today that I breathe much better when Brian is out of town."

Caroline's symptoms are clear indications of the interaction of her psyche and her body, her mindbody. Most of us take this connection for granted, in the sense that few people are surprised to hear of such a reaction to a significant event such as Caroline's. What we forget to remember, though, is the *automaticity,* the high-speed reflexive nature, of these physical responses. They occur without our planning them, and often it takes the observation of an outsider to bring the connection of the response of our bodies to our minds into consciousness.

If an individual is not high in the Mindfulness dimension, there is a stronger probability that the mindbody concept is still at a less conscious level or has not been a strong focus of attention. One of the ways in which you can use your scores on the PSI with regard to the Mindfulness factor is to reflect upon the way your physical being experiences and expresses anxiety, conflict, or stress. Spending time with yourself, by yourself, in purposeful reflection can add dimensions to your own awareness that might surprise you. Caroline and I discussed her breathing. She began to practice mindful breathing in the presence of difficult situations when she would have previously held her breath until the difficult interaction passed. From her meditation practice at the Buddhist retreats she attended and the focused breathing that was already part of her repertoire, Caroline gradually caught sight of herself trying to catch her breath under stress, and she learned, consciously at first, to release her breathing and make it more relaxed. Once she was able to breathe normally, she was then able to retain clarity in the midst of conflict and deal much more effectively with the situation. The Mindfulness factor describes the energy associated with these psychophysiological processes, and can provide a stimulus for understanding the role they play in everyday activities.

A score in the moderate range on the Mindfulness factor indicates that you may share many of the same concerns and habits with those who are in the high range, but from more of an educational point of view, with an eye toward generally healthful eating and use of traditional as well as alternative sources of health-related information. You most likely exercise either alone or with family members for pleasure as well as peace and relaxation. Fast food doesn't scare you, and you might, for example, occasionally take the children to McDonald's or indulge in sugar-coated doughnuts.

If you score in the moderate range of Mindfulness, personal relationships are a source of pleasure to you and you may enjoy meditation and self-reflective discussion in ongoing activities with a partner. Sexuality, for example, can be enjoyed as a physical expression of intimacy as well as of deep friendship. A moderate score on Mindfulness may also be correlated with the pleasures associated with techniques of breathing, exercise, and self-expression through music, poetry, or dance. A feeling of transcendence can be mixed with a focus on the here-and-now and being-in-the-moment.

Low Score

I F YOU score in the low range on Mindfulness, you might pursue athletic and physical exercise such as walking or hiking as pleasurable on their own with no necessary reference to larger meaning. Assuming demands of the job don't necessitate eating at your desk every day, breakfast or lunch in the workplace can be a time of relaxation and sociability with minimal concern for content in terms of nutrition or preparation.

A score in the low range on Mindfulness indicates that you probably use food for energy, preferring basic meat and potatoes or bacon and eggs to organically grown or non-animal-based alternative foods. You may love to eat, but eating and nourishment are not imbued with special meaning. Rather, mealtimes are simply part of ongoing daily activity or an opportunity to dine with family or friends, enjoying the sociability of the moment. You may spend time with your family and children in a relaxed fashion, participating in activities such as helping with homework, watching TV together, or playing board games. You may also spend some time in the day-to-day conflicts associated with family life. In either case you may find that it would be useful to focus some of your energy on more conscious attention to physical and psychological dimensions of living. As a low scorer on the Mindfulness factor, you pursue activities like attendance at arts events, film, and sporting activities for enjoyment and relaxation. You derive pleasure sexually or emotionally from the physical expression of being together with someone you care for, but without the need for psychic exploration. Some people report that the enjoyment of social and intimate activities can be enhanced with increased effort in terms of mindful behavior.

Martin knocks on my door at eight o'clock in the morning. He has already been out walking his dog, and is now ready for a game of tennis. "It's a beautiful day," he beams. "I have to coach soccer for my son's peewee league this afternoon, but wanted to get some exercise first." We play, sweat a lot, shower, and then head out for some breakfast at the local diner. Aware that I'm not as quick on the court as I would like, I order one egg, lightly scrambled, and dry toast, juice, and coffee. Martin is less circumspect. He orders two large muffins, two eggs over easy, bacon, a large glass of juice, and coffee with cream.

Martin and I have a great time together. His approach to life and his spiritual center are not oriented to scoring high on the Mindfulness factor. In fact, Martin's quick mind and keen intellect show up as extremely high on the Intellectuality factor. His considerable mental energy—reflected in his love of and passion for thought—shows where one of his spiritual centers lies. This example also demonstrates one of the strong features of the PSI. Remember, the key concept is to appreciate the overall pattern that describes an individual's personal and unique experience of sacred moments. A high score or a low score on Mindfulness, or any of the factors, is less important than the way in which it reflects your own distribution of spiritual energy.

With a low score on the Mindfulness factor, your spiritual and worshipful activities tend to be focused on the here-and-now. You use self-reflection, introspection, and meditation for self-understanding and psychological insight. Your symbolic thought tends to be oriented toward interpersonal relationships, both present and past, with little emphasis on a transcendent context of meaning.

CHAPTER NINE

Extrasensory Perception

The spirituality factor of Extrasensory Perception (ESP) covers a wide range of experiences and alternative ways of knowing about the self and its relation to the world. In this context, ESP can refer to such mundane and relatively commonplace occurrences as receiving a phone call from someone you were just thinking about, or meeting a person about whom you have been talking. We've all heard, countless times, "Oh, isn't that funny, I was just thinking about you. I had a feeling I would bump into you." Obviously, not everyone has these kinds of experiences, but for those who do, the sense of certainty associated with this knowledge is unquestioning.

At the other end of the ESP scale are experiences that are less common, the origins of which are difficult to explain. Some people report prophetic dreams, prescient percepts, and near-death (NDE) or out-of-body experiences.[1] These experiences are reported by the individual as part of conscious experience, even though they sometimes have a dreamlike quality. An ancient Chinese proverb describes a man who wakes from a dream in which he was a butterfly, and is not sure whether he is a man who has dreamed he was a butterfly or a butterfly who is dreaming that he is a man. Often, if someone reports a vivid dream that feels real, the sense of conviction carries the same power as the report of an NDE or out-of-body phenomenon. Here is an example of a memory of an event that occurred fifteen years previously, vividly and beautifully described by Ashley, a nineteen-year-old college freshman who was four years old at the time:

I believe I crossed the line, and then returned. While my parents unpacked in our Florida hotel room, my babysitter took me [age four] and my two sisters, Jennifer, six, and Julie, two, to the pool. My babysitter placed me on the steps of the shallow end, and went to watch Jennifer do tricks in the deep end. Confidently, I entertained myself by swinging on the railing and prancing along the second step from the bottom. Then I slipped. I immediately panicked, but desperately tried to swim to the edge of the pool. It was only when my fingers scraped along, but could not grasp, the rough surface of the cement around the edges of the pool that I knew I was in serious trouble. I started to cry underwater, and tried, in vain, to scream for my parents—"Mommy, Daddy"—but the words were muted by the water that enveloped me . . . the realization that I could not be heard tortured me . . . I could not escape, and I was not being rescued. Soon the water that was choking me was replaced by a glow that seemed to encompass me. I was in my own world. I stopped thrashing around in the water and arrived in a new place where everything was peaceful and calm, and everyone was cheerful and happy. I could not distinguish people, but I could feel the presence of beings; I was not alone.

After having been without breath or heartbeat for ten minutes, I was revived by a stewardess who had recently been trained in CPR. I have recovered fully, but my outlook on life has never been the same. Having come so close to death gives me a completely different way of approaching life . . . I don't fear much, and I don't fear death, for one reason: I believe I experienced it. Today I have a calm within me that seems to protect me from fear.

The above example is a classic near-death report, articulate and expressive and all the more compelling because the person lived through this event at such a young age. I spoke with this young woman's parents and with the guest of the hotel who had been at the pool that day and saved Ashley's life and who verified the facts of the case. She had been without breath for at least eight to ten minutes! Her mother also told me that her daughter's memory of being taken to the hospital by ambulance was accurate. And, yes, her attitude toward life took a much different path from that of her siblings.

How are we to understand these kinds of unusual and transformative experiences in light of the concept of spiritual intelligence? Are these mental events spiritual? Are they hallucinations, fantasies, elaborated memories? Why do so many of the reported near-death experiences share similar descriptive elements—the white light, the peacefulness and feeling of bliss or ecstasy, the long tunnel, the conversations with departed loved ones or some kind of life review?

In a series of fascinating studies, Michael Persinger of the Behavioral Neuroscience Programme at Laurentian University in

Ontario tries to show that these experiences and the mental activity associated with them are a function of the architecture and organization of the brain.[2] Persinger describes the fact that a lack of blood supply—and hence lack of oxygen (hypoxia)—to certain regions of the temporal and parietal lobes of the brain stimulates usually quiescent neurons to begin firing. The lack of blood supply can be a result of trauma to the head; ingestion of pharmacologic agents such as hallucinogenic drugs; meditation; drowning; or the firing of electrical impulses through the brain as a result of an epileptic seizure. In some cases, the firing of neurons in the memory center (hippocampus) is accompanied by a life review; in some, a release of natural opiates (endorphins) contributes to the feeling of pleasure and bliss.

In order to test these hypotheses in an ethical manner, Persinger and his colleagues use very weak magnetic current and stimulate the brain in both temporal lobes (above the ears) simultaneously or one at a time, in order to try to replicate the effects of electrical and other stimulation, in a controlled way. Their results show that the timing and effects of this stimulation are correlated with the verbal reports in many of the volunteers for the study. Seventy-three percent report feeling "dizzy or odd"; 24 percent—and particularly those for whom the stimulation was in the right temporal lobe—describe "the presence of someone";[3] and 26 percent say they feel "as if I had left my body." Many other feelings are reported, but it is significant that the verbalizations associated with the NDE and out-of-body experience are so well represented.

This research is noteworthy, I think, because it is a step toward showing the experimental induction of a near-death experience, locating it in a specific region of the brain, and demonstrating a neurophysiological mechanism by which these events can take place. Other research about the effects of magnetism on mental states confirms the relationship of this kind of stimulation and psychic consequences. In these experiments, magnets are passed over the cortex (front and side) as a means of elevating mood in depressed patients.[4]

Persinger believes that these mental experiences often associated with near-death or out-of-body experiences can be induced by many other means, including drugs, meditation, and epileptic seizures (hyper-religiosity is a symptom of temporal-lobe epilepsy). He also states that in his view the specific form the experiences assume is determined by—or at least strongly influenced by—the cultural context in which they occur. Physiologically, these responses are in some sense universally replicable, just as the reaction to certain drugs is a response that can be generalized. Culturally, the responses may take on specific forms. For example, if a near-death experience is naturally or experimentally induced in an individual who has a strong Christian identification, it would not be surprising to hear references to biblical figures or even to Jesus himself; if, however, the experience is induced in a member of a pantheistic tribal culture, references might be made to a spirit world that contained unmanageable supernatural forces.

The question for us is, because the near-death and out-of-body experiences—and even feelings of the ecstasy of mystical union— are localized in portions of the brain and are a function of biological underpinnings, does that mean that they are not spiritual? Are we better served to consider them simply a feature of the neurologic functioning of our temporal or parietal lobes and associated brain structures like the hippocampus (for memory) and the amygdala (for emotional power and significance)?

In my view, there is no question that we need to understand brain architecture and to accept the notion that mind requires a biological base on which to stand and function. This does not mean, however, that mental phenomena can be reduced to biological processes. This is the critical junction between brain and mind.

Without brain structure—the biological basis of life—there is no possibility of the existence of mind. The mystery is how consciousness and mental experience emerge out of the assemblage of billions of neurons with their billions of interconnections. The whole of mind is clearly more than the sum of brain, its neurological parts. To reduce our most sacred experiences to biochemical interactions is the same as reducing Shakespeare to a series of linguistic signs and symbols.

As an analogy, let's consider what happens if a group of horsehairs is stretched to a tensile pressure of xx pounds per square inch, then pulled across a series of wound wires, graduated in size, which themselves are stretched to a tensile limit of yy pounds per square inch. The motion creates sound vibrations that reach first the outer and then the inner ear. In a representative sample of human beings, the result can be a painful or pleasurable experience, depending on whether the horsehairs are being pulled by a kindergartener or by Isaac Stern, producing either a painful screech or a "syndrome" known as the Beethoven Effect. This phenomenon is, I submit, widespread and potentially demonstrable with millions of people. The result of this hypothetical experiment is just as consistent as the mental effects of the various pharmacological agents that researchers such as Persinger invoke to substantiate (justifiable) claims for the universality of the organization of the human brain.

Is the music beautiful if it is played by an accomplished musician? Is the mystical moment spiritual and transformative? Does our awareness that we are going to die provide a perspective on our relationship to humanity? I think the answer is yes to all of these questions. I also think that knowing some of the underlying physiological mechanisms which provide the material from which these experiences emerge is both useful and relevant in helping us understand the functioning of our biological selves. With the knowledge of how the brain functions physiologically, we can repair damaged cognitive systems and better comprehend how the development of mental capacities occurs. Mind is not possible without the supporting physiology of brain, but the two are not synonymous.

The distinction between mind and brain is a time-honored one. *Mind* is often used as a synonym for *soul,* that mysterious and elusive life force that constitutes the essence of our being human. Persinger describes what he considers to be some of the neurological underpinnings that are part of our sense of enduring self, our souls. Like many, he views a belief in the preservation of the self or the soul after death primarily as a source of anxiety reduction in the face of imagined mortality, or in the moment when the body faces its neurophysiological limits and "death is highly probable."[5]

For thousands of years, however, the question of the existence and immortality of the soul has been at the heart of philosophical and theological speculation, as well as a critical feature of the enduring power of religion and all forms of spirituality. The question resonates from Plato, who sends Socrates' speculations about the two forms of existence, one "seen," the other "unseen" (as noted in chapter 2) across the ages. Aristotle, too, was very clear in his assertion that the soul was the essence, the "whatness," of being human.

Moreover, since the possession of knowledge must precede its exercise, the soul may be defined as *the initial actuality of a natural body endowed with the capacity of life.* Soul is the essential whatness of a thing in the sense of its definitive meaning, the essential and enduring character of a body possessing the capacity of life. If the eye were an independent organ, sight would be its soul, for it is in terms of sight that the essential whatness of the eye must be defined.[6]

René Descartes, the French philosopher, is, as much as anyone, responsible for the view we have of ourselves that separates soul (mind) from body. He locates the seat of the soul in a physiological setting, the pineal gland:

> . . . it is only the innermost part of the brain, which is a certain very small gland, situated in the middle of its substance, and so suspended over the passage through which the animal spirits of the anterior cavities communicate with those of the posterior that the slightest movement on its part can do a great deal to alter the course of these spirits, and reciprocally, that the slightest change in the course of the spirits can do a great deal to alter the movement of this gland.[7]

Interestingly, Descartes' ideas about the pineal gland and the soul sound remarkably—prophetically—like a description of the thalamus, the basic information traffic center (nerve center) of the brain. Two respected current neurological texts describe the thalamus this way:

> The thalamus is the gateway to the cerebral cortex. All sensory inputs (except olfaction) pass through the thalamus before they reach the cortex. Similarly, motor inputs to the cerebral cortex pass through the thalamus.[8]

Or:

> The thalamus processes most of the information reaching the cerebral cortex from the rest of the central nervous system.[9]

What I am suggesting here is that it is possible to analyze the basis of mental functions in terms of its physiological components, but we must not be led astray by thinking that the two phenomena are equivalent. The ancients, in their wisdom, described *soul* as the essence of being human. Later philosophers like Descartes, in the spirit of rationalism and empiricism, focused on the *mechanisms* of mind, creating the bifurcation, the split in concepts, that we are now finally beginning to overcome.

This discussion of the relationship of mind to body, of brain to soul, underscores the fact not only that this issue is part of our existential heritage, but also that we must be careful not to fall into reductionism—making our most sacred, meaningful, and spiritual moments equivalent to the efficient or inefficient firing of neurons in the brain. Even though they require a biological substrate in order to exist at all, I believe that near-death experiences, mystical epiphanies, and the emotional transport of the Fauré *Requiem* all qualify as spiritual events grounded in our spiritual intelligence. In this fashion and for these reasons, the Extrasensory Perception factor denotes a set of real spiritual experiences.

The ESP spiritual factor encompasses the more unusual and less rational or easily explained ways of knowing. Many people, when pressed, admit that they guide their lives (particularly major moral and existential dilemmas) by their intuitions, their "gut feelings," of what the right choice may be in a difficult situation. As the Gallup polls suggest, every week millions of Americans and untold numbers of people around the globe gather together to worship some form of Divine Force, and embrace the notion of knowledge based on faith, belief, and internal conviction.[10] Consequently, the impact of these other forms of knowledge on daily life, which for some is a repository of a good deal of spiritual energy, would be reflected in high scores on the ESP factor. For people who may mistrust or be frightened or unaware of the power of this mode of being in the world, the scores on the ESP factor would correspondingly fall in the low range.

The knowledge associated with Extrasensory Perception can affect your life in many ways, at work, in your family and personal relationships, as well as in the form of worship or sacred ritual that you find meaningful. High scores imply that you are familiar with this form of being in the world, and may have found opportunities to apply the perceptions that seem to come from other than the five senses. Low scores imply that your approach to daily events is governed by a more practical, objective point of view.

High Score

A HIGH SCORE on the ESP factor may have direct implications for your life in the workplace. You may, for example, find that your business decisions are based on intuition as much as on considered reasoning. Often it is necessary, in the face of a very close and nearly evenly balanced judgment call, to be able to "trust your gut," your innate sense of what will work in a given situation. In a moment of crisis, perhaps in a courtroom or in an operating room where a decision is required that will affect the lives of others for years to come, a background of factual knowledge and experience come together in a moment of insight that is a new creation. There are reports that some people even use their dreams to solve problems, both personal and intellectual, in a process termed "lucid dreaming"—a form of dreaming in which the dreamer is aware of dreaming and consciously selects a difficult issue to resolve.[11]

Steve, a lawyer whose skill at handling custody disputes is considerable, called me one day to consult at a hearing in which his client was accused of hitting his wife and being a danger to his children. The husband sought custody, claiming for his part that the wife was manic-depressive and that her wild mood swings were destroying their marriage and making her unfit as a mother. The judge looked at the husband and asked, "Did you hit her?" "Yes, Judge, I did hit her. That was nine years ago. I slapped her too hard. She was, you know, in my face, screaming at me. It was wrong, and I haven't hit her since. Now I just walk away." Further testimony corroborated the husband's claims about his wife concerning her wild and erratic behavior, and her general neglect of the children. The judge gave custody to the father.

I asked Steve why he had let the husband say, so directly and with so little qualification, that he had hit his wife. General courtroom strategy would usually dictate a more circumspect contextualization of the event—not to falsify it, but to shape it in hopes of softening the impact. Steve replied, "I'm not sure, really. I didn't plan to have my client testify like that beforehand. But I know him, and I know this judge, and seeing the wife here in court and watching her behavior . . . I don't know, I just had a feeling."

"I just had a feeling. . . ." This is the code for the enactment of the level of knowledge that the ESP factor appears to tap. We hear it all the time. Some people call it intuition, hunch, feeling, or sixth sense. Whatever we call the process, it is clearly something other than a logical, completely rational way of knowing.

In your family setting, a high score on the ESP factor may underscore the use of your "third eye" or "inner ear" for understanding the needs and mental states of family members. Somehow, mothers and fathers know when something is wrong with one of their children. Even though today we often learn, tragically too late, of parents who were completely unaware of the trouble their children were in, or the activities they were planning, in many other cases the Extrasensory Perception that occurs in families is striking. If you score high on this factor, you will probably encourage alternative ways of knowing in your family, for example in using intuition as opposed to formal diagnostic tests, where the health and well-being of loved ones is concerned. High scorers on the ESP factor demonstrate a consciousness of a nonlogical connection to other people. Their relationships with family members and intimate partners are suffused with a sense of knowing the other person's inner world in an empathic, almost automatic, process.

In the arena of spirituality and worship, a high score on the ESP factor usually indicates a feeling of connection to an ultimate Energy Source that accounts for the ability to intuit reality at many different levels. This state of mind is described by poets and mystics as the feeling of oneness or existence on the astral plane:

> *God*
>> *loves the soul so deeply*
>> *that were anyone to take away from God*
>> *the divine love of the soul*
> *that person would kill God*
>
> *So too*
> *it is a joy to God*
>> *to have poured out*
>> *the divine nature and being*
>> *completely into us*[12]

The mystics mean by Spiritual Marriage no rapturous satisfactions, no dubious spiritualizing of earthly ecstasies, but a life-long bond "that shall never be lost or broken," a close personal union of will and of heart between the free self and that "Fairest in Beauty" Whom it has known in the act of contemplation.[13]

Moderate Score

A MODERATE score on the ESP factor often shows up in a business setting as a tendency to temper risk-taking and intuitive decision-making with close analysis and a recognition of the economic requirements of any situation. You may be willing to consider the concept of psychological variables affecting the stock market and business, but you also have a strong need for mathematically derived empirical evidence to support any particular business choice.

Moderate scorers on the ESP factor show an interest in, even a tolerance of and curiosity about, other ways of accessing knowledge besides through the traditional five senses. This interest is further encouraged if your partner intuits some source of information or feels some prescience about a life event that in fact materializes. You are also open to discussing the possibilities of other realms of existence, even though you yourself may not be 100 percent certain that such realms exist. The scientific evidence that is coming back from the Hubble telescope, for example, of the existence of other planets in other solar systems strikes you as plausible and prepares you for the belief in extraterrestrial life.

You acknowledge the possibility of alternative realities that we can only know at the edges and lightly feel the brush of against our daily lives, but with a moderate score on the ESP factor, you generally take a practical approach to spirituality. You may well have a commitment to the probability of the immortality of the soul, but you are also troubled by the nonscientific quality of this concept.

Low Score

A LOW SCORE on the ESP factor highlights your focus at work on the practical task, the job at hand, with little interest in or behavior toward anything other than the basic five senses. Attention to the more intuitive side of decision-making strikes you as unnecessarily risky and not showing good business judgment. Business realities, for you, are governed by logical and well-tested theories based on sound economic principles.

A low score on the ESP factor is often correlated with a deep commitment to family and to the realities of day-to-day life: going to work, getting children up and off to school, helping with homework and housework. Your marital relationship can be experienced as a deep and powerful stabilizing force in your life and sense of well-being. For the low scorer on the ESP factor, aspects of personal and intimate relationships may be enjoyable, including the emotional, physical companionship, and the sharing of ideas with an emphasis on the here-and-now of practical duties and pleasurable activities.

The commitment to family and the need for deep interpersonal bonding, whether for high, moderate, or low scorers, may not always be satisfied and fulfilled. If one member of a couple, for example, scores high on the ESP factor and the other scores low, without mutual respect and appreciation of each other's way of being in the world, conflicts can ensue and profound misunderstandings can take place. A high or low score does not guarantee any particular form of psychological behavior. Rather, the scores serve as guides to understanding the distribution of spiritual energy and focus of attention.

In terms of the dimension of spirituality and worship, a low score on the ESP factor emphasizes practical ethics with a focus on the treatment of people by people, as opposed to dependence on the intervention of some kind of outside force or Divine Energy Source. Rational and scientific principles are how you gauge the usefulness of ritual and spiritual behaviors. For example, knowledge that spiritual activity can lead to prolonged life in cancer patients, or facilitate postoperative recovery, may be the determining factor for you in engaging in some form of institutionally based worship.

In general, the spirituality factor of Extrasensory Perception must be understood as more than an attraction to the mystical or occult, a view that is often associated with discussions of this concept. The ESP factor includes and describes some of the most powerful of all life activities, such as mystical union with the One, near-death experiences, or the feeling of overwhelming joy and beauty on hearing an inspired rendition of Beethoven's Ninth Symphony. Appreciation of the power of this dimension of spirituality and its interrelationship with the other spiritual factors enhances our comprehension of the far-reaching strength of spiritual intelligence as it functions throughout our lives.

CHAPTER TEN

Community

The essence of the Community factor of the PsychoMatrix Spirituality Inventory is the concept of group. Other forms of spiritual experience may involve other people or individual behavior, but unlike community, they are not defined by the presence of and concern for others. The psychic energy that a group provides can hardly be underestimated. From singing in gospel choirs to organizing labor unions, the sense of connection to others in a group can be invigorating, exciting, and create a feeling of purpose and meaning. The spirited exuberance of group activity needs no documentation. Can we, however, consider this phenomenon as part of spiritual intelligence? As Robert Watts Thornburg, dean of Marsh Chapel and chaplain to Boston University, posed the question in one of our conversations, "Is there a difference between team spirit and Holy Spirit?"

Being part of any group, whether as the cast member of a play, singing in an opera, or scoring the winning soccer goal, can all be sources of pleasure and joy. But how can we understand the relevance of these communal experiences to a spiritual notion of community? There is no doubt of the emotional power of group activities and gatherings. For me, the distinction between thousands experiencing excited awareness at a concert, or while watching a favorite baseball team, and the spiritual dimension of community described by the PSI is a difference based on the context of meaning.

Exciting, passionate group experience in the arts, politics, or athletics occurs frequently and forms a basis of communal activity. From a spiritual perspective, however, community participation is based on the notion of compassion. Compassion implies a consciousness of the needs and concerns of others, and administering to those needs becomes a moral act. Attending to others and placing their needs ahead of oneself is often described as "the right thing to do." In so doing we enlarge the scope of our particularity, and find the transcendent reality behind daily activity through communal life.

This idea of community need not be rarefied or unapproachable. The Community factor does not require heroic or remarkable feats of human kindness, or saintly acts of compassion. Sending letters to the editor of the local paper about pressing social issues and concerns; working for a political candidate who you believe will make a difference in the quality of life for his or her constituents; supporting the work of charities by sitting on boards and making contributions of mind and/or money; finding ways to improve the lot of the less fortunate by enlisting those sitting on the sidelines; speaking out at PTO meetings in order to improve the overall quality of education for your own children and the children of others: all of these are representative samples of behavior that I include in the Community spiritual factor.

The compassion that often surfaces during the holiday season becomes an excellent vehicle for community involvement. Some families, for example, may choose to spend part of every Thanksgiving or Christmas with their children at a halfway house or soup kitchen, providing care and nurturance to the less fortunate. A priest in upstate New York wrote back that he had received his results on the PSI. "In general," he said, "the report described me pretty accurately. I was surprised by my low score on the Community factor, until I realized that this is an area of my ministry that I have been intending to develop. With all of my other duties, I have let my contact with the community slip. This is a good reminder for me to make sure I accomplish something I had been intending to do." He also requested a shipment of twenty-five additional PSIs for use with his spirituality group at the church.

Some people have favorite causes that occupy their time and energy throughout the year, such as fighting for clean air and water, or combating prejudice through curriculum development in the schools. The global community created by the Internet has astounding power to create positive communal force. A series of rock concerts called Net Aid took place in three different stadiums including Wembley in England and Giants Stadium in the United States. These concerts were designed along the lines of the Farm Aid and Comic Relief concerts, which raised millions for the homeless and the needy. In this case, however, the concerts were broadcast on the World Wide Web, and raised tremendous sums of money that were then donated to a multitude of charitable organizations. Politicians and devoted members of the lay community may fight for increases in funding to develop quality programs. These initiatives may be in the areas of education; Medicare and social security; health-care reform that would guarantee health insurance to the millions of currently uninsured in America alone; support for basic biomedical research; and protection of the environment. These efforts are examples of the sources of spirituality that can be demonstrated in the arena of Community.

High Score

A HIGH SCORE on the Community factor conveys the sense of bonding with other people that stimulates a feeling of purpose and meaning in life. At home, Community essentially equals family life. One often hears people say that in spite of external success or failure, "it is my family that gives my life meaning and reminds me what I am working for." Family is the quintessential expression of community. In fact, the extension of intimate family relationships into society at large is precisely what the spirituality factor of Community measures.

Roger Gottlieb, a professor of philosophy at Worcester Polytechnic Institute, describes how spirituality through community participation takes an individual beyond the self and into a larger, transcendental context of action and responsibility. He presses for involvement in the critical social issues of the day:

> If spirituality means, among other things, moving beyond my isolated ego, then resistance [to evil and suffering] is that movement. For in acts of resistance I go beyond my isolation, my self-concern, my very sense of myself as fully separate. And that sense of moving beyond my ego takes me not only into connection with the suffering Others who are human, but with the more-than-human as well.[1]

Community always involves a group outside the self, and the path to community takes many turns as it winds through individual lives in unpredictable ways. In the following portrayals, we see two very different journeys to a similar goal. The dynamic of the Community factor is particularly relevant here because the interplay of other spiritual forces creates a background against which this factor is played out.

Bill grew up in Indiana, the son of an affluent businessman and his socialite wife. Bill attended college in the San Francisco Bay Area where he met and fell in love with Barbara. She had spent years as a labor union organizer working under the leadership of Cesar Chavez on behalf of the migrant farm workers. When he first came to see me for psychotherapy, Bill had moved with Barbara to the East Coast, where he was working as a labor organizer in a local hospital workers' union. He was extremely successful in this position. In fact, Bill's commitment and dedication earned him the respect of workers who had grown up in blue-collar families, far from his own social origins. His ability to empathize with the plight of less fortunate people created bonds for him in the community of the union, and Bill began to prepare himself for career advancement in the labor movement.

The problem was that whenever Bill visited his family for Thanksgiving or Christmas, he found himself in the middle of bitter, vitriolic fights, particularly with his father, who threatened to disinherit him if he continued his union organizing. Bill and Barbara stood fast in their ideological commitment, but the conflict was taking a toll on Bill and on his marriage. He struggled with the possibility that perhaps his father was right—that he was wasting his life on futile activities. He was also particularly concerned about the potential loss of his inheritance, since he and Barbara were beginning to discuss having a family.

As he and I reviewed his history, Bill realized that his view of life had changed radically from that of his upbringing. His family lived a protected and privileged life in a gated community, and spent their leisure time at a gated country club. Bill, in contrast, had opened himself up to the needs and sufferings of the world, and spent his energies trying to right what he considered the injustices of American corporate life. He had turned his back on the upper middle class, or, rather, taken them on in open battle through his dealings with union grievances. Even though there were compelling family pressures trying to force him back into his "proper" station in life, Bill was holding fast to his beliefs and to his identity in the labor movement.

Bill scored in the high range on the Community factor of the PSI, reflecting his deep involvement in promoting the welfare of those less fortunate than himself. His consciousness of the needs of others showed a sense of caring that he felt was misunderstood by his parents, the people he most expected would have his best interests at heart. In our work together, Bill tried to understand whether his choice of vocation was neurotic or sincere. In other words, his keen mind struggled with the issue of whether his role in the union was generated by feelings of rebellion against his father, by psychological identification with his wife, or by genuine compassion for others.

My discussions with Bill about his responses to the PSI indicated that he experienced his work as a calling, a psycho-spiritual imperative that drove him with passion and dedication. After many conversations with his father and mother, heated, spirited, and finally reflective, his parents began to appreciate the sincere basis of their son's choice. Interestingly, Bill also scored high on the Divinity factor, a score that didn't surprise him in the least. He noted that "I now understand what some clergy mean when they say they are doing God's work. It's not that I believe in a specific God, but when I accomplish something in the union, I really feel connected to a force much larger than myself."

A combination of high scores on the Community and Divinity factors has not been unusual in the research findings. Many individuals who are connected to their communities as a vocation or an avocation express this awareness of transcendence as a sense of integrating themselves in a group consciousness that is larger than the sum of its individual parts.

Another dynamic between factors is that of a high or moderate score on Childhood Spirituality and a high or moderate score on Community. This combination highlights the potential for positive early experience in childhood correlating with group involvement in the community in later life.

Bill chose a life path with a heavy focus on his connection to the community. Although his choice was diametrically opposed to the path his parents would have chosen for him, he finally achieved some measure of peace with them. In terms of the choices one makes in life, there are as many stories as people. We'll look now at two more individuals who also scored in the high range on the Community factor, but who arrived at this point by a significantly different route.

Joe's dad was an inner-city Presbyterian minister in the 1940s. He came up through the ranks, and finally achieved recognition from within the local religious hierarchy when they elected him to the position of minister in charge of community relations. He led marches against racism and McCarthyism, and when Joe and his brother came along, they cut their teeth on folk songs while attending services at which their father gave impassioned sermons. Joe's dad even flirted with socialism for awhile, thinking that this ideology could substantiate his arguments about better relationships in his multicultural parish. Joe was well aware of the evils of racism, intolerance, and social disintegration that were regularly discussed at his dinner table. Joe earned a Ph.D. at a local divinity school and, like his father, took a post with an inner-city church that was desperate for an infusion of new blood.

Joe married Julie, a woman who shared his general philosophical outlook of moral behavior and social justice, but who, unlike Joe, had never been an activist and wasn't particularly interested in any social movement. After the second of their two children was born, Julie decided to go to law school. It had always been her dream to be a lawyer. Her attitude toward the church, however, was less than cordial. She deeply resented the time that the demands of the ministry took from her husband's family involvement. Julie also felt strongly that Joe was wasting the Ph.D. he had worked so hard to achieve. She became even more dispirited and resentful when Joe announced he was going to take a frontline ministry, working with wayward youth and teenage mothers in order to be part of the ongoing life of the working community, and to participate more actively in the lives of those whom he considered his flock.

Joe was never in conflict about his life's mission. His involvement with average people, many of whom were working class, was imparted to him through his love and respect for his father, and he looked forward to carrying on the family tradition. Interestingly, when Joe and Julie took the PSI, they both scored high on the Community factor. I asked them about the similarity. Joe's involvement was expected; Julie's was more of a surprise inasmuch as she had never voiced strong interest in the community. She stated that she, too, had sympathy for the plight of those less fortunate, but she preferred to work in the political arena. She had, for example, been so outraged by the flagrant pollution and lack of environmental awareness on the part of some local manufacturers that she'd contacted the local office of the Environmental Protection Agency to complain and initiate an investigation. Julie was also considering a run for state representative, a position she hoped would enable her to bring about some meaningful form of social change.

Because of the strength of their relationship and the growing tension between them, Joe and Julie sought marital counseling. I met with them and reviewed the PSIs they had each taken as a means for initiating dialogue on spiritual issues and commitments. Julie scored high on the Trauma and Childhood Spirituality factors as well as the Community factor. She had been raised in a religious home in which community service was valued and encouraged. She also had watched her parents, both heavy smokers, suffer the ravages of lung cancer and die painful deaths. Julie followed the state and federal litigations against the tobacco companies with tortured fascination.

As I reviewed their PSI results with them and discussed the implications of the similarities and differences, Joe and Julie were reminded of their deep mutual commitment to their communities, albeit in different forms. Julie's anger with Joe's ministry activities lessened as she realized that he was following essentially the same path she had chosen. Their spiritual energy was more synchronized than they had been willing to admit. In this case the PSI provided the basis for a spiritual dialogue that brought the couple closer than they had been in years.

In both of the above examples, we see how similar scores on the PSI can be the result of very different pathways. The PSI, however, is a useful stimulus for the kind of dialogue necessary to achieve a greater understanding of different life forces that impact each of us. In these vignettes we see how conflicts can be addressed openly and usefully with the understanding that this measure provides.

Low Score

A LOW SCORE on the spirituality factor of Community does not necessarily imply isolation, or indifference to the existence of others. Many people are very gregarious and outgoing, and thrive in the company of both men and women. The difference is that the sense of connection these individuals feel is based more on sociability and culture than on a desire to reach out to help and nurture. Many people who are low on the Community factor prefer to keep their spirituality to themselves, or to orient their spiritual intelligence toward a personal relationship with a Divine Energy Source, rather than in a community, congregation, or group setting.

At home and with family, a low score on the Community factor may well be correlated with the pursuit of pleasurable activities, more solitary in nature, but nonetheless satisfying. Working on projects with family members, raking leaves, painting bedrooms, cooking a new and exciting recipe, or playing a hard game of singles with a friend at the local tennis courts are activities consistent with a low score on the Community factor. The following example describes the interaction of different spiritual energies highlighted by such a result on the PSI.

Lenny and his wife, Susan, came to see me to discuss the potential dissolution of their marriage. Lenny is a university professor of renown in a local Ivy League school. He was an active participant in the civil rights movement in the sixties, and went to Alabama to register voters shortly after the notorious murder of three northern students in Mississippi in 1964. His politics were solidified by his opposition to the war in Vietnam, and he has been a spokesperson for liberal causes and points of view for nearly forty years. He is still an active teacher, and his students love him. He attends political meetings of one kind or another every week. When I asked Lenny to consider taking the PSI, he cast a cynical eye toward me and said, "Okay, if you want me to. But for your information I am a devout atheist, recently converted from agnosticism."

Lenny's wife, Susan, is multitalented and has been working as a writer. Investigative journalism is her specialty, but recently she has rekindled her passion for music, especially modern jazz. Four years ago she decided to forgo her activities as a writer and take up jazz piano in a serious way. Spending long hours in lessons and practice, Susan has perfected her technique to the point where she will soon be performing with a drummer and a bass player. Lenny is pleased at his wife's newfound interest and accomplishment, but feels abandoned even further in their marriage. For years he had been encouraging Susan to continue to attend rallies and political demonstrations with him, which she did, but more to be with him than to become involved herself. She had no trouble espousing Lenny's political views, but she did have difficulty with the constant flow of people in and out of their house and their lives.

Susan's idea of fun is to go out with Lenny and listen to jazz in a local club, or to stay home and practice a new piece on the piano, while Lenny reads, and writes comments on, one of his students' dissertation drafts. When I asked Susan if she would be willing to try the PSI, she smiled and said, "Sure, but God is in the ivories, so don't expect too much in the way of spirituality from me. I've seen, through my reporting, what really happens to people in the world; the pain, suffering, poverty, and deception by people with power is sometimes more than I can bear."

The results of the couple's PSIs were fascinating. Lenny was high on the Community factor, while Susan was predictably low. Both were low on the Intellectuality factor, indicating not a lack of intellectual activity—quite the opposite for this very bright and gifted couple—but a lack of energy directed toward the intellectual approach to spirituality. Both were low on the Divinity, Mindfulness, and Extrasensory Perception factors. The significant differences in their PSI scores centered on the Trauma and Childhood Spirituality factors, with Susan scoring high on Trauma, and Lenny on Childhood Spirituality.

The high score on Trauma in Susan's profile turned out to be associated with the fact that she had spent much of her adolescence caring for an emotionally disturbed mother. She was present when the ambulance arrived to take her mother to a psychiatric ward after a failed suicide attempt, and just at the point when psychotropic medication helped control her mother's symptoms, her father developed a heart condition and had to be taken care of by his daughter, because his wife was still too weak to help out. Susan tried to escape by going away to college, but while she was there, the agony of the human condition seemed to exert a magnetic attraction on her, and she found herself at political rallies—where she met Lenny—and began writing about the plight of the farm workers in California, as well as on the civil rights movement, for the school newspaper. Her subsequent career as an investigative reporter took her to myriad situations in which powerless people were, in her opinion, being deceived, exploited, and killed. By the time I met her, Susan was burnt out, seeking refuge in her art, and disconnecting from the world she had known, a world that included Lenny.

From his side, Lenny's life had been relatively trauma-free. His parents, aged but still active, lived in San Francisco, and Lenny spoke to them and his three younger brothers every week. He was clearly aware of the suffering that society and circumstances visited on a large portion of the earth's population, and he could defeat in debate just about anyone who doubted the legitimacy of his political views. Blessed with his own personal good health and that of his wife, Lenny had not yet experienced trauma personally or with anyone in his family.

Lenny, whose score on Childhood Spirituality was very high, described his early life as one in which community service and the care of others were of highest priority. His parents were Irish immigrants who struggled to make a living of any kind in the dark days of the Depression. They arrived from Ireland and were taken into the bosom of a large extended family that had preceded them to the United States. From a young age, Lenny learned the sense of responsibility for others that his parents drilled into him as a lesson of survival. His family also raised Lenny as a Catholic, but his skeptical mind and rebellious nature quickly substituted concern with social justice for a concern about mortal sins. He disagreed with the Catholic Church's position on many issues, including homosexuality and birth control, and finally decided that the kingdom of God was just not for him. Lenny poured his spiritual passion into his political activism, and was chronically disappointed that he could no longer share this basic dimension of who he is with Susan.

The three of us worked very hard on the issues stirred up and reactivated by the couple's participation in the PSI. There were many tearful and pleading moments when each desperately tried to convince the other to return to the way things used to be: Lenny begging Susan to return to the political arena with him; Susan adamantly refusing to be drawn back into a world that overwhelmed her and filled her with painful and unresolved memories. Lenny and Susan finally decided to walk their own diverging paths. They are still friends, but the strain of opposing worldviews was more than their union could tolerate. I consider our work together successful in the sense that both Lenny and Susan acted from conscious choice rather than impulse. They can now pursue life in a manner that could lead each to personal fulfillment, even though it is not with each other.

In conclusion, it is noteworthy that the Community factor evokes a variety of interesting and revealing responses. A rabbi, writing to me after she had taken the PSI, told me how much the report had reflected her own style of spirituality. She remarked that her low score on the Community factor reminded her that, having become focused on her own young family and their pressing needs of the moment, she needed to reengage with her congregation. A busy executive, in his response to the low Community score on his profile, sent me an e-mail stating that he was glad to see that he didn't have to feel guilty about a low score. He wrote that that was just the way he preferred to exercise his spirituality, particularly after a long week at the office beseiged by hundreds of demands from his staff and employees. As I have repeatedly emphasized, there is no evaluation built into any of the spirituality profiles that the PSI generates. You take from it what is useful. You can incorporate the information into your life in a way that makes sense for you and has the potential for enhancing your relationship with others and to your own spirituality.

Each of the spirituality factors lends its own power to the mix that I am calling spiritual intelligence. I have found that no matter what the scores on any particular factors, discussions of ultimate and life-changing issues invariably follow from the use of the PSI, both in the clinical setting and in everyday environments. The need to explore, understand, and resolve spiritual questions and conflicts affects us all; and in the situations I present here, the satisfaction of this desire reaffirms the relevance of spiritual intelligence to our daily lives.

CHAPTER ELEVEN

Intellectuality

The spiritual factor of Intellectuality denotes an energy associated with thought, understanding, and dialogue in relation to ultimate questions and concerns. Your Intellectuality factor scores indicate the degree to which you think about, reflect on, study, and converse with others about sacred or spiritual matters. In applying this dimension of your spiritual intelligence to basic life situations, you can obtain a clearer picture of the degree to which intellectual inquiry plays a role in your life in general, and the way in which you might apply this interest and aptitude to specific areas of spiritual activity.

As we have discussed, one of the intelligences that Howard Gardner postulates is termed "existential intelligence" and psychologist Robert Emmons uses the term spiritual intelligence to denote attention to "ultimate concerns." The Intellectuality factor of the PSI captures the energy devoted to questioning the nature of existence, the meaning of life, and possible theoretical rationales for the existence of evil in the world. Clearly, one can be intelligent and receive a low score on this factor. High or low refers to the focus of ones intellect on these specific issues, not to conventional arenas of intellectuality.

Spiritual intelligence, as it is expressed through the Intellectuality factor, serves to address some of the fundamental moral questions of our day. This process encourages, through thought and reflection, the active participation of the powers of mind, and can result in an approach to spirituality unlike any other, namely the rational, objective, and reasoned approach to painful and disputed issues. Intellectuality connotes a strength of mind that enhances the other pathways through which spirituality reaches our consciousness.

High Score

HAVING interest in discussions of spiritual topics at the dinner table or at family gatherings is a sign of someone who scores high on the Intellectuality factor. Whether it is at a Christmas dinner, a Passover Seder, or Thanksgiving after everyone is stuffed with turkey and the trimmings, people who score high on the Intellectuality factor invariably find themselves in the middle of conversations and dialogues about spiritual or moral issues. This discussion may take the form of analyzing the priest's sermon from the Mass at church that day, or finding moral issues reported in the daily paper as worthy of dinnertime discussion.

Driven by the force of Intellectuality, these encounters can be exhilarating and enlightening, or filled with bitterness and acrimony. Conversations about the war in Vietnam during the sixties and seventies, for example, were fierce battles over deeply held moral convictions: love of country and national duty versus the imposition of national will on another country that, according to some, needed no intervention and posed no real threat to our national security. Countless arguments at home, at sit-ins, and in the media took place over whether American national interest meant exercising a military action that led to the destruction of American lives and American ideals. Parents and their children, responding to powerful forces of intellectual energy, often spent years trying to repair the torn family fabric from such troubled times.

A high score on the Intellectuality factor can also have direct implications for activities and attitudes toward work. In some companies the spiritual dimensions of intellectuality are shared at weekly meetings—breakfast meetings sometimes. Recently, for example, I was invited to attend one of these meetings at a well-known Boston law firm, in which a lively discussion of sacred texts took place. The texts that are examined include selections from the Bible, the Koran, and sometimes the Talmud, in which fine points of religious law are studied. These lawyers from different faiths meet together with an invited guest or speaker, or sometimes just draw upon their own expertise to discuss, argue, learn, and generally enjoy the intellectual stimulation. Some colleagues who score in the moderate range on the Intellectuality factor also share their strong intellectual curiosity, even though their specific interest in spiritual matters or sacred texts is limited.

Low Score

A LOW SCORE on the Intellectuality factor does not, of course, imply or suggest a lack of interest in learning or study. It may mean that dialogue and inquiry are oriented more toward secular or professional issues than toward specifically spiritual ones. For example, many inter- and intra-office professional-development meetings or continuing-education seminars are attended by professional people who must meet the requirements of staying current in their fields. In addition, these conferences and seminars are a source of new learning, and are pleasurable activities in themselves. Many CEOs of large and small corporations alike include such meetings as a means of enhancing performance, which at the same time serve to nourish the minds of employees. The role of Intellectuality is obviously quite wide. In some instances it provides access to the spiritual dimension of life for people who otherwise might never approach this area of life experience. The following vignette displays the power of Intellectuality and its relation to some of the other spirituality factors.

Intellectuality in Personal Relationships

RECENTLY my wife and I were invited for dinner to the home of a couple we were meeting for the first time. The husband, Matthew, a former professional chemist, now worked part-time in the science department of a local university. The conversation began with the usual get-acquainted banter, but soon turned to more serious issues when we touched on the topic of spirituality. "I'm not particularly spiritual," Matthew said, "but I do wonder about the existence of a universal morality. If what is considered good is simply a question of what the cultural context I live in happens to be, then something like slavery might be considered acceptable; but if I assume there is a universal good, then I risk imposing my beliefs on others."

After going back and forth in the dialogue, we were treated to a tour of their home, which sat in the middle of the mountains and had beautiful views of the setting sun. The couple had recently moved here, and were understandably proud. On the second floor, where Matthew had his office work space, I encountered a room lined with floor-to-ceiling bookshelves and filled with books, some modern, some quite ancient.

"These are my father's books," Matthew explained. "He died recently, and this is his library. My father was a rabbi in a small town for thirty years, and he loved books. Here, take a look at this seventeenth-century edition of the Talmud that he found in an old bookstore. I went to temple every week and listened to all his sermons, but he considered me lost to the faith when I became a scientist and started questioning the validity of some of the miracles that are described in the Bible. I don't consider myself religious. I only attend synagogue on the High Holy Days, and I can't ever remember actually praying, even when my wife was sick in the hospital with an illness no one could diagnose. But you know what? Every summer when my children and their families come to the mountains for vacation, I pick one question to discuss, whether about the existence of an ultimate good, or the one I used last summer about the beginning of time. I can't even really call myself spiritual," he continued, "but these questions always bothered me."

I explained that from my perspective, this newfound friend could indeed consider himself spiritual. Matthew's deep and enthusiastic commitment to learning about and questioning even the most sacrosanct of religious or spiritual teachings was a spiritual act. Because of his passion and his interest, he brought meaning to his life. It is the search, as much as the arrival, that defines us. I went on to explain my understanding of spirituality and the various factors, making it quite clear to him that he had just achieved a very high rating on—at least—the factor of Intellectuality.

Matthew said he was interested in taking the complete Inventory, and his outcome was fairly predictable based on our previous conversation. His score on the factor of Intellectuality was indeed high, and his score on the factor of Childhood Spirituality was also high. These scores were consistent with the picture he had painted of himself, and he acknowledged that the Inventory produced an accurate snapshot of his spiritual consciousness.

Matthew's wife, Karen, was somewhat in the background the night we were there. A bright and engaging woman, she seemed to prefer to let her husband do most of the talking when it came to his interest in pursuing ethical and cosmological questions. Karen seemed drawn to the topic of spirituality, though, and at our visit I could sense, behind her eyes, an energy that she kept to herself. When I offered Karen the opportunity to take the PSI, she seemed a little reluctant at first, but then agreed after a little prodding from Matthew. Her outcome was fascinating.

On the factor of Intellectuality, Karen scored in the low range, indicating that reading and study in the area of spirituality were not of prime interest to her, or a favorite activity. She also scored low on Childhood Spirituality, in direct contrast to her husband. Interestingly, her score on the Divinity factor was unusually high, as were her scores on the factors of Trauma and Extrasensory Perception. I was intrigued not only by the differences between her pattern and her husband's, but by the actual dimensions themselves, and I asked her about it. "Tell me about your experience with Trauma," I said. What followed was unexpected.

Karen proceeded to relate a riveting tale about the experience she had during the birth of her third child. Matthew was away on business, and she began her labor somewhat early. A friend drove her to the hospital, but couldn't stay with her. Her labor progressed normally; then, during the delivery the obstetrician noticed that the umbilical cord was wrapped around the baby's neck, threatening to asphyxiate the child if they continued with a standard delivery through the birth canal. Karen began to panic. She was alone and frightened, barely comforted by her doctor's attempt to calm her with the reassurance that the cesarean section he was preparing was not unusual, and would save the baby. Karen was clearly in no position to argue or discuss, and she desperately wished her husband were nearby.

The surgery began. Karen asked to be awake so that she would be able to be conscious during the delivery. After four and a half minutes—a lifetime in this circumstance—Karen's blood pressure began to drop for some unknown reason. Her heart actually stopped for thirty seconds, and it was necessary to use the electrical stimulator paddles to revive her. When her heart finally started beating normally, the operation proceeded, and the baby was born, a healthy eight-pound, six-ounce girl.

Karen was slow to come around after the ordeal. She seemed to be in another world, and by the time Matthew arrived and heard the story, she had a look on her face he had never seen. "Thank God you're okay," said Matthew. "You nearly died, but now we have a beautiful new daughter." "I did die," replied Karen. "I know this sounds crazy, but I felt myself leave my body. I could see and hear everything that was going on in the operating room. I even saw the white light they talk about in all the magazines." "It's going to be all right," Matthew replied as he tried to reassure his wife—and himself—that she would soon be back to normal. "The white light is nothing more than oxygen deprivation, so don't worry about it. I spoke to the doctor. He said all your vital signs are completely normal and you're going to be okay. You're going to be okay, I know it."

Karen never spoke about her near-death experience again, fearing that she would be thought crazy and weird—or that it would be trivialized. When the PSI items stimulated the memories of that traumatic time, Karen began to sob. She felt Matthew wouldn't understand, and that he would accuse her of nonscientific or non-rational thinking.

When he saw the scores on the Inventory factors, however, Matthew seemed to take a different kind of interest in his wife's experience. He had been comforting her during her tears, but now he was asking questions that revealed an interest in what she had gone through. With the objective and independent evidence in front of him, Matthew was able to share an understanding he had never approached. With her newfound validation, Karen could discuss the transformations that had occurred in her life as a result of that remarkable time. She had developed a kind of sixth sense with her children, and was known for her remarkable intuition of being aware if they were ever in any danger or subject to any threat. She had given up her traditional religious practices of Judaism when she was in college, but, following the birth of her third child, she was continually aware of a Divine Energy Source that she often spoke about with her children. Karen's interest in thinking about religious or ultimate questions was small in comparison to her deep conviction of the interconnectedness of all living beings, a conviction she expressed in modulated and self-effacing ways.

This story of the path down which the exploration of one of the seven spirituality factors can lead signals the way in which the self-awareness associated with taking the PSI can be used. We can see that Matthew is resting comfortably in the high range on the Intellectuality factor, but the way in which he uses his intellectual curiosity about ultimate issues had never been applied, *in the way that she needed,* to his most intimate relationship, the one with Karen. For Matthew this insight was unexpected but was—given his tendency toward the joy of understanding—most welcome. He realized that he had never fully discussed the spirituality that made the most sense to Karen, and a new door of intimacy opened in their marriage.

For Karen, once it dawned on her that she wasn't crazy or just imagining what had happened to her, she was able to discover new understanding and comfort in the context of her relationship with her husband. Her return from "the other side" had been a reality long held deep within, with few opportunities for expression. While the intellectual aspects of her experience were not particularly important or interesting to her, she learned that couching her conversations with Matthew in rational scientific terminology could help her bridge the gap that had been created between them since the birth of their daughter. From my point of view, it was fascinating to see how a low score on the spiritual factor of Intellectuality could ultimately lead, in a very bright and articulate woman, to the existence of deeper realities waiting to be revealed.

Intellectuality in Spirituality and Worship

I F YOUR scores are in the high range on the spiritual factor of Intellectuality, you may find yourself being active in church or temple study groups, or participating in study weekends devoted to the elucidation of difficult religious or spiritual texts. You may even offer to give a reading and interpretation of some aspect of the Bible or some passage in Buddhist teachings to the company at hand. In other words, the intellectual component of worship is integrated into your spiritual experience and is supported by the community of participants who share your spiritual life. Inquiry into the meaning of life and the direction of ultimate concerns feels comfortable to you, and easy to pursue. To those around you, the joy and pleasure you take from discussions about the existence of God or the fate of the universe are infectious, and lead to new friendships.

A moderate score on the Intellectuality factor can lead you toward learning in a wide variety of fields—not only spirituality, but also the arts, politics, and science. You will probably also feel comfortable in participating in seminars and discussion groups that raise questions of ultimate concern, but you are also likely to enjoy conferences that are associated with professional continued education. This middle-of-the-road position is a comfortable one for many people, and can provide a satisfying response to the concerns of intolerant extremism.

A low score on the Intellectuality factor may imply the focus of your intellectual powers on any number of subjects, just not the general area of spirituality, which you may think of as too lacking in scientific evidence to be taken seriously. Your intellectual pursuits may be in the area of science, current events, and the arts, but seldom in the world of spirituality, except to challenge conventional spiritual views that you think lack scientific or objective evidence. A low score on the Intellectuality factor does not imply an anti-intellectual attitude.

For both high scorers and low scorers on the factor of Intellectuality, it is important to keep in mind that strong positions can sometimes lead to a lack of tolerance or patience with other points of view. The compatibility of science with spirituality is a topic we have discussed previously, and is one that can yield useful conversations if kept in proper perspective.

Whatever the score, the factor of Intellectuality is a significant dimension of the experience of spirituality, and contributes the activity of a conscious, critical mind to the process. A common stereotype of spirituality is that it reflects a rather tender-minded and nonthinking approach to issues of ultimate meaning and the fate of individuals or groups of human beings. When intellectual focus is brought to bear on the topic of spirituality, however, the outcome is as thrilling and as meaningful as any intuitive knowledge gleaned from directly perceiving the mysteries of the universe. Once again, a word of caution. Always remember that no factor or score on any factor should be considered in isolation. Each must be viewed as part of a dynamic whole, in which all factors operate in conjunction with each other. The power of the spirituality factors and using them in the context of the Psycho-Matrix Spirituality Inventory lies in the dynamic relationship and creative tension of the seven facets of spirituality that comprise the consciousness of each of us.

CHAPTER TWELVE

Trauma

Traumatic events, particularly if they occur in childhood, can have such a deep effect on personality and behavior that they lie buried under the cover of guilt, shame, and suppression. The growth of spirituality in such situations can often be arrested, leaving a blind spot in one's life. As you reflect on your Trauma scores and their corresponding correlations with various components of your life, you can make choices that reflect a direct implementation of your spiritual center. You might be able to apply the findings directly from one part of your life to another, or you may choose to prepare yourself for change. Some people use the findings on their own, while others share them with a trusted, sensitive friend, a valued loved one, or a trained clinician. In your hands and those of such a third person, the factor scores and their interpretations can provide insight and understanding into your spiritual and life choices.

Trauma in Relationships

THE POWER of the dimension of Trauma may be seen clearly in the following example. Natasha, a student in my class at Harvard called "Why People Change: The Psychology of Influence," was dedicated to the study of her own individual development and the related psychological theory that helped her understand the life cycle in which she found herself. Natasha is a woman in her early forties. She was an excellent student, which was all the more impressive inasmuch as she had been in the United States only ten years, having fled a communist regime in eastern Europe, where, she said, "I didn't know there was such a thing as feelings, or that people had them. Everyone in my country is angry and mean. At the store, if you ask a price, they say, 'What is the matter with you? Can't you see for yourself?'"

Reading psychological literature was an enlightening experience for Natasha, and she proudly told me of her accomplishments of straight A's in her other courses. When the class took the PSI, I went over her results with her. Natasha was crushed, thinking her low scores on every factor but Trauma represented a resounding failure. She then described the general views on spirituality in her country of origin, namely that such matters were considered politically incorrect, bourgeois, and subversive; they were never taught in school and discouraged at home.

I assumed that her country's hostile attitude toward spiritual values was her own attitude as well, and was being reflected in her profile. As we spoke, however, a more comprehensive picture emerged. In addition to the cultural milieu in which she grew up, it turned out that Natasha's father had left when she was quite young. Her mother had remarried within the next year, hoping to restore a sense of family. Unfortunately, she married an alcoholic who abused her as well as Natasha and her brothers.

Natasha's mother never protected her. In fact, because Natasha loved to wander out to gaze at the river nearby, her mother tied her, like a pet on a tether, to the legs of the kitchen table. Now, many years and miles from this nightmare, Natasha returns to her home for occasional "vacations." Following the most recent one, she told me that she'd managed only an hour with her mother before she started to cry. "I realized that I wanted her to hug me or even for me to hug her, but she couldn't do it and neither could I."

Inspection of Natasha's scores on the PSI and discussion of their meaning for her showed a picture consistent with a terrified childhood, lacking love, respect, and nurturance, in a culture that provided no spiritual alternatives for anyone in need of solace or sanctuary. It was as if the early experience of trauma in her life had left her few options to develop other facets of her spiritual personality. Because of her strong will and ability, she poured her psychic and intellectual energy exclusively into academic endeavors.

Our conversation began a spiritual dialogue in which Natasha told me she had briefly joined a religious sect, from which she dropped out when the rigidity of its members began to stir psychic trauma from her past. The dialogue stimulated by the PSI also carried over into Natasha's personal life, and opened the doors to exploring her own psychic and spiritual needs.

She brought the spiritual conversation into her marriage as well, and encouraged Ivan, her husband, who was also from her home country, to participate with her in the process of uncovering their spiritual lives in a safe and loving fashion. My recent discussions with Natasha indicate that she and Ivan are, through psychotherapy, working out their problematic relationship with an analysis of traditional psychodynamic forces. Their therapy also includes the new, previously threatening dimension of their lives, the dimension of how they see the priorities of life played out in their daily activities and their relationship. Discussion of life's ultimate meaning and purpose has opened uncharted waters for Natasha and Ivan and even encouraged them to consider starting a family, a concept that had been taboo for years.

For Natasha and Ivan, taking the PSI provided a stimulus for spiritual dialogue that served an important function because, like many people, they were reticent or unfamiliar with language appropriate to describing spiritual experiences associated with physical or emotional conditions. They were also frightened that discussing spiritual issues would activate traumatic memories and recollections. The means by which the PSI can actually validate, without judgment, an individual's spiritual experience is extremely useful. Personal experience should not need validation. It is common, however, to hear people report that seeing the words on paper has the effect of legitimizing the experience—or at least the expression of the experience—of spirituality. No matter what specific dimension of spirituality is being addressed, the reality and validation associated with the PSI encourage a willingness to share personal feelings.

Individual Trauma

THE REPORT from the PSI anchors the information outside the individual, which provides both psychological protection and the psychological undeniability of responding to something "out there," externally anchored. I told Nancy, a friend of mine who is the extremely bright and no-nonsense CEO of a financial services company in Chicago, about the PSI and the work I was doing and asked her if she wanted to take the test and receive a personal spiritual profile. "Sure, I'll take it," Nancy said. "But I'm warning you, I'm not spiritual in the least." We went to lunch to discuss her results. As Nancy had "warned" me, she scored in the low category on six of the seven spiritual factors. On the Trauma factor, however, her score was extremely high. "Nancy, tell me about your experience with illness," I said. The remainder of our luncheon was dominated by a profound and emotional discussion about the bone-marrow transplant she had survived several years ago—a fact I had known, but the power of which I had never fully appreciated.

For Nancy, her illness and her triumph over it was a deeply spiritual experience—spiritual because it was personally transformative and connected her to individual and transcendent sources of strength and clarity of thought she had never dreamed possible. To have dismissed this courageous woman from spiritual dialogue because of her reluctance to call this remarkable experience "spiritual" would have been a mistake. Instead, with the PSI, I was able, quickly and efficiently, to help her access her spiritual core and thereby create a new level of understanding between us.

Trauma is one of the most immediate and salient factors of the PSI, the factor of witnessing or experiencing emotional or physical illness in oneself or in others, or the actual loss of a loved one through death. My research has also shown that Trauma is dynamically related to other factors, particularly Divinity. This active interrelationship between factors is to be expected, not only because no aspect of spirituality exists in isolation, but also because certain psychological and psycho-spiritual forces seem to require this connection.

In the face of significant trauma, many respondents have described a feeling or experience of being closer to God or some Transcendent Energy Source; while others have distanced themselves from the association of the trauma with any larger context of meaning. A recent study of cancer patients demonstrated that those who scored higher on a spiritual well-being questionnaire had higher quality-of-life scores after treatment. This questionnaire tapped beliefs that patients felt their suffering had some meaning, that God was part of their lives, that their lives had been meaningful prior to the illness.

Some people, however, distance themselves from the kinds of energy sources to which many other suffering individuals cling for hope and reassurance. Even though they may be in considerable pain, these individuals prefer to try to keep their suffering within manageable bounds by committing themselves to alternative activities such as work or family. Sometimes such people report that they have moved from a position of deep connection with larger spiritual contexts to a position of distance, mistrust, and cynicism. A patient of mine, Barbara, is one of those who report a loss of connection to the Divine. "I lost everything when my husband finally left after years of drinking, abuse, and chasing women," she sobbed in my office. "I lost my religion, too." "Do you ever go to church now?" I asked. "No," came the tearful reply. "I try to go to church, but I just sit there and cry, and I have to leave."

While temporarily overcome with feelings of hopelessness and despair, these individuals do sometimes go on to lead productive lives, pouring their spiritual energy into any number of activities that can keep them busy and active and away from pain. Some, sadly, may end up crippled by their loss of faith and overcome by feelings of helplessness at the prospect of reestablishing a meaningful connection to life.

High Score

I F YOU SCORE in the high range on the Trauma factor, there is often an increased sense of bonding between family members. Sometimes, in the face of tragic loss, a wife will feel overprotective toward a husband, or a mother will feel overprotective toward a child or to surviving children. There is a strong sense of the value of personal connection and the transitory nature of existence. Some responses to trauma are also remarkable in their clarity of vision.

It is hard to imagine anything more horrible or traumatic than dropping your seventeen-year-old daughter off at Columbine High School in the morning, only to learn, several hours later, that she was one of the fifteen children cut down by the bullets of two deranged classmates. To make the event even more incomprehensible, both of the perpetrators had successfully completed anger-management and community-service programs for earlier offenses, complete with counselors and psychotropic medication. How is it possible for parents to tolerate the psychic assault, or to integrate into their consciousness such an overwhelming trauma?[1]

How can we explain the reaction of Rachel Scott's parents to their daughter's murder in the Littleton, Colorado, massacre at the Columbine High School in April 1999, upon being interviewed several days after the tragedy? "We know that she is in a better place, that she fulfilled her purpose here and did what God had intended her to do: to show us the way to light our lives by her example. We also feel how much pain the parents of those boys must be feeling. They suffered the loss, like we had, but they have the extra agony of the guilt and responsibility."

The automatic psychological explanation is that these parents are in denial. The shock of their loss is so overwhelming, the argument goes, that they have distanced themselves from their pain, anger, and despair. This psychic distance serves to dull the pain and enables them to speak of forgiveness, show compassion, and transcend the horror of their lives. But the parents state that their faith in God is what has seen them through this dark hour.

Individual differences in response to this horrible event were great. There certainly were, and still are, angry and outraged protests. The response of Rachel's parents serves to substantiate our findings, through the PSI, that one of the outcomes of an intense trauma is an increased feeling of closeness to some larger force in the universe, call it God, Higher Power, or Universal Energy. In psychometric terms, high scores on the Trauma factor are often coupled with high scores on the Divinity factor.

The other side of the dynamic between Trauma and Divinity is a high score on Trauma correlated with a *low* score on Divinity. In some cases trauma is intense and may occur early in life, as in the situation of child abuse, while in others there may have existed a positive family history of spiritual or religious affiliation or consciousness, but some unplanned or unavoidable physical or emotional trauma may have occurred. In both scenarios, the findings usually show that Trauma scores are high and Divinity scores are low. This pattern reflects a pragmatic, worldly orientation to life, with little sympathy—or sometimes little understanding—of the Divinity dimension of spirituality.

Often, feelings of anger and outrage are directed toward God—or the equivalent—in the form of literal disbelief: "How could any God have let this happen? This child's death is so unfair. He was innocent and had done nothing to deserve this fatal disease. How can I believe in a God who would let innocent and beautiful children die such a meaningless death?" I am reminded of Elie Wiesel's statement that when he saw innocent children hanged in the concentration camps, it was then that he knew God had died. So traumatic was the experience that for ten years after his liberation, he could not speak a word about it.

It is also not uncommon to see high scores on Trauma, high Divinity, and Intellectuality on the same profile. Once again we look at the dynamic interaction between factor scores to find the best interpretation for that individual. One of the physicians who participates in the Massachusetts General Hospital Chaplaincy program produced this exact profile. As we talked about her spirituality, she was very clear in her analysis: "I have my own history of illness in my family. That's one of the reasons I became a doctor, to see if I could help relieve the suffering of others. But I know I am not alone when I work with terminally ill patients. I feel a surrounding presence like no other, and my patients and their families feel it, too. This sense of connection strengthens my own spirituality, a world in which I feel comfort and in which I enjoy pursuing intellectual understanding through study."

The response of this physician to seeing her profile demonstrates an important feature of the PSI. The Inventory provides an accurate and rapid means of describing one's spirituality to self or others. Think of the results as a kind of "spiritual snapshot." Often there are no surprises. We hear comments like "Yeah, that's pretty much me; that's how I see the world." From such comments and self-reflections, though, can come some of the most vivid and moving personal histories, filled with memory, conflict, hope, and disappointment, which people feel the permission and encouragement to share after taking the PSI. This doctor, surrounded on a daily basis by trauma and suffering, was not surprised by her results. She was surprised, however, to realize the emphasis she placed on this dimension of spirituality, along with her sense of integration of the three spiritual energy centers in her life.

Moderate and Low Scores on Trauma

THE TRAUMA factor, by definition, pertains to painful and difficult life experiences. The examples I used were those based on a high score, because the effects on the rest of one's spiritual consciousness can be seen most clearly. For those who scored in the moderate range, or were fortunate enough to score in the low range on Trauma, you can assess the impact of these events in your life by extrapolating from the high score examples. Physical and psychological pain are such uniquely subjective experiences that I thought it would be better to leave the application of the scores in the mid and lower range to the discretion and judgment of each reader.

CHAPTER THIRTEEN

Childhood Spirituality

The spiritual world of the child is most often bound up with the notion of God as taught by parents, grandparents, and clergy, or is based in a media-related experience like theater or movies of Jesus or other biblical stories. Sometimes children are drawn to ultimate questions because a death or trauma has befallen their family and forced the question of God or afterlife upon them. The stages through which religious thinking passes in childhood (and beyond) has been an interesting area of research in its own right, and an overview of the stages of religious thinking is referenced in the notes at the end of this book.[1] The spiritual world of children is hence a fascinating one, one through which we all have passed, and one that is to some extent captured by the factor of Childhood Spirituality.

Robert Coles, psychiatrist and devoted researcher of the world of children, set out on a quest to investigate children's spirituality, and came to the following insight:

. . . psychologically God can take almost any shape for children. He can be a friend or a potential enemy; an admirer or a
critic; an ally or an interference; a source of encouragement or
a source of anxiety, fear, even panic . . . Often, children
whose sternly Christian, Jewish, or Moslem parents don't hesi-
tate to threaten them with the most severe of religious stric-
tures can construct in their thoughts or dreams a God who is
exemplary yet lenient, forgiving, and encouraging . . .[2]

The images of God that are impressed on children's psyches
form the foundation on which spirituality is built. This is one of
the reasons it is so important to use an instrument like the PSI,
which assesses spirituality based on self-report rather than on a
predetermined notion of practice or belief.

The factor of Childhood Spirituality is designed to gauge the
range and frequency of childhood spiritual experiences. In times
of personal difficulty and mortal fear, such as when facing open-
heart surgery, many people revert to their earliest religious or
spiritual concepts. The prayers of those in the midst of crisis
sound more like the clear and simple language of young children
than the sophisticated language of poetry. Some people who take
the PSI relate their Childhood Spirituality in terms of positive—or
negative—memories of being taken to church with their parents,
sometimes forcibly, sometimes willingly. Some share fond and
warm stories of family and religious holiday gatherings, or of their
first experience with death at a grandparent's funeral. Other children remember discussions of ethical behavior and moral teaching
independent of traditional religious instruction. For some, however, Childhood Spirituality is virtually nonexistent. Their parents
may have been nonpracticing or also disaffected members of a particular denomination who themselves imparted little in the way of
childhood activities or discussion centered on religious or spiri-

tual themes. In some cases these individuals report that they have dedicated themselves to the principle that their own children not suffer the same lack of knowledge they had, and these parents are deeply involved with Sunday school and religiously based communal activities with their children.

As with the other spirituality factors, scores on Childhood Spirituality can in no way be construed to be evaluative: a high score implies only that the experience of spirituality in childhood was frequent and maybe even important. Only further discussion with a person about the outcome of his or her PSI can elicit thoughts and feelings about whether this form of spirituality was welcome or detested, a source of comfort or of guilt and self-recrimination.

My research suggests that scores on the factor of Childhood Spirituality have relevance to daily life in terms of making spiritual decisions in accordance with, or in opposition to, early training and exposure. The dynamic of this factor is particularly noticeable in conjunction with family and raising one's children.

One of the most important spiritual dimensions of child-rearing is establishing the ground for ritual. Ritual, a repeated sacred behavior, connects past with present and provides a framework for memory. The child's spiritual experience, embedded in ritual, is easier to find emotionally at any age. The rituals associated with the unique festival behavior in any family are ready examples. The songs, smells, activities, and expectations are retained through the generations by means of ritual, and children are the new participants who are ushered into the community through ritual. Scores on the Childhood Spirituality factor usually imply the presence or absence of ritual in one's life. Often, when young couples have children, even if their own childhood had a lack of ritual (or sometimes because of that lack) they are quick to adopt or create rituals that will establish the sacred space of their own family.

High Score

A HIGH SCORE on the factor of Childhood Spirituality may show up at work or at school as an emphasis on the spiritual aspects of learning. Many teachers are now including in their curricula a focus on the spiritual dimension of life, helping children find language and modes of expression for their questions of ultimate concern. These teachers come from a background of either fullness or emptiness of explicit spiritual experience, and in their classrooms they seek to continue their own history, or create a new one for and with their students.

People who score high on the Childhood Spirituality factor often show their interest and commitment by expressing interest in children's belief in an afterlife, their conceptions of God, the meaning of death, and the reason for violence in schools. Because individuals who score high are aware of the power of spiritual thinking on young children, they are willing to discuss events like the terrible massacre at Columbine High School in 1999, or to devote time to curricula oriented toward understanding prejudice and genocide, like "Facing History and Ourselves," an international curriculum designed to help youngsters become articulate about the darkest aspects of society.

In the family setting, a high score on the Childhood Spirituality factor refers to frequent and possibly meaningful spiritual experiences early in life, with an interest in passing on similar experiences to your own children. You may have been read to from the Bible or other sacred texts by parents or grandparents, and you are eager to make sure that this activity is included in your present family. Your score is an indication that you probably attended religious school or religious services as a young child, with the clergy in your life speaking often of God and other religious, moral, or ethical themes directly to you or in your presence. High scorers on the factor of Childhood Spirituality feel strong ties to family via spiritual or religious experiences such as holidays, sacred periods like Ramadan, Lent, or Passover, and life events involving spiritual activity such as weddings, funerals, and family gatherings at holidays.

In terms of worship, some high scorers on Childhood Spirituality continue their attendance at the churches and temples of their parents or grandparents. These people are often willing to use time-tested spiritual precepts with little modification or "modernization." They are likely to raise their own children in established patterns with a strong sense of tradition.

Moderate Score

A MODERATE score on the factor of Childhood Spirituality indicates an appreciation of the power and importance of children's belief in God or some Divine Energy Source. The search for the meaning of life is tempered with a focus on the ethics and moral considerations associated with a variety of situations. A moderate score on the factor of Childhood Spirituality relates to family relationships that were involved with spiritual or religious interactions between children and their parents or grandparents, which may have included the reading and discussion of religious texts. At the same time, many of these discussions, for example around the dinner table, may have focused on the social and ethical considerations of political realities as much as on the consideration of sacred dimensions of life.

The dimension of personal and intimate relationships reflects the moderate score in terms of ties to family and loved ones through religious holidays. At the same time, these ties are strengthened through the celebration of such secular life events as birthdays and anniversaries.

Moderate scorers on the factor of Childhood Spirituality are mixed in their history of worship and spirituality. They have spent time in the traditional mold of spiritual observance, but have also been willing to consider alternatives to traditional methodologies of integrating sacred thought and activity into their lives.

Ruth is one of these moderate scorers. She loved going to Mass every Sunday morning at eleven o'clock with her grandfather. Her family lived on the second floor of a three-family triple-decker in East Boston, and their parish church was two blocks away. Her grandfather lived with her grandmother on the first floor, and as far back as she can remember, Sunday mornings were exciting for her as her mother helped her into her best clothes and she walked downstairs to find the wonderful, portly man whose English was mostly Italian. She looked up at him and smiled as they walked hand-in-hand to the service.

The Mass filled Ruth with a sense of awe and joy. For one thing, the church was huge—especially for a little girl of six. The pageantry was dramatic, and the service was long enough that she could snuggle into her grandfather's side and look at the stained-glass windows. But what Ruth remembered most was the music. She knew every hymn and prayer by the time she was seven, and the rich resonance of the organ filled her with joy and made her tingle all over. After Mass, Ruth and her grandfather returned to their home and enjoyed a sumptuous Italian dinner with the whole family.

When she married and had children, Ruth wanted desperately to give them the kind and quality of spiritual experience she had enjoyed as a child. Her husband, Bob, got a new job in California, and the couple and their three children moved to Santa Rosa for five years, where Bob was the CFO of a start-up Internet company.

Displaced from her roots, Ruth tried to create a spiritual environment for her family, but Bob simply wasn't interested, and was frankly opposed to the idea at times. He cited the fact that as a child he had been forced to attend religious services by his strict and authoritarian parents, who made him miss many social and athletic events in which he might have participated. Bob vowed that he would give his children complete latitude in determining their spiritual life, and consequently he waited for them to approach him with their interests and questions.

By the time Bob was relocated back to the Boston area, this difference in personal experience, as reflected in their Childhood Spirituality scores, had become a source of bitter conflict between the couple. Ruth called and asked if they could come to see me for therapy, and at our first meeting I was impressed by the depth of antagonism this issue had created. Ruth felt that Bob was being unreasonable and consciously stubborn; Bob felt that Ruth was forcing spirituality down his and their children's throats.

With the PSI as an aid, I showed Ruth and Bob what I thought was the critical issue. We examined their scores in the context of their early experience with spirituality, and although each of them scored in the high range, the meaning and import was obviously quite different. Ruth and Bob eventually began to see that neither of them was acting out of spite or stubbornness. The fact was that their spiritual styles had been shaped by their early experiences, and they had both made conscious vows to themselves. In Ruth's case, her vow was to re-create, as nearly as possible, her early spiritual experiences for their children. Bob, for his part, resolved never to repeat or do anything that might resemble early spiritual experience, to give his children freedom to choose, but with no input from him.

Ruth and Bob finally agreed to disagree. He came to understand, almost to respect, his wife's spiritual needs, and no longer made snide remarks to her in front of the children. Ruth pursued her spirituality with their son and daughter, while Bob maintained his distance. Instead he focused his energy on activities with the children that included the sports he loved and the theater he enjoyed. An imperfect resolution, but, under the circumstances, a realistic one.

Low Score

I N A SCHOOL or work setting, a low score on the factor of Childhood Spirituality may be connected to a focus on ethical and socially acceptable behavior, but with no emphasis on a history of spiritual or religious concepts. In the family context, a low score on Childhood Spirituality implies a relative absence of religious activities in childhood—either positive or negative in nature. There may have been many ethical and moral discussions with family, but with little if any formal ritual instruction or expression. Family interaction may have included some religious holidays, such as Christmas, Easter, or Passover, but these events were probably more cultural and ethnic than religious or spiritual in terms of discussion of religious or sacred texts and exploration of the tenets of the faith.

In your personal and intimate relationships, a low score on the Childhood Spirituality factor suggests that your ties to family and loved ones may be extremely dedicated and strong, but that the celebrations that hold the most significance would tend to be more on the order of birthdays, weddings, and anniversaries rather than Christmas or Easter, which represent an emphasis on cultural participation as opposed to spiritual experience.

The dimension of spirituality and worship for low scorers on the factor of Childhood Spirituality is highlighted primarily by an absence of church or temple attendance with family members during childhood, and little attention paid to sacred or ultimate issues. Many of the people who scored low on the Childhood Spirituality factor remembered little in the way of ritual when a family member died. As one man told me, "After my father died, we had a cremation, and I went back to work two days later. My brother and sister had been planning a memorial service to which we were hoping to invite relatives and friends, but we never quite got around to it." Some low scorers have made a conscious attempt to rectify what they perceive as a lack in their lives. They fill their world with an abundance of activity with their own children, taking them to communal spiritual experiences in places of worship, or spending time building tradition with a variety of family activities oriented toward religious themes.

Marc was horrified the first time he visited his father in the hospital. He received a call at work as next of kin that his father had suffered a massive coronary and was alive only by definition. Marc sensed that death was hovering over his father's hospital bed, and he began to panic. This was his first experience with a trauma of this proportion since his mother had left him and his father when Marc was thirteen. The doctors in the cardiac care unit of the teaching hospital were cordial and informative about his father's medical condition, telling the young, terrified man more than he wanted to know about his father's prognosis and the probability of success for one treatment approach over another. He and his father had lived together for fourteen years, a team against the world. His father, bitter after his wife left, withdrew emotionally, socialized rarely, and taught Marc that self-reliance was the key to survival. The two had become each other's world, and now Marc felt his partner and teammate slipping away.

In the waiting area near the critical care unit, one of the senior physicians saw Marc looking particularly distraught. "Where is the rest of your family?" the doctor asked gently. "This is us," said Marc. "My father's family is not close to him, and they live in Washington State. My mother left when I was a teenager, and I'm an only child and all he's got." "His chances are not good," the doctor practically whispered. "I know," said Marc. "That's what's got me scared. We don't know any priests or reverends or anyone like that. I've never been to a funeral, because my father never thought I needed to see one, and I don't know what to do or if I should contact a cemetery, or even which one. The people at the hospital asked me if I wanted to sign a paper to have my father's organs donated in the event that he should expire. Expire! Can you believe these stupid euphemisms?" At this point Marc dissolved in tears.

With no early training or guidance, Marc was, like many others, caught unawares in the midst of trauma. His education as an architect had been extensive, but he knew little about the rituals that guide people through crises. He had no information about how to approach the huge questions he faced, both the pragmatic issues of managing his father's imminent demise, and the spiritual questions of how this experience could be integrated into his psychic world. With the help of the hospital chaplain and the kindly intervention of his father's cardiologist, Marc was finally able to deal with the practical issues surrounding his father's death, which came four days later.

Shaken by his loss, confusion, and terror, Marc told me his story. The funeral was painful and he had few guidelines for managing his feelings of grief. Over the next six months, Marc and I worked on the questions that his father's death had raised. At my suggestion, he took the PSI. His low score on the Childhood Spirituality factor and his high score on the Trauma factor reflected the events I've described here. Marc also scored low on the Divinity factor. He explained that he and his father had left their church when his mother left home, and had thenceforth stayed away from anything resembling a spiritual approach to life. Marc did, however, retain an intellectual curiosity about spirituality. He scored in the high range on the Intellectuality factor, and in fact it turned out that he had taken a college course in comparative religion, one that had been among his favorites.

Marc told me one day that he had decided to investigate the local Buddhist community. He had read the Tibetan Book of the Dead shortly after his father died, had been very moved by it, and had found comfort in the reading. A young woman who was a member of the Buddhist group had invited him to participate, and he was planning his first meeting there. At our last visit, Marc told me that he finally felt grounded in the world and that he was beginning to feel a connection to an unnameable something larger than himself.

My work with Marc reinforces my confidence in the value of addressing the issues that the PSI raises. As an indication of a person's spirituality style, the PSI is extremely useful and opens doors to dialogue and understanding. The specific factor of Childhood Spirituality invariably unlocks memories and recollections. Some are nurturing; some are bittersweet. All are deeply ingrained in individual history and have left a permanent trace on the individual consciousness. In my view, it is important and useful to share and reflect upon these memories. Once understood, they can become a foundation for constructing a spiritual self.

I submit that every child has some concept of God or a Divine Energy Source. The documentation of these early beliefs, visions, concepts, and fears is one part of the Childhood Spirituality factor. By understanding our spiritual history and building on it or correcting it, we can integrate early needs and experience into our current lives.

CHAPTER FOURTEEN

Conclusion

*In the study of ideas, it is necessary to remember that insistence
on hard-headed clarity issues from sentimental feeling, as it were
a mist, cloaking the perplexities of fact. Insistence on clarity at
all costs is based on sheer superstition as to the mode in which
human intelligence functions. Our reasonings grasp at straws
for premises and float on gossamers for deductions.*
—Alfred North Whitehead, *Adventures in Ideas*

We are reminded in the above quote that the
new study of complex, emotionally charged,
and tradition-laden ideas must not be held to a
standard of precision that would smother a new
avenue of understanding or an unanticipated insight. Consequently, in my efforts to articulate this new ground of spiritual

intelligence, I ask for latitude in my exploration and the generosity of consideration of a new point of view.

At the beginning of the twentieth century, William James examined religion from a psychological and neurological perspective and came to the conclusion that the characteristics of the religious life include a belief that the visible world is part of a spiritual universe; that union with that universe is our true end; and that prayer with that spirit—be it God or law—and the resulting spiritual energy produces psychological and material effects within the phenomenal world.[1]

At the beginning of the twenty-first century, my investigation into the nature of spiritual experience and practice seeks an empirical method for understanding similar phenomena to those William James described. This work, however, begins from a different premise, namely that by examining the spiritual life of average individuals, rather than those James called "geniuses in the religious line," it is possible to understand these experiences from a broader perspective. James studied and wrote about the religious elite. In this century, as I have stated earlier, each of us has the power and permission to become his or her own spiritual guru. As a result, whether or not we have all had similar spiritual instruction, the unique qualities of our personal spiritual experience remain distinct.

One of the reasons I began this study was to document not only the wide variety of ways in which we live our spirituality, but also to search for the commonalities that may exist and could therefore serve to bind rather than separate us from each other. Think of the Tower of Babel. In that biblical account, the tower could not be completed because its builders were thrown into confusion when God caused them to speak in different tongues. The important fact, though, was that everyone was talking. The task, then, becomes how to figure out the structure and meaning of each language, and compare and contrast the outcome. With this new method it is possible to communicate with others who at first seem radically different and unapproachable; but who can open treasures of internal life that I find remarkable in their clarity and passion.

The spiritual dimension of life is inseparable from the question spiritual intelligence asks about the meaning and purpose of our being alive, here on this planet, and also the terror of our *not* being here:

> [Spirituality] speaks to the most fundamental need of all. That is the need to know that somehow we matter, that our lives mean something, count as something more than just a momentary blip in the universe.[2]

Another compelling image of this preoccupation with the meaning of our existence is portrayed by Annie Dillard:

> We who are here now make up about 6.8 percent of all people who have appeared to date. These, our times, are, one might say, ordinary times, a slice of life like any other. Who can bear to hear this, or who will consider it? . . . One R. Houwink, of Amsterdam, uncovered this unnerving fact: The human population of earth, arranged tidily, would just fit into Lake Windermere, in England's Lake District.[3]

The unacceptability of the destruction of the self has been a subject of concern since the beginning of recorded consciousness, and may be understood as the basis for the invention of the concept of soul. Death has frightened and haunted people for thousands of years, and has been the subject of shamanistic ritual, the origin of religious ideology, and the very stuff of the philosophic enterprise.[4]

Spiritual intelligence enables us to grapple with the ultimate questions of existence. At the same time, it connects us to the ongoing flow of experience. Any question separates us from being in the world. In order to ask a question, we must step back and relinquish our unconscious connection to the context of experience. That separation is the source of the anxiety that is directly linked to death, the ultimate separation. I suggest that our spirituality makes it possible for us to tolerate the anxiety of death and separation, and simultaneously makes it possible for us to establish the connections to the world and to each other that give life joy and purpose.

The findings of the research with the PsychoMatrix Spirituality Inventory indicate that each of us develops a personal and idiosyncratic way of using and expressing spiritual intelligence. As we have seen, spiritual experience can be described in seven categories, which I have defined as the Seven Spiritual Factors. The finding that these factors exist is exciting for me, and gives me a language with which to approach people and learn about their spiritual thoughts, feelings, practices, and experiences.

I have also learned that one must always keep all seven factors in mind in order to describe a person's spirituality accurately. Like a fingerprint, the unique pattern or gestalt of a person's spiritual profile is distinct from all others, but shares with them common structural elements. The shape of the pattern is important. Is someone high on the Intellectuality factor? If so, this score indicates that a strong component of his spiritual energy is devoted to learning and reflecting about spiritual matters. Does this person also have a high score on the Mindfulness factor? If so, then orientation to healthful living, including food and exercise, probably highlights a focus of her spiritual energy.

Equally important to understanding an individual's spirituality by looking at the high and low points of his or her spirituality profile, in which all seven spiritual factors are viewed at once, is that the factors must be understood as interacting with and acting upon each other. In other words, I have found that there is a dynamic relationship between factors, which can create an effect that is more than the sum of the contributions of each factor taken on its own.

One of the most common and profound interactions of spiritual factors is the dynamic between Trauma and Divinity. A high score on Trauma indicates strong personal experience with psychological or physiological illness, either in the self or in a loved one. The extreme case of Trauma is the death of a close person. In response to trauma—and this is the dynamic aspect that must be appreciated—a person may be drawn toward God, a Divine Energy Source, or nature and animal life. Alternatively, a person may, in the face of Trauma, be driven away from such sources of spiritual nourishment in bitterness, disappointment, and cynicism. In the examples cited in the previous chapters, I have tried to show the ways in which the exploration of these interactive processes can uncover the deeper meaning of spirituality for any individual.

Going Forward

ONCE YOU have taken your PsychoMatrix Spirituality Inventory, calculated your results, and examined your profile in the dynamic terms we have been discussing, the question arises, "Okay, now what?" "What do I do with the information? How can this new understanding help me?"

The uses to which the spirituality profile can be put are many. First, it is well worth knowing where you currently stand with regard to your own spirituality. This knowledge helps you see yourself in non-evaluative, descriptive terms. Rather than chiding yourself for not being spiritual in all ways at all times, you can see yourself in more realistic terms as an individual who experiences spirituality in a particular fashion. My guess is that you will look at your profile and say, "Yes, that seems to describe my approach to spirituality."

You may see in your inventory a dimension of spirituality that you would want to change. Remember the examples of the priest and the rabbi who wanted to spend more of their spiritual energy on their experience with Community? Perhaps you, too, will take the opportunity to focus specifically on the desired dimension. Let's suppose, for example, that you want to increase your time and spiritual energy in relation to Community. What can you do?

Changing your involvement with community consciousness can take many forms. Specifically you can seek out friends and mentors whose lives in the community appeal to you and use their experience to guide and influence your behavior. You could also begin to find resources in the community on your own, through political activities, your children's school, religious affiliations, and social organizations that might have an appeal. You can visit any of the thousands of Web sites that have a spiritual content, such as **beliefnet.com** and others. The Web site that hosts the Psycho-Matrix Spirituality Inventory can also help you learn new ways to apply your knowledge.

At **www.psychomatrix.com** you will find the PSI. You can take the Inventory online, have it scored automatically, and receive a personal report summarizing your outcome—the short version of what you have already learned here. In addition, the Web site provides opportunities for spiritual growth and the enhancement of spiritual intelligence. Through a series of narrowing questions, the site will help you focus on the dimensions of spirituality that are of interest to you, and help you explore them in some detail. For example, if you score in the low category on Mindfulness and would like to begin to attend to the development of this dimension of your spirituality, you might click on "meditation" on the site and begin to learn about it from an intellectual point of view; and then be led to a variety of meditation practice techniques, ending with referrals to meditation resources and people in your own community. Finally, should you have specific unanswered questions, you can interact with a skilled counselor chosen by PsychoMatrix to discuss your particular concerns.

Another way in which the results of your PSI can be useful to you is to stimulate spiritual dialogue. Many times, when both members of a couple, or members of the same family, take the PSI, they receive "permission" and are encouraged to discuss matters often left unsaid. Many personal and apparently psychological conflicts are really differing spiritual points of view, the open discussion of which can bring new life—and sometimes acrimony—to relationships. With the stimulus of the PSI, however, the possibility of resolving some of these issues is at hand.

Finally, the PsychoMatrix Spirituality Inventory provides a language for spirituality. Many people simply do not have the words for describing or discussing their spiritual experiences. When one is searching for phrases or reflecting on whether to share what may feel like an unacceptable or embarrassing out-of-body experience, having the terms and concepts at hand can make all the difference in the world. For large groups of students or people not used to discussing spiritual issues, the PSI is an efficient and pleasurable way to open discussion and facilitate dialogue.

Research into the nature of spiritual intelligence is just beginning. At this point, the methods are still rough and in need of new research to further understand what I believe is a fundamental human capacity. The PSI is being used in ongoing research to try to document the effects of the activation of spiritual intelligence and its effect on the mind/body. One study with prisoners who participate in programs of emotional awareness training shows that scores on the PSI factors of Mindfulness and Community increase at a statistically significant level following intervention.

Another study is using the PSI as part of a national investigation into the uses of alternative health care by people recovering from long-term mental illness.[5, 6]

Currently, a study on the effect of using the PSI in a setting of integrated medicine applications with cancer patients is proposed. In this study, I hypothesize that the discovery of meaning in personal suffering is indeed an important factor that can then influence one's own life span.[7] I will also be using the PSI in my new international study on the nature and meaning of work in the twenty-first century. Opportunities for new and exciting research on spiritual intelligence abound. The PsychoMatrix Spirituality Inventory is a promising methodology to be used in pursuing this knowledge.

I believe more firmly than ever in the proposition that each of us possesses spiritual intelligence. I am amazed and reassured by the many varieties of expression of this human capacity for spirituality—not so much in the mode of a study of comparative religion or comparative spiritual experience, but by the creative and innovative ways that so many people find to activate and live out of their own spiritual centers. The humility one feels in the presence of this powerful force can be staggering. I am grateful to all who have shared with me their spiritual knowledge, perplexities, fears, remarkable life events, and compassion.

Notes

PREFACE

1. James Gleick has articulated the notion of Chaos Theory as the basis for unseen yet powerful and inexorable influence of life systems on each other. Though it may seem at first a bit farfetched and superficial, the theory begins to make more sense when one considers large amounts of time or feels the unpredictable and accidental influences that one life has on another. At the most mundane yet profound level, how often have we said, "If I hadn't met him at just that moment . . ." or "One more millimeter and I would have been in a wheelchair"? How many experiences are recounted in terms of a life-changing event that occurred just in time—or, sadly—just a second too late.

2. See Kepecs and Wolman, in which it is demonstrated experimentally that the conscious perceptual world is a thin veneer covering a vast repository of information. While this is obviously not a new theory, the use in this study of subliminal stimulation created by showing pictures of their therapists to patients, and pictures of teachers to their students, elicits a depth of feeling and cognitive association significantly different from conscious reports.

3. This quote is from Kushner, *Invisible Lines of Connection*. Kushner has written extensively on the role of the spiritual, and in a way that beautifully underscores the spiritual nature of everyday life, as well as the transcendent possibilities available to us all.

ACKNOWLEDGMENTS

1. Everett Fox, *Now These Are the Names,* is a quote from Exodus outlining the genealogy of the Israelites as they leave Egypt for freedom in the Promised Land. Fox's translation of the Five Books of Moses has become a modern classic of scholarship and poetic interpretation.

INTRODUCTION

1. PsychoMatrix is an educational research and psychological testing company that I founded in 1996. Though my original plan was to provide personality testing to large groups and organizations, and to study personality interactions in the formation of personal relationships, I found myself drawn to the challenge of research on the area of spirituality—as described in the following chapters. PsychoMatrix has also developed a Web site, psychomatrix.com, where one can actually take the Spirituality Inventory online and, upon completion, immediately receive a confidential, personal spiritual profile and report.

2. Many recent surveys and articles document the devastation that AIDS has brought to Africa in particular, but also to other highly populated and undersanitized and undereducated populations. See especially James Carroll, "Stopping Africa's AIDS Nightmare," *Boston Globe,* Jan. 22, 2000; World Health Organization, *AIDS Epidemic UPDATE,* May 11, 2000; and CDC Nation Center for HIV, STD, and TB Prevention, *Daily News UPDATE,* 19 April 2000.

3. My personal thanks to Professor Gardner for his thoughtful and insightful comments on an earlier version of the manuscript of this book. He has brought this area of scholarship and clinical application before the public like no other; and he has also developed a theory of intelligences that speaks to the actual experience of educators who have known for eons that different children learn different things differently—with successful results when they are approached properly.

4. No one has articulated better than James Agee the extreme caution and concern for privacy that one must exercise in doing investigative research or reporting. In his book *Let Us Now Praise Famous Men*, Agee writes:

. . . it is in some fear that I approach these matters at all and in some confusion. And if there are questions in my mind how to undertake this communication, and there are many, . . . if I am clumsy, that may indicate partly the difficulty of my subject, and the seriousness with which I am trying to take hold what I can of it. . . . For in the immediate world, everything is to be discerned, for him who can discern it, and centrally and simply, without either dissection into science, or digestion into art, but with the whole of consciousness, seeking to perceive it as it stands: so that the aspect of a street in sunlight can roar in the heart of itself as a symphony, perhaps as no symphony can: and all of consciousness is shifted from the imagined, the revisive, to the effort to perceive simply the cruel radiance of what is."

CHAPTER ONE. SPIRITUALITY TODAY

1. These are the classic voices of the American Transcendentalists at the end of the nineteenth and the beginning of the twentieth century. They are not to be missed. For an excellent overview of the development and course of American spirituality from the end of the nineteenth century to the present, see Eugene Taylor, *Shadow Culture*.

2. An indispensable compendium of the thought that shaped the intellectual view of spirituality and religion at the turn of the last century. The consummate psychologist, James focused on the subjective experience of religion: "If the inquiry be psychological, not religious institutions, but rather religious feelings and religious impulses must be its subject." James knew also that the psychological or biological analysis of religion was dangerous: ". . . some of you may think it a degradation of so sublime a subject and may even suspect me of deliberately seeking to discredit the religious side of life." I, too, have had a similar experience of being accused of studying a subject—spirituality—in a fashion that does violence to its sacred nature by using an objective measure such as the PSI.

3. The 2000 presidential campaign gives a clear example of how the language (at least) of religion played itself out. The Republican side featured George W. Bush stating—in response to a reporter's questions—that Jesus Christ was the philosopher who had most influenced him, and that "finding Christ" was the beginning, for him, of the road back from alcoholism. Both Bush and John McCain aligned themselves with the religious

position of right-to-life groups and the traditional Republican stance on the difficult question of abortion; and McCain, in a more private moment, revealed how he had rediscovered God on the walls of his cell in a North Vietnamese prison camp. Al Gore, self-defined as a born-again Christian and a Southern Baptist, made it perfectly clear that in his view, religion needed to inform our culture particularly through the (unassailable) route of the philosopher. For his choice as a running mate, Mr. Gore chose Joseph Lieberman, the first Jewish vice presidential candidate, whose strong vocal moral convictions are rooted in his religious beliefs and observance. See Kenneth Woodward, "Finding God," *Newsweek,* 7 February 2000; Michael Novak, "Faith in Search of Votes," *New York Times,* 19 December 1999; and Gustav Niebuhr, "God and Man and the Presidency," *New York Times,* 19 December 1999.

4. George Gallup, Jr., *The Next American Spirituality: Finding God in the Twenty-first Century* (Chariot Victor, 1999). The new look in American religion and spiritual practice is widely noted in the media, but the Gallup organization continues to make meaningful observations from their samples. David Butler, John Long, and John Yemma, "America 2000: Measuring the Nation," *Boston Globe,* 21 November 1999. The authors quote both the Gallup findings on religious attitudes and the findings of a study conducted by the University of Michigan on attendance at religious services. Gallup, for example, reports that 70 percent of Americans favor daily spoken prayers in the classroom, 74 percent would allow schools to display the Ten Commandments, and 40 percent favor teaching creationism instead of evolution in public schools.

5. A beautifully written piece, filled with conflict, adventure, humor, and love.

6. For a nice discussion of this topic, showing the relationship of breath to spirit, see Diana Eck, *Encountering God,* in which she traces Eastern and Western notions.

7. See Wuthnow, *After Heaven,* a yin/yang discussion of the two strands of spiritual life, basically the classic philosophical analysis of Being and Becoming in modern terms, nicely presented in terms of the relationship of journey to community. Also, "Two Nations Under God."

Book review (28 January 1999) in *Salon,* an online magazine of political/literary reviews, discussing the two strands of American spirituality: fundamentalists (who use religious fundamentalism for political agendas) and the "hodge-podge of baby boomer wanderers moving from one eclectic spiritual home to another."

8. For an excellent analysis of the Augustine transformation of spiritual conversation, see Patricia Hampl, introduction to Philip Zaleski, ed., *The Best Spiritual Writing of 1998.*

9. Madonna is one of those quoted in an excellent *Psychology Today* article by David Elkins on the relationship of spirituality and mental health practices, with a nice image of the role of the therapist as shaman.

10. In the liner notes to his excellent CD *Solo,* (Sony, 1996), Yo-Yo Ma speaks of the spiritual journey, through music, across the Silk Road linking East and West. Note the similarity in concept to Wuthnow's seeker-and-dweller metaphor in this description.

11. This song, by one of America's most musical and resonant talents, is surprising in its evocative power. Upon seeing the music video for the first time, I was mesmerized by the images and passion of the madness of the "fire" that is part of our current world, and which has been part of the American consciousness for as long as anyone living can remember.

12. For a fascinating and intriguing inquiry into the nature and power of artificial intelligence, and some remarkable predictions of the future, see Ray Kurzweil, *The Age of Spiritual Machines,* in which he predicts, among other things, that before the end of this century, computers will possess computing power equal to or greater than the power of the human brain.

13. McLuhan, writing over thirty years ago, would probably be nodding in prophetic recognition at the development of the Internet.

14. Nelson Mandela is a man who knows more than almost any other of the power of communal dedication to a vision of interconnected transformation in human relationships.

15. See Parker J. Palmer, "Evoking the Spirit in Public Education," an excellent article focused on bringing a sense of the sacred into the schools.

16. See the article by James Glanz, "Survey Finds Strong Support for Teaching Two Origin Theories," *New York Times,* 11 March 2000, as well

as his article on the current controversy over teaching the Big Bang theory, "Science vs. the Bible: Debate Moves to the Cosmos," *New York Times,* 10 October 1999.

17. See the excellent article by Scott Canon, "Kansas Board Split on Whether Creationism Belongs in Schools," *Boston Globe,* 13 June 1999.

18. Mark Edington, consulting editor at *Daedalus,* the journal of the American Academy of Arts and Sciences, gives an insightful account of this conference in his article "How the 'God Question' Divides Us," in the *Boston Globe,* 23 May 1999.

19. Patricia Hampl, introduction to Zaleski, *The Best Spiritual Writing of 1998.*

20. Sigmund Freud, *The Future of an Illusion.* Freud's classic work on the phylogenetic/psychological origin and function of religion.

21. Gould, *Rocks of Ages.*

22. Ibid.

CHAPTER TWO. PERSONAL VIEW

1. On March 12, 2000, my cousin Itzick was murdered in his home. He knew the man who killed him—an acquaintance to whom Itzick had been kind. That was his way. The killer, high on drugs and looking for money to buy more, ended the life of a loving soul.

2. This Platonic dialogue is one of the classics of Western philosophical thought, and helps substantiate Alfred North Whitehead's claim that "the history of European philosophy can be considered an extended footnote to Plato."

3. See Elkins, "Spirituality: It's What's Missing," and the book on the placebo by Anne Harrington, *The Placebo Effect,* as well as Walter Brown's "The Placebo Effect" and "Mind Over Medicine" by Howard Brody.

4. We studied over 350 families in the probate and family court in Middlesex County, Massachusetts. In addition to the support from the judges in the court, notably Hon. Sheila McGovern and Hon. Laurence Perera, I was joined in this research by my friends and colleagues Keith Taylor, Ph.D., who collaborated on design, data collection, and interpretations, and Marcus Lieberman, Ph.D., whose methodological expertise made the study possible by providing a structure for the massive amounts of data we

collected and analyzed. Results of this study can be found under: Wolman, R. and Taylor, K., "Psychological Effects of Custody Disputes on Children." *Behavioral Sciences & the Law,* Vol. 9(4), 1991, 399–417.

5. Elkins (see note 3), and also see D. Lukoff, et al., "From Spiritual Emergency," which discusses the place of spiritual crisis in the nomenclature of the Diagnostic and Statistical Manual (DSM-IV) of the American Psychiatric Association. In addition, Stephen Post, in "Physicians and Patients Spirituality," addresses some of the issues raised when caregivers begin to struggle with the limits of their involvement in the spiritual lives of their patients.

6. In Drew Westen's *Psychology, Mind, Brain and Culture,* arguably the premier textbook of psychology of the last century, the subject of spirituality is not mentioned, and the role of religion is relegated to a few pages. In a personal conversation with Professor Westen, he assured me that the next edition would include a section on spirituality, the research related to its function in the human psyche, and its influence on healing.

7. For a discussion of the issues involved in the self-report form of testing, see Block, "A Contrarian's View of the Five-Factor Approach to Personality Description," and Westen, "A Clinical-Empirical Model of Personality."

CHAPTER THREE. INTELLIGENCE

1. Howard Gardner's theories of multiple intelligences have become household phrases. His work is outstanding for its challenge to classical theory and for its relevance to daily life. In his latest book, *Intelligence Reframed* (1999), Gardner discusses the inclusion of a new "naturalist" intelligence, and the notion of existential intelligence.

2. These researchers have done fascinating and important work in the area of emotional intelligence, and the concept was made popular by the excellent presentation in Goleman's 1995 book, *Emotional Intelligence.*

3. Sternberg and Detterman, *What Is Intelligence?,* gives an excellent historical overview of the development of the conception of intelligence.

4. From Binet's classic 1909 work on intelligence, *Les idées modernes sur les enfants.*

5. Sternberg and Detterman, *What Is Intelligence?*

6. Interestingly, the invention of the SAT tests was inspired by Henry Chauncey, an assistant dean of Harvard University, and James Bryant Conant, president of the university. Together the two sought a scientific method to find qualified students for the incoming classes at Harvard College who would otherwise have been overlooked because of geographic or social isolation. The "Census of Abilities" project was to use a series of multiple-choice mental tests to determine, on the basis of the scores, essentially what everyone's role in society would be. The organization created for this purpose and of which Chauncey was the first president was christened the Educational Testing Service.

7. Sternberg's 1990 book on intelligence as metaphor is one of the classic presentations by this pillar of the intelligence theorists community and should be examined carefully.

8. The work of Roger Sperry and, later, Michael Gazzaniga is some of the most fascinating in all of neurology and neuropsychology. The question of lateralization of thinking continues to be hotly contested, but there is little dispute that right brain and left brain do function differently in important and meaningful ways.

9. Jean Piaget, the famous Swiss child psychologist has had an enormous influence on developmental psychology, particularly in terms of his "stage theory," which suggests that mental development can only occur in the appropriate stage of growth, and that mental development follows a "genetic" or unfolding process.

10. Gardner's classic definition of intelligence.

11. See specifically his *Intelligence Reframed*.

12. Although the concept of emotional intelligence has been most popularized by Goleman in his book *Emotional Intelligence,* these researchers have been studying the phenomenon for some time, and their research is very much worth reading to gain insight into the complexity of the problem, and the creative ways they have found to study differential emotional responses and understanding.

13. Goleman's accessible and excellent presentation was a welcome addition to the field insofar as it alerted people to the function of emotion in intellectual endeavors, widened the scope of the discussion on who is

"smart," and showed how this form of intelligence has enormous impact on all of our lives.

14. See Mayer et al.'s excellent paper on this topic, "Competing Models of Emotional Intelligence."

15. Daniel Goleman has taken his view of emotional intelligence into the world of business and commerce and may be seen on PBS, lecturing to businesspeople on the value and function of emotional intelligence in the workplace.

16. LeDoux, an articulate and informed neuroscientist, is the author of *The Emotional Brain,* an important treatise on the physiologic role of emotion in the functioning of the brain—and subsequently of the mind.

17. Hubel is internationally known for his contributions to the neurophysiology of vision.

18. Damasio is the author of the fascinating *Descartes' Error,* an account of the interaction of reason and emotion in the human brain and the unnecessary split in consciousness that is implied by the French philosopher's theory of mind.

19. Gardner, *Intelligence: Multiple Perspectives.*

20. Yo-Yo Ma, the brilliant cellist, keeps moving himself and his music to the cutting edge of experience and interconnection. "I learned the communication between composer, performer, and listener. Bobby McFerrin said, 'You don't learn to improvise by practicing more. Trust yourself, know yourself, be yourself, don't judge yourself on stage.'"

21. See Stephen Jay Gould, "Evolution: The Pleasures of Pluralism," in which he discusses the dimensions of this problem.

22. Steven Pinker and other evolutionary psychologists have found a willing audience for their view that basically "that's the way we are," a view that can explain everything from infanticide to the Clinton-Lewinsky debacle.

23. In this regard, see Gould and Lewontin, "The Spandrels of San Marco," and also the works of Lewontin on the subject of genetic transmission, *Not in Our Genes* and *Biology as Ideology.*

24. See Pinker et al., "Evolutionary Psychology," for a fascinating debate between Pinker and Gould.

25. Kant's work continues to inspire with its contemporary relevance.

26. Lewontin, *The Triple Helix*.

CHAPTER FOUR. SPIRITUAL INTELLIGENCE

1. The number of books and articles on the nature of testing that demonstrate the effects of training is growing daily. Add to this phenomenon the rise in the business of college test preparation spearheaded by the Kaplan Group and elaborated by the *Princeton Review*, demonstrating that students can change their test scores in a positive direction through adequate test-taking preparation—so much so, in fact, that the Scholastic Aptitude Tests have been renamed the Scholastic Achievement Tests.

2. Emmons, *The Psychology of Ultimate Concerns*.

3. Zohar and Marshall, *SQ Connecting with Your Spiritual Intelligence;* Kurzweil, *The Age of Spiritual Machines*.

4. Michael Persinger is doing fascinating work on the nature of mystical and religious experiences and their localization in the brain.

5. Geneticist Kenneth Kendler's work should be examined for a fuller understanding of this concept.

6. Rose has jumped into the fray with Gould and Pinker, with a humanistic and wise point of view.

7. Gardner, *Multiple Intelligences*.

8. Gardner, *Intelligence Reframed*.

9. Kohlberg and Gilligan are two psychologists whose work in the measurement of moral development has influenced the field like few others, Kohlberg through his original work which, as it turned out, was based entirely on the moral development of males; and Gilligan for her insightful leap forward in her book *In a Different Voice,* in which she investigated the nature of moral development in girls and young women.

10. Emmons, *The Psychology of Ultimate Concerns*.

11. David Abram, in his phenomenological treatise *The Spell of the Sensuous* beautifully describes the work of Merleau-Ponty and its relationship to understanding our place in the world.

12. Alfred North Whitehead, the brilliant philosopher, understood the phenomenological as well as the mathematical nature of reality.

13. Rabbi Kushner continues to be one of the luminaries of contemporary spiritual thought. A combination of a consciousness that emanates from the mystics of 1265 C.E. and the consciousness of 1965 C.E., he has had a profound effect on the spiritual renaissance of thousands, and has been a strong influence on me personally.

14. Selzer, *Raising the Dead*. His *Letters to a Young Doctor* is also well worth reading.

15. Gardner, personal communication with the author, January 2000.

16. Suzuki, *Nurtured by Love*.

17. Once again I am indebted to Howard Gardner for this insight and distinction.

18. *Amae* is a concept that the West has considered pathological as a fusion and merging of boundaries—with the exception, of course, of some of the religious experiences of ecstasy and transubstantiation that are the backbone of the experience of the true believer.

19. See the Siegel and Weinberger research on merging.

20. See S. Taylor's research, which demonstrates the relationship between finding meaning in suffering and actual longevity. These concepts were also beautifully articulated by Victor Frankl in his classic work on man's search for meaning.

21. Torgovnik, *Primitive Passions*. An excellent analysis and description of the subterranean life of us all.

22. Baldwin, *Edison*.

23. Roberts, *The Nature of Personal Reality*.

24. Gay, *Mozart*. The description of Mozart's composing as one complete, seamless activity is a little romanticized, according to Gay, but there is no doubt that he could just sit down and write a complete work if the occasion necessitated it. In those moments the music did simply flow from his brain to his pen.

CHAPTER SIX. TAKING THE PSI

1. The thirty-nine items not included in the scoring form part of the context for the inventory and were statistically close enough to achieving factor status that further research will determine their ultimate usefulness.

CHAPTER SEVEN. DIVINITY

1. Zohar, *Rewiring the Corporate Brain*.

2. Michelle Conlin, "Religion in the Workplace." *Business Week*, 1 November 1999. See also Tobler, "Making Work Meaningful," and Brown, "Corporate Soul."

3. Sacha Pfeiffer, "Lawyering with a Heart." *Boston Globe*, 28 November 1999.

4. Rabbi Susan Harris, personal communication, January 2000.

5. *Business Week* article on spirituality in the workplace.

6. Weltner, "In the Spiritual Dimension," *Boston Globe*, May 7, 1998.

7. S. Taylor et al., "Psychological Resources." These findings do not, in my opinion, constitute evidence for the value of total denial or living in a delusional state. I am grateful to Drew Westen (personal communication, February 2000) for the insight that the distribution of acceptance versus denial and finding meaning is probably more like a "bell curve," in which both extremes, of denial and of hard-hearted realism, appear nonconducive to optimal outcome.

CHAPTER EIGHT. MINDFULNESS

1. The National Institutes of Health has created a division that was first called, the Office of Alternative Medicine. The name has now been changed to the National Center for Complementary and Alternative Medicine. Andrew Weil, M.D., has coined the term "Integrative Medicine" for his program at the University of Arizona, a name used by other centers including the Integrative Medicine Center at Memorial Sloan-Kettering Cancer Institute in New York City.

2. See Eisenberg, "Trends in Alternative Medicine Use in the United States," and "Unconventional Medicine in the United States," fascinating and counterintuitive studies by the director of the Alternative Medicine Program at Beth Israel Hospital in Boston.

3. See Ramachandran and Blakeslee, *Phantoms in the Brain*, p. 56.

CHAPTER NINE. EXTRASENSORY PERCEPTION

1. There is actually a service in New York City to which anyone can send a prophetic vision or dream—say of an airline disaster. The commu-

nication is time-stamped, so that if the event occurs and the claim of pre-science is made, there will be verification.

2. Persinger, "Near-Death Experiences and Ecstasy," and "Subjective pseudocyesis."

3. There is a body of neurological research suggesting that the right hemisphere of the brain, the side associated with feeling and intuition, is also associated with images of a more threatening nature. Persinger's findings seem to support this hypothesis. In this regard, see Corballis, "Are We in Our Right Minds?"

4. Pascual-Leone, et al., "Rapid rate transcranial magnetic stimulation of left dorsolateral prefrontal cortex in drug resistant depression"; and George et al., "Mood improvement following daily left prefrontal repetitive transcranial magnetic stimulation in patients with depression."

5. Persinger, "Near-Death Experiences and Ecstasy."

6. Aristotle, *The Way of Philosophy*.

7. Descartes, René, "The Seat of the Soul."

8. Afifi and Bergman, *Basic Neuroscience*.

9. Kandel et al., *Principles of Neural Science*.

10. Gallup and Lindsay, *Surveying the Religious Landscape*. See also Gallup, *The Next American Spirituality*.

11. The reader is directed to the fascinating work of LaBerge (*Lucid Dreaming*) and others on this topic.

12. Eckhart, "The Divine Love of the Soul."

13. Underhill, "The Rapture of Divine Love," in *Mysticism*.

CHAPTER TEN. COMMUNITY

1. Gottlieb, *Spirituality and Resistance*.

CHAPTER TWELVE. TRAUMA

1. The massacre of innocent children at Columbine High School in Littleton, Colorado, in 1999 was shocking in its proportion, premeditation, and loss of innocence on the part of the American public. Subsequent school violence in which a six-year-old shot another kindergartener and twelve- and thirteen-year-olds hold their classmates at bay with loaded

pistols taken from home only serve to remind us of the violence that we have perpetrated on ourselves.

CHAPTER THIRTEEN. CHILDHOOD SPIRITUALITY

1. See Wilber, et al., for a fascinating presentation of the developmental stages of spiritual thought.

2. Coles, *The Spiritual Life of Children;* and *The Moral Intelligence of Children*.

CHAPTER FOURTEEN. CONCLUSION

1. James, *The Varieties of Religious Experience,* 529. In some sense this present work may be viewed as an homage to James, although I start from a different premise.

2. Kushner, "You've Got to Believe in Something," *Redbook,* December 1987. Harold Kushner, no relation to Lawrence Kushner, but also a rabbi, is best known for his moving book *When Bad Things Happen to Good People*.

3. Dillard, *For the Time Being*. This compelling and brilliant book must not be missed.

4. Unamuno, *Tragic Sense of Life*. In his insightful and troubling treatise, Miguel de Unamuno, the Spanish philosopher, posits the issue as follows: "It is impossible for us, in effect, to conceive of ourselves as not existing, and no effort is capable of enabling consciousness to realize absolute unconsciousness, its own annihilation. . . . We cannot conceive ourselves as not existing."

5. Unpublished study by Casarjian, Wolman, and Philips: "Effects of Emotional Literacy Training on Incarcerated Prisoners."

6. Farkas and Rogers, "Rehabilitation for Persons with Long Term Mental Illness."

7. See S. Taylor et al., "Psychological Resources, Positive Illusions, and Health." This fascinating study with AIDS patients documents the positive effects of belief on longevity, as well as the discovery of meaning in suffering.

References

Abram, D. *The Spell of the Sensuous*. New York: Pantheon, 1996.

Afifi , A. K., and R. A. Bergman, *Basic Neuroscience*. 2nd edition. Baltimore and Munich: Urban and Schwartzenberg, 1986.

Agee, J., and W. Evans. *Let Us Now Praise Famous Men*. Boston: Houghton Mifflin, 1969.

Aristotle. *The Way of Philosophy*. Translated by P. E. Wheelwright. Macmillan College Publishing Company, 1960.

Baldwin, N. *Edison: Inventing the Century*. New York: Hyperion, 1995.

Barkow, J., L. Cosmides, and J. Tooby, eds. *The Adapted Mind: Evolutionary Psychology and the Generation of Culture*. New York: Oxford University Press, 1995.

Ben-Gurion, D. Invited address, Brandeis University, Waltham, Mass. 1962.

Binet, A. *Les idées modernes sur les enfants*. Paris: Flammarion, 1909.

Block, J. "A Contrarian's View of the Five Factor Approach to Personality Description." *Psychological Bulletin* 117 (1995); 187–215.

———. "Going Beyond the Five Factors Given: Rejoinder to Costa and McCrae (1995) and Goldberg and Saucier (1995)." *Psychological Bulletin* 117, no. 2 (1995): 226–29.

Brody, H. "Mind Over Medicine." *Psychology Today,* May 2000.

Brown, T. "'Corporate Soul': Meaning Behind the Buzz Words." *Harvard Management Update*. Boston: Harvard Business School Publishing, 1988.

Brown, W. "The Placebo Effect." *Scientific American,* January 2000.

Casarjian, R., R. Wolman, and J. Philips, "Effects of Emotional Literacy Training on Incarcerated Prisoners." Unpublished manuscript, June 2000.

Cella, D., et al. "A Case for Including Spirituality in Quality of Life Measurement." In *Oncology*. Society of Behavioral Medicine annual meeting, March 1999.

Cohen, A., and P. Mendes-Flohr, eds. *Contemporary Jewish Religious Thought*. New York: Charles Scribner's Sons, 1987.

Coles, R. *The Moral Intelligence of Children*. New York: Random House, 1997.

————. *The Spiritual Life of Children*. Boston: Houghton Mifflin, 1990.

Conlin, M. "Religion in the Workplace." *Business Week,* 1 November 1999.

Cooper, L. A. "Strategies for Visual Comparison and Representation: Individual Differences." In *Advances in the Psychology of Human Intelligence,* edited by R. J. Sternberg. Vol. 1. Hillsdale, N.J.: Erlbaum, 1982.

Corballis, M. "Are We in Our Right Minds?" In *Mind Myths,* edited by S. Della Sala. New York: John Wiley & Sons, 1999.

Costa, P. T. and R. R. McCrae. "Solid Ground in the Wetlands of Personality: A Reply to Block." *Psychological Bulletin* 117, no. 2: 216–20.

Cytowic, R. *The Man Who Tasted Shapes*. New York: Putnam, 1993.

D'Aguili, R. "Philosophy and Psychology of Consciousness." *American Psychologist,* February 1997.

Damasio, A. R. *Descartes' Error: Emotion, Reason and the Human Brain*. New York: Avon Books, 1994.

Descartes, R. "The Seat of the Soul." In *Essential Works of Descartes,* translated by L. Bair. New York: Bantam Books, 1961.

Dillard, A. *For the Time Being*. New York: Vintage, 1999.

Domar, A. D., and H. Dreher. *Healing Mind, Healthy Woman*. New York: Henry Holt, 1996.

Eck, D. L. *Encountering God*. Boston: Beacon Press, 1993.

Eckhart, M. "The Divine Love of the Soul." In *Meditations with Meister Eckhart,* edited by Matthew Fox. Santa Fe: Bear & Co., 1983.

Eisenberg, D., R. Davis, et al. "Trends in Alternative Medicine Use in the United States, 1990–1997: Results of a Follow-up National Survey."

Journal of American Medical Association 280, no. 18 (11 November 1998): 1569–75.

Eisenberg, D., R. Kessler, et al. "Unconventional Medicine in the United States: Prevalence, Costs, and Patterns of Use." *New England Journal of Medicine*, 28 January 1993.

Elkins, D. "Spirituality: It's What's Missing in Mental Health." *Psychology Today*, September–October 1999.

Emerson, R. W. "The Over-Soul." In *The Best of Ralph Waldo Emerson*. Roslyn, N.Y.: Walter J. Black, Inc. 1969.

Emmons, R. *The Psychology of Ultimate Concerns: Motivation and Spirituality in Personality*. New York: Guilford Publications, 1999.

———. "Religion and Personality." In *Handbook of Religion and Mental Health*, edited by H. Koenig. San Diego: Academic Press, 1998.

Farkas, M., and E. S. Rogers. "Rehabilitation for Persons with Long Term Mental Illness" (U.S. Department of Education Application Control Center CFDA No. 84-133B). Boston: Center for Psychiatric Rehabilitation, Boston University, 1999.

Fox, E. *Now These Are the Names*. New York: Schocken Books, 1986.

Frankl, V. *Man's Search for Meaning*. Boston: Beacon, 1992.

Freud, S. *The Future of an Illusion*. London: Hogarth Press, 1957.

Friedman, R. E. *Who Wrote the Bible?* New York: Summit Books, 1987.

Fuchs-Kreimer, N. *Parenting as a Spiritual Journey*. Woodstock, Vermont: Jewish Lights Publishing, 1996.

Gallup, G., Jr. *The Next American Spirituality: Finding God in the Twenty-first Century*. New York: Chariot Victor, 2000.

Gallup, G., Jr., and D. M. Lindsay. *Surveying the Religious Landscape: Trends in U.S. beliefs*. New York: Morehouse Publishing Co., 2000.

Gardner, H. *Frames of Mind: The Theory of Multiple Intelligences*. New York: Basic Books, 1993.

———. *Intelligence Reframed*. New York: Basic Books, 1999.

———. *Multiple Intelligences: The Theory in Practice*. New York: Basic Books, 1993.

Gardner, H., et al. *Intelligence: Multiple Perspectives*. New York: Rinehart and Winston, 1996.

Gay, P. *Mozart*. New York: Viking, 1999.

Gazzaniga, M. *Nature's Mind*. New York: Basic Books, 1992.

George, M., E. Wasserman, et al. "Mood improvement following daily left prefrontal repetitive transcranial magnetic stimulation in patients with depression: A placebo-controlled cross-over trial." *American Journal of Psychiatry* 154 (1997): 1752–56.

Gilligan, C. *In a Different Voice*. Cambridge: Harvard University Press, 1993.

Glazer, S., ed. *The Heart of Learning: Spirituality in Education*. New York: Penguin Putnam, 1999.

Gleick, J. *Chaos: Making a New Science*. New York: Viking Penguin, 1987.

Goldberg, L. R., and G. Saucier. "So What Do You Propose We Use Instead? A Reply to Block." *Psychological Bulletin* 117, no. 2: 221–25.

Goleman, D. *Emotional Intelligence*. New York: Bantam Books, 1995.

Gordon, J. S. *Manifesto for a New Medicine*. New York: Addison-Wesley, 1996.

Gottlieb, R. *Spirituality and Resistance: Finding a Peaceful Heart and Protecting the Earth*. New York: Crossroad Press, 1999.

Gould, S. J. "Darwinian Fundamentalism." *New York Review of Books* 44, no. 10 (12 June 1997): 34–37.

———. "Evolution: The Pleasures of Pluralism." *New York Review of Books* 44, no. 11 (26 June 1997): 47–52.

———. *Leonardo's Mountain and the Diet of Worms*. New York: Harmony Books, 1998.

———. *Rocks of Ages: Science and Religion in the Fullness of Life*. New York: Harmony Books, 1999.

Gould, S. J., and R. C. Lewontin. "The Spandrels of San Marco and the Panglossian Paradigm." Proceedings of the Royal Society of London, 1979.

Hampl, P. Introduction to *The Best Spiritual Writing of 1998*, edited by P. Zaleski. San Francisco: Harper, 1998.

Harrington, A. *The Placebo Effect: An Interdisciplinary Exploration*. Cambridge: Harvard University Press, 1997.

Hebb, D. O. *The Organization of Behavior: A Neuropsychological Theory*. New York: John Wiley, 1949.

Hubel, D. *Eye, Brain and Vision*. New York: Scientific American Library, 1988.

"Intelligence and Its Measurement: A Symposium." *Journal of Educational Psychology* 12 (1921): 123–47, 195–216.

James, W. *The Varieties of Religious Experience: Being the Gifford Lectures on Natural Religion Delivered at Edinburgh in 1901–1902*. New York: Random House Modern Library, 1994.

Jensen, A. R. *Bias in Mental Testing*. New York: Free Press, 1980.

Joseph, R. *Neuropsychiatry, Neuropsychology, Clinical Neuroscience*. Baltimore, Md.: Williams & Wilkins, 1996.

Kamenetz, R. *The Jew in the Lotus*. San Francisco: Harper, 1995.

Kandel, E., J. Schwartz, and T. Jessell. *Principles of Neural Science*. 3rd edition. Norwalk, Conn.: Appleton and Lange, 1991.

Kandinsky, W. *Concerning the Spiritual in Art*. New York: Dover, 1977.

Kant, I. *Critique of Pure Reason*, translated by Kemp Smith. New York: St Martin's Press, 1958.

Kendler, K., et al. "Religion, Psychopathology, and Substance Use and Abuse: A Multimeasure, Genetic-Epidemiologic Study." *American Journal of Psychiatry* 154, no. 3 (March 1997): 322–29.

Kepecs, J. G., and R. N. Wolman. "Preconscious perception of the transference." *The Psychoanalytic Quarterly* 41, no. 2 (1972): 172–94.

Koenig, H., ed. *Handbook of Religion and Mental Health*. San Diego: Academic Press, 1998.

Kohlberg, L. *Essays on Moral Development*, Vol. 1. San Francisco: Harper and Row, 1981.

Kornfield, J. *A Path with Heart*. New York: Bantam Books, 1993.

Kosslyn, S. M. *Image and Mind*. Cambridge, Mass.: Harvard University Press, 1980.

———. May 1999 *Harvard University Gazette*.

Kübler-Ross, E. *On Death and Dying*. New York: Simon & Schuster, 1975.

Kuhn T. S. *The Structure of Scientific Revolutions*. 2nd edition. Chicago: University of Chicago Press, 1970.

Kurzweil, R. *The Age of Spiritual Machines*. New York: Penguin, 1999.

Kushner, L. *God Was in This Place, and I, i Did Not Know.* Woodstock, Vt.: Jewish Lights Press, 1991.

———. *Invisible Lines of Connection.* Woodstock, Vt.: Jewish Lights Press, 1996.

———. *River of Light.* Chappaqua, N.Y.: Rossel, 1981.

LaBerge, S. *Lucid Dreaming.* New York: Ballantine Books, 1985.

LeDoux, J. *The Emotional Brain.* New York: Simon and Schuster, 1996.

Lemann, N. *The Big Test: The Secret History of the American Meritocracy.* New York: Farrar, Straus and Giroux, 1999.

Lerner, M. "Spirituality in America." *Tikkun* 6, no. 13 (November 1998): 33.

Lesser, E. *The New American Spirituality.* New York: Random House, 1999.

Lewis, W. *Why People Change: The Psychology of Influence.* New York: Holt, Rinehart and Winston, 1972.

Lewis, W. C., R. N. Wolman, and M. King. "The Measurement of the Language of Emotions." *American Journal of Psychiatry* 127, no. 11 (May 1971).

Lewontin, R. *Biology as Ideology: The Doctrine of DNA.* New York: HarperCollins, 1991.

———. *Not in Our Genes.* New York: Pantheon, 1984.

———. *The Triple Helix: Gene, Organism, and Environment.* Cambridge: Harvard University Press, 2000.

Longfellow, H. D. "The Soul of the Voice." In E. Hubbard, *Elbert Hubbard's Scrapbook.* New York: M. Wise & Co., 1923.

Lukoff , D., F. Lu, and K. Turner. "From Spiritual Emergency to Spiritual Problem: The transpersonal roots of the new DSM-IV category." *Journal of Humanistic Psychology* 38, no. 2: 21–50.

Lustick, I. S. *For the Land and the Lord: Jewish Fundamentalism in Israel.* New York: Council on Foreign Relations, 1988.

Lykken, D. "The Genetics of Genius," In *Genius and Mind: Studies of Creativity and Temperament,* edited by A. Steptoe et al. New York: Oxford University Press, 1998, 15–37.

McLuhan, M. and Q. Fiore. *The Medium Is the Message.* New York: Bantam Books, 1967.

Ma, Y. "Finding Your Voice." Commencement Address, Williams College, Williamstown, Mass., June 1998.

————. Liner notes to *Solo*, compact disc, Sony Records, 1996.

MacLeod, C. M., E. B. Hunt, and N. N. Matthews. "Individual Differences in the Verification of Sentence-Picture Relationships." *Journal of Verbal Learning and Verbal Behavior* 17 (1978): 493–507.

Mandela, N. "Globalizing Responsibility." Address, 1999, Aspen Institute/Nobel 2000.

Mayer, J., D. Caruso, and P. Salovey. "Emotional Intelligence Meets Traditional Standards for an Intelligence." Unpublished manuscript.

Mayer, J., P. Salovey, and D. Caruso. "Competing Models of Emotional Intelligence." In *Handbook of Human Intelligence*, edited by R. J. Sternberg. 2nd edition. New York: Cambridge University Press, 2000.

Merleau-Ponty, M. *Phenomenology of Perception*. London: Routledge & Kegan Paul, 1962.

Moore, T. "Spiritualities of Depth." *Tikkun* no. 13 (November 1998): 40.

Newberg, A., and E. D'Aquili. "Neuropsychology of Spiritual Experience." In *Handbook of Religion and Mental Health*, edited by H. Koenig. San Diego: Academic Press, 1998.

Niebuhr, G. "Alternative Religions as a Growth Industry." *New York Times*, 25 December 1999.

O'Brien, D. "Outfoxing the Hedgehogs: *The Moral Animal: Why We Are the Way We Are: The New Science of Evolutionary Psychology* by Robert Wright; *The Ethical Primate: Humans, Freedom and Morality* by Mary Midgley." *Commonweal*, 2 June 1995.

O'Brien, T. *The Things They Carried*. Boston: Houghton Mifflin, 1990.

Olsen, T. *Silences*. New York: Delacorte Press, 1978.

Oser, F. "The Development of Religious Judgment." In *New Directions for Child Development* no. 52, *Religious Development in Childhood and Adolescence*, edited by F. Oser and G. Scarlett. San Francisco: Jossey-Bass, Inc., 1991.

Ozick, C. "Remember the Sabbath Day and Keep It Holy." In *The Best Spiritual Writing of 1998*, edited by P. Zaleski. San Francisco: Harper, 1998.

Palmer, P. J. "Evoking the Spirit in Public Education." In *Educational Leadership: The Spirit of Education* 56, no. 4 (December 1998/January 1999).

Pascual-Leone, A., et al. "Rapid rate transcranial magnetic stimulation of left dorsolateral prefrontal cortex in drug resistant depression." *Lancet* 348 (1996): 233–37.

Persinger, M. "Near-Death Experiences and Ecstasy: A Product of the Organization of the Human Brain." In *Mind Myths,* edited by S. Della Sala. West Sussex, England: John Wiley & Sons, Ltd., 1999.

―――. "Subjective pseudocyesis in normal women who exhibit enhanced imaginings and elevated indicators of electrical lability within the temporal lobes." *Social Behavior and Personality* 24, no. 2 (1996): 101–11.

Pfeiffer, S. "Lawyering with a Heart." *Boston Globe,* 28 November, 1999.

Piaget, J. *The Language and Thought of the Child,* translated by M. G. Bain. London: Routledge & Kegan Paul; New York: Harcourt Brace, 1926.

―――. *The Origins of Intelligence in Children.* New York: International Universities Press, 1952.

―――. *The Psychology of Intelligence.* Totowa, N.J.: Littlefield Adams, 1972.

Pinker, S., et al. "Evolutionary Psychology: An Exchange." *New York Review of Books,* 9 October 1997.

Pinker, S., *How the Mind Works.* New York: Norton, 1997.

―――. "Why They Kill Their Newborns." *The New York Times Magazine,* 2 November 1997.

Plato. "The Phaedo." In *The Dialogues of Plato,* translated by B. Jowett. New York: Random House, 1937.

Post, S., C. Puchalski, and D. Larson. "Physicians' and Patients' Spirituality: Professional Boundaries, Competency, and Ethics." *Annals of Internal Medicine* 132 (4 April 2000): 578–83.

Raaheim, K. *Problem Solving and Intelligence.* Oslo: Universitetsforlaget, 1974.

Ramachandran, F. S., and S. Blakeslee. *Phantoms in the Brain: Probing the Mysteries of the Human Mind.* New York: William Morrow & Co., 1998.

Rizzuto, A. "Religious Development: A Psychoanalytic Point of View." In *New Directions for Child Development* no. 52, *Religious Development in*

Childhood and Adolescence, edited by F. Oser and G. Scarlett. San Francisco: Jossey-Bass, Inc., 1991.

Roberts, J. *The Nature of Personal Reality.* New York: Buccaneer, 1993.

Rose, S. *The Making of Memory.* London: Bantam, 1992.

―――. "Why Pinker Is Wrong: It takes more than dodgy genes to produce a compulsive shopper." *The Independent,* 19 January 1998.

Sacks, O. *An Anthropologist from Mars.* New York: Knopf, 1995.

"Spirit of Education." *Educational Leadership* 56, no. 4 (December 1998/January 1999).

Salovey, P., et al. "Emotional States and Physical Health." *American Psychologist* 55, no. 1 (January 2000): 110–21.

Scarlett, W. G. "Spiritual Development: Lessons from Lincoln." Unpublished manuscript, 1999.

Selzer, R. *Raising the Dead.* New York: Penguin, 1993.

Siegel, P., and J. Weinberger. "Capturing the 'Mommy and I Are One' Merger Fantasy: The Oneness Motive." In *Empirical Studies of Psychoanalytic Theories,* edited by R. Bornstein and J. Masling. Washington, D.C.: APA Press, 1998.

Siegler, R. S. "Unities Across Domains in Children's Strategy Choices." In *Perspectives on Intellectual Development: The Minnesota Symposia on Child Psychology.* Vol. 19. Edited by I. M. Perlmutter. Hillsdale, N.J.: Erlbaum, 1986.

Snow, R. E., and D. F. Lohman. "Toward a Theory of Cognitive Aptitude for Learning from Instruction." *Journal of Educational Psychology* 76 (1984): 347–76.

Spearman, C. *The Abilities of Man.* London: Macmillan, 1927.

Steinmetz, H. "Structure, Function and Cerebral Asymmetry: In "Vivo Morphometry of the Planum Temporale." *Neuroscience and Behavioral Reviews* 20, no. 4 (Winter 1996): 587–91.

Sternberg, R. J. *Intelligence, Information Processing, and Analogical Reasoning: The Componential Analysis of Human Abilities.* Hillsdale, N.J.: Erlbaum, 1977.

―――. *Metaphors of Mind: Conceptions of the Nature of Intelligence.* New York: Cambridge University Press, 1990.

————. *Handbook of Human Intelligence.* New York: Cambridge University Press, 1982.

Sternberg, R. J., and D. K. Detterman, eds. *What Is Intelligence? Contemporary Viewpoints on Its Nature and Definition.* Norwood, N.J.: Ablex Publishing Corp., 1986.

Sternberg, R. J., and C. Smith. "Social Intelligence and Decoding Skills in Nonverbal Communication." *Social Cognition* 3 (1985): 168–92.

Suzuki, S. *Nurtured by Love.* New York: Exposition Press, 1969.

Taylor, E. *Shadow Culture: Psychology and Spirituality in America.* Washington, D.C.: Counterpoint, 1998.

Taylor, S., et al. "Psychological Resources, Positive Illusions, and Health." *American Psychologist* 55, no. 1 (January 2000): 99–109.

Tobler, A. "Making Work Meaningful." *Harvard Management Update.* Boston: Harvard Business School Publishing, 1997.

Torgovnick, M. *Primitive Passions: Men, Women and the Quest for Ecstasy.* New York: Alfred A. Knopf, 1997.

Unamuno, M. de. *Tragic Sense of Life.* New York: Dover Books, 1954.

Underhill, E. *Mysticism.* New York: World Publishing, 1970.

Walters, J., and H. Gardner. "The Development and Education of Intelligences." In *Essays on the Intellect,* edited by F. Link. Washington, D.C.: Curriculum Development Associates/Association for Supervision and Curriculum Development, 1985.

Weltner, L. "In the Spiritual Dimensions," *Boston Globe,* 7 May 1998.

Westen, D. "A Clinical-Empirical Model of Personality: Life after the Mischelian Ice Age and the Neo-Lithic Era." *Journal of Personality* 63, no. 3 (September 1995): 495–524.

————. *Psychology, Mind, Brain and Culture.* New York: John Wiley & Sons, 1999.

Whitehead, A. N. *Adventures in Ideas.* New York: Mentor, 1933.

————. *Symbolism: Its Meaning and Effect.* New York: Putnam/Capricorn Books, 1959.

Whitman, W. "I Sing the Body Electric." *Walt Whitman: The Complete Poems,* edited by Francis Murphy. New York: Penguin Books, 1975.

Wilber, K., et al., eds. *Transformations of Consciousness: Conventional and Contemplative Perspectives on Development.* Boston: Shambhala, 1986.

Wilson, E. O. "Biological Basis of Morality." *The Atlantic Monthly,* June 1998.

Winnicott, D. W. "Transitional Objects and Transitional Phenomena." *International Journal of Psychoanalysis* 34, no. 2 (1953).

Winnicott, D. W. *The Maturational Process and the Facilitating Environment: Studies in the Theory of Emotional Development.* New York: International Universities Press, 1965.

Wolman, R., and K. Taylor. "Psychological Effects of Custody Disputes on Children." *Behavioral Sciences and the Law.* 9, no. 4 (1991): 399–417.

Wolman, R. N., W. C. Lewis, and M. King. "The development of the language of emotions: Bodily referents and the experience of affect." *Journal of Genetic Psychology* 121 (1972): 65–81.

————. "The development of the language of emotions: Conditions of emotional arousal." *Child Development* 72, no. 12 (1971).

Wright, R. *The Moral Animal: Evolutionary Psychology and Everyday Life.* New York: Pantheon, 1994.

Wuthnow, R. *After Heaven: Spirituality in America Since the 1950s.* Berkeley: University of California Press, 1998.

Zohar, D. *Rewiring the Corporate Brain: Using the New Science to Rethink How We Structure and Lead Organizations.* London: Berrett-Koehler, 1997.

Zohar, D., and I. Marshall. *SQ: Connecting with our Spiritual Intelligence.* New York and London: Bloomsbury Publishing, 2000.

Index

About the Author

RICHARD N. WOLMAN, PH.D., has been a member of the faculty at Harvard Medical School for more than twenty-five years.